Jane Barlow

Strangers at Lisconnel

Second Series of Irish Idylls

Jane Barlow

Strangers at Lisconnel
Second Series of Irish Idylls

ISBN/EAN: 9783744725026

Printed in Europe, USA, Canada, Australia, Japan

Cover: Foto ©Thomas Meinert / pixelio.de

More available books at **www.hansebooks.com**

STRANGERS AT LISCONNEL

A SECOND SERIES OF IRISH IDYLLS

BY

JANE BARLOW

NEW YORK
DODD, MEAD AND COMPANY
1895

To

M. L. B.

Is fada me beō do ḋíaiḋ.

CONTENTS

CHAPTER I.
                                                        PAGE

OUT OF THE WAY.................................. 1

CHAPTER II.
JERRY DUNNE'S BASKET..................... 14

CHAPTER III.
MRS. KILFOYLE'S CLOAK..................... 31

CHAPTER IV.
A GOOD TURN.................................. 53

CHAPTER V.
FORECASTS.................................. 80

CHAPTER VI.
A FAIRING.................................. 112

CHAPTER VII.

	PAGE
MR. POLYMATHERS.................................	139

CHAPTER VIII.

HONORIS CAUSA....................................	168

CHAPTER IX.

BOYS' WAGES......................................	211

CHAPTER X.

CON THE QUARE ONE...............................	235

CHAPTER XI.

MAD BELL...	271

CHAPTER XII.

A FLITTING.......................................	303

CHAPTER XIII.

A RETURN...	324

CHAPTER XIV.

GOOD LUCK.......................................	340

CHAPTER I

OUT OF THE WAY

To Lisconnel, our very small hamlet in the middle of a wide bogland, the days that break over the dim blue hill-line, faint and far off, seldom bring a stranger's face; but then they seldom take a familiar one away, beyond reach, at any rate of return before nightfall. In fact, there are few places amid this mortal change to which we may come back after any reasonable interval with more confidence of finding things just as we left them, due allowance being made for the inevitable fingering of Time. We shall find some old people who have aged under it, and some who, as certain philosophers would hold, have grown younger again. The latter may be seen just beginning, perhaps, to sit up stiff on a woman's arm, or starting for a trial crawl over mother earth; and of them we remark that there is another little Ryan or Quigley; while the former stay sunning themselves so inertly, or totter about so shakily, that we notice at once how much old Sheridan, or the Widow Joyce, has failed since last year. These babies and grandparents often associate a good deal with one another at the stage when the old body is still capable of "keepin' an eye on the child," and the child still resorts to all fours if it wants to get up its highest speed. But this companionship does not last long in any given case. Very soon the expanding and the contracting sphere cease to touch closely. On the one hand, the world widens into more spacious tracts for nimbler and bolder ranging over, with all manner of remarkable things growing and living upon it, to be gathered and captured, or at least sought and chased, among pools and hillocks and swampy places. On the other, it shrinks to within the limits of a few dwindling furlongs and perches, traversed ever more feebly, until at length even the nearest stone, on which the warm rays can be basked in, seems to have moved too far off, and the flicker-haunted nook by the hearth-fire becomes the end of the whole day's journey.

Thus the generations, as they succeed one another, wave-like preserve a well-marked rhythm in their coming and going—play, work, rest—not to be interrupted by anything less peremptory than death or disablement. This wag-by-the-wall swings and swings its bobbed pendulum without pause, but one swing is much like the other, and their background never varies. Little Pat out stravading of a fine morning on the great brown-wigged bog, and, it may be hoped, enjoying himself thoroughly, is taking the same first steps in life as young Pat his father, now busy cutting turf-sods, and old Pat, his grandfather, idly watching them burn, with a pipe, if in luck, to keep alight. And the Lisconnel folk, therefore, because the changes wrought by human agency come to them in unimposing forms, are strongly impressed by the vast natural vicissitudes of things which rule their destinies. The melting of season into season, and year into year, the leaf-like withering and drifting away of the old from among the fresh springing growths, are ever before their eyes, and the contemplation steeps them in a sense of the transitoriness of things good and bad. Even the black soil they tread on may next year flutter up into a vanishing blue column through a smoke-hole in somebody's thatch. They carry this sense with a light and heavy heart. In like manner they make the very most of all unusual events. They find materials for half-an-hour's talk in the passage by their doors of one of those rarely coming strangers, who do appear from time to time, as frequently, indeed, as anybody would expect, having surveyed the thoroughfare that links us with humanity. For if we follow it southward, where, like the unvanishing wake of some vessel, it streaks the level plain, that is lonely as a wide water, but stiller, we pass by Dan O'Beirne's forge, now neighbourless, and through humble Duffclane, and on to Ballybrosna, our Town; but we must go many a mile further to reach anything upon which you would bestow that title. Or, if we turn northward, we only find it seaming another ample fold of bogland, outspread far and far beyond Lisconnel before a grey hill-range begins to rise in slow undulations, crested with furze and broom. Here we smell turf-smoke again, and see a cabin-row that is Sallinbeg, and hence the road strikes north-westward in among the mountains, where a few mottled-faced sheep peer down over it from their smooth green walks, but do not care to trust their black velvet legs upon it. And then, by the time that the air has become sea-scented, the road climbs to the top of a hill, and stops there abruptly, as if it had been travelling all the while merely to look at the view. The truth is that the funds for its construction would go no further, and, in consequence, wayfarers coming along by the shore still have to tread out a path for themselves across a gap of moorland, if they are bound for Lisconnel.

You may perceive, therefore, that Lisconnel lies out of the way, on the route to no places of importance, and as its own ten or a dozen little houses are, I fear, collectively altogether insignificant, it has small reason to expect many visitors. The Widow M'Gurk said one day that you might as well be living at the bottom of the boghole for any company you got the chance of seeing; but this was an exaggeration. She was vexed when she made the remark, because Mrs. Dooley, old Dan O'Beirne's married daughter, then staying at the forge, had promised to come and inspect a pair of marketable chickens, in anticipation of which Mrs. M'Gurk had wetted a cup of tea and used up her last handful of wholemeal for a cake, that Mrs. Dooley, who was in rather affluent circumstances, might not think them "too poorly off altogether." But, after all, the hours had slipped blankly by, and nobody had arrived. So the widow had ruefully put her teapot to sit on the hob until himself came in—for, properly speaking, she was at this time not yet a widow—and had stepped down her tussocky slope with her double disappointment to Mrs. Kilfoyle.

Mrs. Kilfoyle was knitting at her door and not looking out over the bog, where the flushed light of the sunset drowsed on the black sod in an almost tangible fire-film. Against it the poppies stood up dark and opaque, but the large white daisies had caught the wraith of the glow on their glimmering discs. She had been thinking how not so long ago her son Thady used to come whistling home to her across the bog when the shadows stretched their longest. The sunset still came punctually every evening, but had grown wonderfully lonesome since the kick of a cross-tempered cart-horse had silenced his whistling and stopped his home-coming for ever. Thady's whistling had been indifferent, considered as music, yet it had sounded pleasant in her ears, and Mrs. M'Gurk's trouble seemed to her not very serious. However, she replied to her complaint: "Ah, sure, woman dear, like enough she might be here to-morra."

"And if she is, she'll be very apt to not get e'er a chuck or a chucken off of me—not the feather of a one," said Mrs. M'Gurk, resentfully, "plenty of other things I have to do besides wastin' me time waitin' for people that don't know their own minds from one minyit to the next, and makin' a fool of meself star-gazin' along the road, and ne'er a fut stirrin' on it no more than if it was desolit wildernesses."

She would not for the world have alluded to her expenditure of more material resources, and accordingly had to explain her vexation by putting a fictitious value upon her time, which, in reality, was just then drearily superabundant.

"Sure," suggested Mrs. Kilfoyle, "the poor woman maybe was kep' at home some way, and she wid ivery intintion to be comin'. I declare, now, you'd whiles think things knew what you was manin' in your mind, and riz themselves up agin it a' purpose to prevint you, they happen that conthráry."

As Mrs. M'Gurk's experience did not dispose her to gainsay this proposition, and she was nevertheless disinclined to be mollified by it, she likewise had recourse to generalities, and said:

"Deed then it's welcome anybody is to stop

away if they're wishful, hindered or no. Long sorry I'd be to have people disthressin' themselves streelin' after *me*." And she added, rather inconsistently, the remark already mentioned: "But the likes of this place I never witnessed. You might as well be livin' at the bottom of the blackest ould boghoule there, for e'er a chance you have to be seein' a bit of company."

"And it's yourself 'ud make the fine sizeable waterask, ma'am," a high-pitched voice said suddenly from within doors, causing Mrs. M'Gurk to start and peer into the dark opening behind her, somewhat taken aback at finding that she had had an unsuspected audience, which is always more or less of a shock. The first object she descried through the hazy dusk was the figure of the old woman known to Lisconnel as Ody Rafferty's aunt, but in fact so related to his father, sitting with her short black dudeen by the delicate pink and white embers, for the evening was warm and the fire low. Ody himself was leaning against the wall, critically examining Brian Kilfoyle's blackthorn, and forming a poor opinion of it with considerable satisfaction. Not that he bore Brian any ill-will, but because this is his method of attaining to contentment with his own possessions.

"Whethen now and is it yourself that's in it, Ody Rafferty?" said Mrs. M'Gurk, as she recognised him. "And what talk have you out of you about waterasks? You're the great man, bedad."

"Me aunt's lookin' in on Mrs. Kilfoyle, ma'am," said Ody, "be raison of Brian bein' off to the Town. And right enough you and me knows what's took him there; and so does Norah Finegan. Och, good luck to the pair of thim."

"Coortin'," said his aunt, who preferred to put things briefly and clearly. "But I was tellin' Mrs. Kilfoyle to not be frettin', for sure God is good, and they'll be apt to keep her in it all's one."

"Goodness may pity you, woman," said Mrs. M'Gurk. "Brian 'ud as lief take and bring home a she *hyenna*, and it ravin' mad, as anybody 'ud look crooked at his mother, I very well know."

"Norah's a rael dacint little slip of a girl," Mrs. Kilfoyle said tranquilly, considering that her son's character needed no certificate. But the old woman only grunted doubtfully, and said: "Och, is she?" For she had been a superfluous aunt so long that she found it hard to believe in anything better than toleration.

"Talkin' of company," said Ody, to change the

subject—which his aunt's remarks often disposed people to do—"Mad Bell's just after shankin' back wid herself; she's below colloguin' wid Big Anne. It's a fine long tramp she's took this time; so if she was in the humour she'd a right to ha' plinty to be tellin' us."

"Well, now, I'm glad the crathur's home," said Mrs. Kilfoyle. "It's lonesome in a manner to think of the little ould bein' rovin' about the world like a wisp of hay gathered up on the win'; for all, tubbe sure, it's her own fancy starts her off."

"I won'er where to she wint this time," said Mrs. M'Gurk.

"You might as well," said Ody, "be won'erin' where a one of thim saygulls goes, when it gives a flourish of its ould flippers and away wid itself head foremost—barrin', in coorse, that Mad Bell's bound to keep on the dhry land at all ivents. But from Sallinbeg ways she come this evenin', singin' 'Garry Owen' most powerful—I know that much."

"Ah, then she might be chance ha' been as far as Laraghmena, and ha' seen a sight of me brother Mick and Theresa," Mrs. Kilfoyle said, with wistful interest. 'For at Lisconnel we still look not a little to the reports brought by stray travellers for news of absent friends, much as we did before the days of penny posts and mail trains. And our geographical lore is vague enough to impede us but slightly in our hopes of obtaining information from any quarter. Only the probability seems to be increased if the new-comer arrives from the direction in which our friend departed.

"Sure she might so," said Ody. "But niver a tell she'll tell onless she happens to take the notion in the quare ould head of her. It's just be the road of humouring her now and agin, and piecin' her odd stories together, you git e'er a discovery, so to spake, of the places she's after bein' in."

The scenes of Mad Bell's wanderings did indeed reveal themselves to her neighbours confusedly and dispersedly in her fitful and capricious narrative, like glimpses of a landscape caught through a shifting mist. As this sometimes distorts the objects that loom within it, so Mad Bell's statements were occasionally misleading. Once, for example, she threw the Quigley family into most distracted concern by her accounts of the terrific "shootin' and murdherin' and massacreein'" she had seen in progress down away at Glasgannon, where Joe Quigley had taken service with a strong farmer ; these disturbances being in reality nothing more than a muster of the county militia.

"But I can tell you how she thravelled a good step of the way home," Ody now continued, "for she tould me herself. The Tinkers gave her a lift in their ould cart. Somewheres beyant Rosbride she met wid them; glory be to goodness 'twasn't any nearer here they were, the ould thieves of sin. Howane'er, *Mrs. M'Gurk* belike 'ud be wishful to see thim comin' along. Fine company they'd be for anybody begorrah. Troth, it's the quare ugly boghoule she'd find the aquil of thim at the bottom of."

Mrs. M'Gurk, however, said protestingly, "Och, wirrasthrew, man, don't be talkin' of the Tinkers. They'd a right to not be let set fut widin tin mile of any dacint place. Thim or the likes of any such rogues."

And Mrs. Kilfoyle said, "I'd liefer than a great deal they kep' out of it. Ne'er a one of the lot of them I ever beheld but had the eyes rowlin' in his head wid villiny. And the childer, goodness help them, do be worse than the grown people."

And Ody Rafferty's aunt said, "Bad cess to the whole of them."

For in Lisconnel nobody has a good word to say of the Tinkers.

The tribe and their many delinquencies have even supplied us with a bit of the proverbial philosophy in which not a little of our local history is epitomised. The saying, "As pat as thievin' to a tinker" is probably quoted among us as frequently as any other, except, perhaps, one which refers to Jerry Dunne's basket. This latter had its origin in a certain event, not like the former in the long-accumulating observation of habits and propensities, and to explain it therefore is to write a chapter of our chronicles. Moreover, the event in question is otherwise not unimportant from a sociological point of view, because it is very likely to have been the first morning call ever made at Lisconnel.

CHAPTER II

JERRY DUNNE'S BASKET

So it is worth while to tell the reason why people at Lisconnel sometimes respond with irony to a question: "What have I got? Sure, all that Jerry Dunne had in his basket." The saying is of respectable antiquity, for it originated while Bessy Joyce, who died a year or so back, at "a great ould age entirely," was still but a slip of a girl. In those days her mother used often to say regretfully that she didn't know when she was well off, like Rody O'Rourke's pigs, quoting a proverb of obscurer antecedents. When she did so she was generally thinking of the fine little farm in the county Clare, which they had not long since exchanged for the poor tiny holding away in the heart of the black bog; and of how, among the green fields, and thriving beasts, and other good things of Clonmena, she had allowed her content to be marred by such a detail as her

Bessy's refusal to favour the suit of Jerry Dunne.

Mrs. Joyce eagerly desired a brilliant alliance for Bessy, who was rather an important daughter, being the only grown-up girl, and a very pretty one, among a troop of younger brethren; so it seemed contrary enough that she wouldn't look the same side of the road as young Jerry, who was farming prosperously on his own account, and whose family were old friends and neighbours, and real respectable people, including a first cousin nothing less than a parish priest. Yet Bessy ran away and hid herself in as ingeniously unlikely places as a strayed calf whenever she heard of his approach, and if brought by chance into his society became most discouragingly deaf and dumb.

It is true that at the time I speak of Bessy's prospects fully entitled her to as opulent a match, and no one apparently foresaw how speedily they would be overcast by her father's improvidence. But Andy Joyce had an ill-advised predilection for seeing things what he called "dacint and proper" about him, and it led him into several imprudent acts. For instance, he built some highly superior sheds in the bawn, to the bettering, no doubt, of his cattle's condition, but very little to his own purpose, which he would indeed have served more advantageously by spending the money they cost him at Moriarty's shebeen. Nor was he left without due warning of the consequences likely to result from such courses. The abrupt raising of his rent by fifty per cent. was a broad hint which most men would have taken; and it did keep Andy quiet, ruefully, for a season or two. Then, however, having again saved up a trifle, he could not resist the temptation to drain the swampy corner of the farthest river-field, which was as kind a bit of land as you could wish, only for the water lying on it, and in which he afterwards raised himself a remarkably fine crop of white oats. The sight of them "done his heart good," he said, exultantly, nothing recking that it was the last touch of farmer's pride he would ever feel. Yet on the next quarter-day the Joyces received notice to quit, and their landlord determined to keep the vacated holding in his own hands; those new sheds were just the thing for his young stock. Andy, in fact, had done his best to improve himself off the face of the earth, and he should therefore have been thankful to retain a foothold, even in a loose-jointed, rush-roofed cabin away at stony Lisconnel. Whether thankful or no, there, at any rate, he presently found himself established with all his family, and the meagre remnant of his hastily sold-off gear, and the black doors of the "house" seeming to loom ahead whenever he looked into the murky future.

The first weeks and months of their new adversity passed slowly and heavily for the transplanted household, more especially for Andy and his wife, who had outgrown a love of paddling in bogholes, and had acquired a habit of wondering "what at all 'ud become of the childer, the crathurs." One shrill-blasted March morning Andy trudged off to the fair down below at Duffclane—not that he had any business to transact there, unless we reckon as such a desire to gain a respite from regretful boredom. He but partially succeeded in doing this, and returned at dusk so fagged and dispirited that he had not energy to relate his scraps of news until he was half through his plate of stirabout. Then he observed: "I seen a couple of boys from home in it."

"Whethen now, to think of that," said Mrs. Joyce with mournful interest, "which of them was it?"

"The one of them was Terence Kilfoyle," said Andy.

Mrs. Joyce's interest flagged, for young Kilfoyle was merely a good-looking lad with the name of being rather wild. "Ah sure *he* might as well be in one place as another," she said indifferently. "Bessy, honey, as you're done, just throw the scraps to the white hin where she's sittin'."

"He sez he's thinkin' to settle hereabouts," said Andy; "I tould him he'd a right to go thry his fortin somewhere outlandish, but he didn't seem to fancy the idee, and small blame to him. A man's bound to get his heart broke one way or the other anywheres, as far as I can see. I met Jerry Dunne too."

"Och and did you indeed?" said Mrs. Joyce, kindling into eagerness again.

Jerry had been absent from Clonmena at the time of their flitting, and they had heard nothing of him since; but she still cherished a flicker of hope in his connection, which the tidings of his appearance in the neighbourhood fanned and fed.

"And he's quit out of it himself," Andy continued, "for the ould uncle of his he's been stoppin' wid this while back at Duffclane's after dyin' and lavin' him a fine farm and a hantle of money, and

I dunno what all besides. So it's there he's goin' to live, and he's gave up the ould place at Clonmena, as well he may, and no loss to him on it, for he sez himself he niver spent a pinny over it beyont what he'd be druv to, if he wanted to get e'er a crop out of it at all, and keep things together in any fashion: he wasn't such a fool." Andy hesitated, as if on the brink of a painful theme, and resumed with an effort: "He's bought Magpie and the two two-year-olds off of Peter Martin. Chape enough he got them, too, though he had to give ten shillin's a head more for them than Martin ped me."

"Mavrone, but some people have the luck," said Mrs. Joyce.

"And Jerry bid me tell you," said Andy, the memory of his lost cattle still saddening his tone, "that he might be steppin' up here to see you tomorra or next day."

At this Mrs. Joyce's face suddenly brightened, as if she had been summoned to share Jerry Dunne's good luck. She felt almost as if that had actually happened. For his visit could surely signify nothing else than that he meant to continue his suit; and under the circumstances, Bessy's misliking was a piece of folly not to be taken into account. Besides that, the girl, she thought, looked quite heartened up by the news. So she replied to her husband: "'Deed then, he'll be very welcome," and the sparkle was in her eyes all the rest of the evening.

On the morrow, which was a bright morning with a far-off pale blue sky, Mrs. Joyce hurried over her readying-up, that she might be prepared for her possible visitor. She put on her best clothes, and as her wardrobe had not yet fallen to a level with her fortune, she was able to array herself in a strong steel-grey mohair gown, a black silk apron with three rows of velvet ribbon on it besides the binding, a fine small woollen shawl of very brilliant scarlet and black plaid, with a pinkish cornelian brooch to pin it at the throat, all surmounted by a snowy high-caul cap, in those days not yet out of date at Lisconnel, where fashions lag somewhat. She noticed, well-pleased, Bessy's willingness to fall in with the suggestion that she should re-arrange her hair and change her gown after the morning's work was done; and the inference drawn grew stronger, when, for the first time since their troubles, the girl began to sing "Moll Dhuv in Glanna" while she coiled up her long tresses.

All that forenoon Mrs. Joyce had happy dreams about the mending of the family fortunes, which would be effected by Bessy's marriage with Jerry Dunne. When her neighbour, Mrs. Ryan, looked in, she could not forbear mentioning the expected call, and was further elated because Mrs. Ryan at once remarked: "Sure, 'twill be Bessy he's after," though she herself, of course, disclaimed the idea, saying: "Och musha, ma'am, not at all." The Ryans were tenants who had also been put out of Clonmena, and they occupied a cabin adjoining the Joyces', these two dwellings, backed by the slopes of the Knockawn, forming the nucleus of Lisconnel.

About noon, Paddy, the eldest boy, approached at a hand gallop, bestriding a donkey which belonged to the gang of men who were still working on the unfinished road. As soon as the beast reached the open-work stone wall of the potato-field it resolutely scraped its rider off, a thing it had been vainly wishing to do all along the fenceless track. Paddy, however, alighted unconcerned among the clattering stones, and ran on with his tidings. These were to the effect that he was "after seein' Jerry Dunne shankin' up from Duffclane ways, a goodish bit below the indin' of the road, and he wid a great big basket carryin', fit to hould a young turf-stack."

The intelligence created an agreeable excitement, which was undoubtedly heightened by the fact of the basket. "Very belike," said Mrs. Ryan, "he's bringin' somethin' to you, or it might be Bessy." And while Mrs. Joyce rejoined deprecatingly: "Ah sure, woman alive, what would the poor lad be troublin' himself to bring us all this way?" she was really answering her own question with a dozen flattering conjectures. The basket must certainly contain *something*, and there were so few by any means probable things that would not at this pinch have come acceptably to the Joyces' household, where the heavy pitaty sack grew light with such alarming rapidity, and the little hoard of corn dwindled, and the childer's appetites seemed to wax larger day by day. She had not quite made up her mind, when Jerry arrived, whether she would wish for a bit of bacon—poor Andy missed an odd taste of it so bad—or for another couple of hens, which would be uncommonly useful now that her own few had all left off laying.

Mrs. Ryan having discreetly withdrawn, Mrs. Joyce stood alone in her dark doorway to receive her guest, and, through all her flutter of hope, she felt a bitter twinge of housewifely chagrin at being discovered in such miserable quarters. The black earth flooring at her threshold gritted hatefully under her feet, and the gusts whistling through the many chinks of her rough walls seemed to skirl derisively. She was nevertheless resolved to put the best possible face upon the situation.

"Well, Mrs. Joyce, ma'am, and how's yourself this long while?" said Jerry Dunne, coming up. "Bedad I'm glad to see you so finely, and it's an iligant place you've got up here."

"Ah, it's not too bad whatever," said Mrs. Joyce, "on'y 'twas a great upset on us turnin' out of the ould house at home. Himself had a right to ha' left things the way he found them, and then it mightn't iver ha' happened him. But sure, poor man, he niver thought he'd be ruinatin' us wid his conthrivances. It's God's will. Be steppin' inside to the fire, Jerry lad; there's a thin feel yet in the win'."

Jerry, stepping inside, deposited his basket, which did not appear to be very heavy, rather disregardfully by him on the floor. Mrs. Joyce would not allow herself to glance in its direction. It struck her that the young man seemed awkward and flustered, and she considered this a favourable symptom.

"And what way's Mr. Joyce?" said Jerry. "He was lookin' grand whin I seen him yisterday."

"'Deed, he gits his health middlin' well enough, glory be to goodness," she said; "somewhiles he'll be frettin' a bit, thinkin' of diff'rent things, and when I tell him he'd better lave botherin' his head wid them, he sez he might as aisy bid a blast of win' to not be blowin' through a houle. Och, Andy's a quare man. He's out and about now somewheres on the farm."

Mrs. Joyce put a spaciousness into her tone wholly disproportionate to their screed of tussocks and boulders; and then paused, hoping that the next inquiry might relate to Bessy.

But what young Jerry said was, "You've got a great run, anyway, for the fowls."

The irrelevance of the remark disappointed Mrs. Joyce, and she replied a little tartly: "A great run you may call it, for begorrah our hearts is broke huntin' after the crathurs, and they strayin' off wid themselves over the width of the bog there, till you've as much chance of catchin' them as the sparks flyin' up the chimney."

"That's unhandy, now," said Jerry. He sat for some moments reflectively ruffling up his flaxen hair with both hands, and then he said, " Have you the big white hin yit that you got from me a while ago?"

"We have so bedad," said Mrs. Joyce, not loth to enlarge upon this subject. "Sure we made a shift to bring a few of the best chickens we had along wid us, and sorry we'd ha' been to lose her, and she a won'erful layer, and after you a-givin' her to us in a prisint that way."

"There was some talk that time," said Jerry, "about me and Bessy."

"Ay, true for you, there was," said Mrs. Joyce, in eager assent, "plinty of talk." She would have added more, but he was evidently in a hurry to speak again.

"Well, there's none now," he said. "Things is diff'rent altogether. If I'd ha' known, I'd ha' kep' the hin. The fact of the matter is I'm about gettin' married to Sally Coghlan, that's me poor uncle's wife's niece. He's after leavin' her what he had saved up. She's a fine figure of a girl as iver you saw, and as good as gould, and the bit of lan' and the bit of money had a right to go the one way. So I was thinkin', Mrs. Joyce, I might as well be takin' home the ould hin wid me—things bein' diff'rent now, and no talk of Bessy. Sally has a great wish for a white hin, and we've ne'er a one of that sort at our place. I've brought a wad of hay in the basket meself, for 'fraid yous might be short of it up here." Jerry gave a kick to the basket, which betrayed the flimsy nature of its contents by rolling over with a wobble on its side.

At this critical moment Mrs. Joyce's pride rallied loyally to the rescue of her dignity and self-respect, proving as effectual as the ice-film which keeps the bleakest pool unruffled by the wildest storm wing. With the knell of all her hope clanging harshly in her ears, she smiled serenely, and said gaily: " Ay bedad, himself was tellin' us somethin' about it last night. Sure, I'm rael glad to hear tell of your good luck, and I wish you joy of it. And will you be gettin' married agin Shrovetide? Och, that's grand. But the white hin now—the on'y thing is the crathur's been sittin' on a clutch of eggs since Monday week. So what are we to do at all?"

"There's hapes of room for the whole of them in the basket, for that matter," Jerry suggested promptly.

"Ah, sure, it's distroyed they'd be, jogglin' along, and the crathur herself 'ud go distracted entirely; sorra a bit of good you'd get of her. But look here, Mr. Dunne, I've got another out there as like her as if the both of them had come out of the one egg, and you could be takin' that instid. It's a lucky thing I didn't set her to sit the way I was intendin'; on'y I niver could get a clutch gathered for her, be raison of the lads aitin' up the eggs on me. Sure, I can't keep them from the little bosthoons when they be hungry."

"'Twould be all the same thing to me, in coorse, supposin' she was equally so good," Jerry admitted with caution.

"Ivery feather she is," said Mrs. Joyce. "I seen her runnin' about there just this minute; you can be lookin' at her yourself."

She went towards the door as she spoke, and was somewhat taken aback to perceive her husband leaning against the wall close outside. How much of the discussion he might have heard, she could not tell. The white hen also appeared within easy reach, daintily resplendent under the sunshine on a background of black turf. And Mrs. Ryan, standing darkly framed in her doorway, was very certain to be an interested observer of events. For the moment Mrs. Joyce's uppermost anxiety was to avoid any betrayal of discomfiture, and she accordingly said in a loud and cheerful tone :

"Och, and are you there, Andy? Jerry Dunne's wishful for the loan of a clockin' hin, so I'm about catchin' him the young white one to take home wid him."

But, to her intense disgust, Jerry, who had followed her with his basket, said remonstrantly : "Whethen now, Mrs. Joyce, the way I understand the matter there's no talk in it of borryin' at all. I'm on'y takin' her back instid of the ould one, and I question would any raisonable body stand me out I don't own her be rights. It's an unjust thing to be spakin' of loans."

Mrs. Joyce was so dumbfounded by this rebuff that she could only hide her confusion by displaying an exaggerated activity in the capture of the hen.

Her husband, however, said blandly, "Och, don't make yourself onaisy, man. Loan or no loan, you needn't be under any apperhinsion we'll be comin' after her wid a basket. Divil a much. Stir yourself, Kitty, and be clappin' her in under the lid. He's in a hurry to get home to his sweetheart wid the iligant prisint he's after pickin' up for her. Ay, that's right, woman alive: give a tie to the bit of string, and then there's nothin' to be delayin' him."

After this everybody said good-bye with much politeness and affability, though withal a certain air of despatch, as if they were conscious of handling rather perishable goods. And when Jerry was beyond earshot, Andy, looking after him, remarked, "I niver liked a bone in that fellow's skin. Himself and his ould basket. The lads 'ill be prisintly comin' in to their dinners."

"D'you know where Bessy is?" said Mrs. Joyce, her heart sinking still lower at the thought of the disappointment, which she had presumably been helping to prepare for her daughter.

"When I seen her a while back, she was out there wid the childer, discoorsin' to Terence Kilfoyle," Andy said contentedly.

"Musha, good gracious, Terence Kilfoyle, and what's *he* come after?" she said in a bitter tone.

"He stepped up wid a couple of pounds of fresh butter and a dozen of eggs. He said he minded Bessy havin' a fancy for duck-eggs, and he thought we mightn't happen to have e'er a one up here. She seemed as pleased as anythin'.

But if you ax *me*, Kitty," he said with a twinkle, "I've a notion he's come after somethin' more than our ould hin."

"He's a great young rogue," said Mrs. Joyce. Yet there was an accent of relief in her voice, and on her face a reflection of her husband's smile.

And Jerry Dunne's basket still occupies its niche in the stores of our proverbial philosophy.

CHAPTER III

MRS. KILFOYLE'S CLOAK

THE opprobrious proverb already mentioned is not the only permanent mark of unpopularity that the Tinkers have earned for themselves at Lisconnel. Their very name has become a term of reproach among us, so that "an ould tinker" is recognised as an appropriate epithet for any troublesome beast or disagreeable neighbour. If they were not case-hardened by long experience, they would surely be mortified sometimes at the reception with which they meet almost wherever they go. The approach of the two queer vehicles in which they now generally travel is watched by displeased eyes all over our country-side, and they are so to speak lighted on their way by the gleam of suspicious or resentful glances. And it must be admitted that their evil reputation has not been bestowed upon them gratuitously. According to Ody Rafferty, "The like of such a clanjamfry of thievin' drunken miscreants, you wouldn't aisy get together, if you had a spring-trap set for them at the Ould Fellow's front door for a month of Sundays. And if himself didn't do a hard day's work the time he was consthructin' them, he niver done one in his life, and that's a fac'." But Ody is apt to be particularly severe in his strictures upon the Tinkers, because he feels an aggravated form of rivalry existing between him and them. For the wiliness which is understood to be Ody's forte also pre-eminently characterises many of the Tinkers' nefarious proceedings, and this makes it seem to him that they not only set their wits against his, but throw discredit upon his favourite quality by the glaring moral defects which they exhibit in conjunction with it. One's pleasure in being described admiringly as "the ould boyo that's in it," is much diminished when one hears the same thing said bitterly of some slieveen who has filched a poor body's meal bag, or run off with a lone 'widdy woman's fowl.

Still, although the Tinkers' name has become a by-word among us through a long series of petty offences rather than any one flagrant crime, there is a notable misdeed on record against them, which has never been forgotten in the lapse of many years. It was perpetrated soon after the death of Mrs. Kilfoyle's mother, the Widow Joyce, an event which is but dimly recollected now at Lisconnel, as nearly half a century has gone by. She did not very long survive her husband, and he had left his roots behind in his little place at Clonmena, where, as we know, he had farmed not wisely, but too well, and had been put out of it for his pains to expend his energy upon our oozy black sods and stark-white boulders. But instead he moped about fretting for his fair green fields and few proudly-cherished beasts—especially the little old Kerry cow. And at his funeral the neighbours said: "Ah bedad, poor man, God help him, he niver held up his head agin from that good day to this."

When Mrs. Joyce felt that it behoved her to settle her affairs, she found that the most important possession she had to dispose of was her large cloak. She had acquired it at the prosperous time of her marriage, and it was a very superior specimen of its kind, its dark-blue cloth being superfine, and its ample capes and capacious hood being double-lined and quilted, and stitched in a way which I cannot pretend to describe, but which made it a most substantial and handsome garment. If Mrs. Joyce had been left entirely to her own choice in the matter, I think she would have bequeathed it to her younger daughter Theresa, notwithstanding that custom clearly designated Bessy Kilfoyle, the eldest of the family, as the heiress. For she said to herself that poor Bessy had her husband and childer to consowl her, any way, but little Theresa, the crathur, had ne'er such a thing at all, and wouldn't have, not she, God love her. "And the back of me hand to some I could name." It seemed to her that to leave the child the cloak would be almost like keeping a warm wing spread over her in the cold wide world; and there was no fear that Bessy would take it amiss.

But Theresa herself protested strongly against such a disposition, urging for one thing that sure she'd be lost in it entirely if ever she put it on, a not unfounded objection, as Theresa was several sizes smaller than Bessy, and even she fell far short of her mother in stature and portliness. Theresa also said confidently with a sinking heart: "But sure, anyhow, mother jewel, what matter about it? 'Twill be all gone to houles and flitters and thraneens, and so it will, plase goodness, afore there's any talk of anybody else wearin' it except your own ould self." And she expressed much the same conviction one day to her next-door neighbour, old Biddy Ryan, to whom she had run in for the loan of a sup of sour milk, which Mrs. Joyce fancied. To Biddy's sincere regret she could offer Theresa barely a skimpy noggin of milk, and only a meagre shred of encouragement; and by way of eking out the latter with its sorry substitute consolation, she said as she tilted the jug perpendicularly to extract its last drop:

"Well, sure, me dear, I do be sayin' me prayers for her every sun goes over our heads that she might be left wid you this great while yet; 'deed I do so. But ah, acushla, if we could be keepin' people that-a-way, would there be e'er a funeral iver goin' black on the road at all at all? I'm thinkin' there's scarce a one livin', and he as ould and foolish and little-good-for as you plase, but some crathur'ill be grudgin' him to his grave, that's himself may be all the while wishin' he was in it. Or, morebetoken, how can we tell what quare ugly misfortin thim that's took is took out of the road of, that we should be as good as biddin' thim stay till it comes to ruinate them? So it's prayin' away I am, honey," said old Biddy, whom Theresa could not help hating heart sickly. "But like enough the Lord might know better than to be mindin' a word I say."

And it seemed that He did; at any way the day soon came when the heavy blue cloak passed into Mrs. Kilfoyle's possession.

At that time it was clear, still autumn weather, with just a sprinkle of frost, white on the wayside grass, like the wraith of belated moonlight, when the sun rose, and shimmering into rainbow stars by noon. But about a month later the winter swooped suddenly on Lisconnel: with wild winds and cold rain that made crystal-silver streaks down the purple of the great mountain-heads peering in over our bogland.

So one perishing Saturday Mrs. Kilfoyle made up her mind that she would wear her warm legacy on the bleak walk to Mass next morning, and reaching it down from where it was stowed away among the rafters wrapped in an old sack, she shook it respectfully out of its straight-creased folds. As she did so she noticed that the binding of the hood had ripped in one place, and that the lining was fraying out, a mishap which should be promptly remedied before it spread any further. She was not a very expert needlewoman, and she thought she had better run over the way to consult Mrs. O'Driscoll, then a young matron, esteemed the handiest and most helpful person in Lisconnel.

"It's the nathur of her to be settin' things straight wherever she goes," Mrs. Kilfoyle said to herself as she stood in her doorway waiting for the rain to clear off, and looking across the road to the sodden roof which sheltered her neighbour's head. It has long been lying low, vanquished by a trouble which even she could not set to rights, and some of the older people say that things have gone a little crookeder in Lisconnel ever since.

The shower was a vicious one, with the sting of sleet and hail in its drops, pelted about by gusts that ruffled up the puddles into ripples, all set on end, like the feathers of a frightened hen. The hens themselves stood disconsolately sheltering under the bank, mostly on one leg, as if they preferred to keep up the slightest possible connection with such a very damp and disagreeable earth. You could not see far in any direction for the fluttering sheets of mist, and a stranger who had been coming along the road from Duffclane, stepped out of them abruptly quite close to Mrs. Kilfoyle's door, before she knew that there was anybody near. He was a tall, elderly man, gaunt and grizzled, very ragged, and so miserable-looking that Mrs. Kilfoyle could have felt nothing but compassion for him had he not carried over his shoulder a bunch of shiny cans, which was to her mind as satisfactory a passport as a ticket-of-leave. For although these were yet rather early days at Lisconnel, the Tinkers had already begun to establish their reputation. So when he stopped in front of her and said: " Good-day, ma'am," she only replied distantly, "It's a hardy mornin'," and hoped he would move on. But he said: " It's cruel could, ma'am," and continued to stand looking at her with wide and woful eyes, in which she conjectured erroneously as it happened—hunger for warmth or food. Under these circumstances what could be done by a woman who was conscious of owning a redly-glowing hearth with a big black pot, fairly well filled, clucking and bobbing upon it? To possess such wealth as this, and think seriously of withholding a share from anybody who urges the incontestable claim of wanting it, is a mood altogether foreign to Lisconnel, where the responsibilities of property are, no doubt, very imperfectly understood. Accordingly Mrs. Kilfoyle said to the tattered tramp:

"Ah, thin, step inside and have a couple of hot pitaties." And when he accepted the invitation without much alacrity, as if he had something else on his mind, she picked for him out of the steam two of the biggest potatoes, whose earth-coloured skins, cracking, showed a fair flouriness within; and she shook a little heap of salt, the only relish she had, on to the chipped white plate as she handed it to him, saying, "Sit you down be the fire there, and git a taste of the heat."

Then she lifted her old shawl over her head, and ran out to see where at all Brian and Thady were gettin' their deaths on her under the pours of rain; and as she passed the Keoghs' adjacent door—which was afterwards the Sheridan's, whence their Larry departed so reluctantly— young Mrs. Keogh called her to come in and look at "the child," who being a new and unique possession was liable to develop alarmingly strange symptoms, and had now "woke up wid his head that hot, you might as well put your hand on the hob of the grate." Mrs. Kilfoyle stayed only long enough to suggest, as a possible remedy, a drop of two-milk whey. "But ah sure, woman dear, where at all 'ud we come by that, wid the crathur of a goat scarce wettin' the bottom of the pan?" and to draw reassuring omens from the avidity with which the invalid grabbed at a sugared crust. In fact, she was less than five minutes out of her house; but when she returned to it, she found it empty. First she noted with a moderate thrill of surprise that her visitor had gone away leaving his potatoes untouched, and next, with a rough shock of dismay, that her cloak no longer lay on the window seat where she had left it. From that moment she never felt any real doubts about what had befallen her, though for some time she kept on trying to conjure them up, and searched wildly round and round and round her little room, like a distracted bee strayed into a hollow furze-bush, before she sped over to Mrs. O'Driscoll with the news of her loss.

It spread rapidly through Lisconnel, and brought the neighbours together exclaiming and condoling, though not in great force, as there was a fair going on down beyant, which nearly all the men and some of the women had attended. This was accounted cruel unlucky, as it left the place without any one able-bodied and active enough to go in pursuit of the thief. A prompt start might have overtaken him, especially as he was said to be "a thrifle lame-futted," though Mrs. M'Gurk, who had seen him come down the hill, opined that "'twasn't the sort of lameness 'ud hinder the miscreant of steppin' out, on'y a quare manner of flourish he had in a one of his knees, as if he was gatherin' himself up to make an offer at a grasshopper's lep, and then thinkin' better of it."

Little Thady Kilfoyle reported that he had met the strange man a bit down the road, "leggin' it along at a great rate, wid a black rowl of somethin' under his arm that he looked to be crumplin' up as small as he could"—the word "crumpling" went acutely to Mrs. Kilfoyle's heart—and some long-sighted people declared that they could still catch glimpses of a receding figure through the hovering fog on the way towards Sallinbeg.

"I'd think he'd be beyant seein' afore now," said Mrs. Kilfoyle, who stood in the rain, the disconsolate centre of the group about her door; all women and children except old Johnny Keogh, who was so bothered and deaf, that he grasped new situations slowly and feebly, and had now an impression of somebody's house being on fire. "He must ha' took off wid himself the instant me back was turned, for ne'er a crumb had he touched of the pitaties."

"Maybe he'd that much shame in him," said Mrs. O'Driscoll.

"They'd a right to ha' choked him, troth and they had," said Ody Rafferty's aunt.

"Is it chokin'?" said young Mrs. M'Gurk, bitterly. "Sure the bigger thief a body is the more he'll thrive on whatever he gits—you might think villiny was as good as butter to people's pitaties—you might so. Shame how are you? Liker he'd ate all he could swally in the last place he got the chance of layin' his hands on anythin'."

"Och, woman alive, but it's the fool you were to let him out of your sight," said Ody Rafferty's aunt. "If it had been me, I'd niver ha' took me eyes off him, for the look of him on'y goin' by made me flesh creep upon me bones."

"'Deed was I," said Mrs. Kilfoyle, sorrowfully, "a fine fool. And vexed she'd be, real vexed, if she guessed the way it was gone on us, for the dear knows what dirty ould rapscallions 'ill get the wearin' of it now. Rael vexed she'd be."

This speculation was more saddening than the actual loss of the cloak, though that bereft her wardrobe of far and away its most valuable property, which should have descended as an heirloom to her little Katty, who, however, being at present but three months old, lay sleeping happily unaware of the cloud that had come over her prospects.

"I wish to goodness a couple of the lads 'ud step home wid themselves this minit of time," said Mrs. M'Gurk. "They'd come up wid him yet, and take it off of him ready enough. And smash his ugly head for him if he would be givin' them any impidence."

"Aye, and 'twould be a rael charity—the mane baste—or sling him in one of the boghoules," said the elder Mrs. Keogh, a mild-looking little old woman. "I'd liefer than nine nine-pennies see thim comin' along. But I'm afeard it's early for thim yet."

Everybody's eyes turned, as she spoke, towards the ridge of the Knockawn, though with no particular expectation of seeing what they wished upon it. But, behold, just at that moment three figures, blurred among the grey rain-mists, looming into view.

"Be the powers," said Mrs. M'Gurk, jubilantly, "it's Ody Rafferty himself. To your sowls! Now you've a great good chance, ma'am, to be gettin' it back. He's the boy 'ill leg it over all before him"—for in those days Ody was lithe and limber—"and it's hard-set the thievin' Turk 'ill be to get the better of him at a racin' match—Hi—Och." She had begun to hail him with a call eager and shrill, which broke off in a strangled croak, like a young cock's unsuccessful effort. "Och, murdher, murdher, murdher," she said to the bystanders, in a disgusted undertone. "I'll give you me misfort'nit word thim other two is the pólis."

Now it might seem on the face of things that the arrival of those two active and stalwart civil servants would have been welcomed as happening just in the nick of time; yet it argues an alien ignorance to suppose such a view of the matter by any means possible. The men in invisible green tunics belonged completely to the category of pitaty-blights, rint-warnin's, fevers, and the like devastators of life, that dog a man more or less all through it, but close in on him, a pitiful quarry, when the bad seasons come and the childer and the old crathurs are starvin' wid the hunger, and his own heart is broke; therefore to accept assistance from them in their official capacity would have been a proceeding most reprehensibly unnatural. To put a private quarrel or injury into the hands of the peelers were a disloyal making of terms with the public foe; a condoning of great permanent wrongs for the sake of a trivial temporary convenience. Lisconnel has never been skilled in the profitable and ignoble art of utilising its enemies. Not that anybody was more than vaguely conscious of these sentiments, much less attempted to express them in set terms. When a policeman appeared there in an inquiring mood, what people said among themselves was: "Musha cock him up. I hope he'll get his health till I would be tellin' him," or words to that effect; while in reply to his questions they made statements superficially so clear and simple, and essentially so bewilderingly involved, that the longest experience could do little more for a constable than teach him the futility of wasting his time in attempts to disentangle them.

Thus it was that when Mrs. Kilfoyle saw who Ody's companions were, she bade a regretful adieu to her hopes of recovering her stolen property. For how could she set him on the Tinker's felonious track without apprising them likewise? You might as well try to huroosh one chicken off a rafter and not scare the couple that were huddled beside it. The impossibility became more obvious presently as the constables striding quickly down to where the group of women stood in the rain and wind with fluttering shawls and flapping cap-borders, said briskly, "Good-day to you all. Did any of yous happen to see e'er a one of them tinkerin' people goin' by here this mornin'?"

It was a moment of strong temptation to everybody, but especially to Mrs. Kilfoyle, who had in her mind that vivid picture of her precious cloak receding from her along the wet road, recklessly wisped up in the grasp of as thankless a thievin' black-hearted slieveen as ever stepped, and not yet, perhaps, utterly out of reach, though every fleeting instant carried it nearer to that hopeless point. However, she and her neighbours stood the test unshaken. Mrs. Ryan rolled her eyes deliberatively, and said to Mrs. M'Gurk, "The saints bless us, was it yesterday or the day before, me dear, you said you seen a couple of them below near ould O'Beirne's?"

And Mrs. M'Gurk replied, "Ah, sure, not at all, ma'am, glory be to goodness. I couldn't ha' tould you such a thing, for I wasn't next or nigh the place. Would it ha' been Ody Rafferty's aunt? She was below there fetchin' up a bag of male, and bedad she came home that dhreeped, the crathur, you might ha' thought she'd been after fishin' it up out of the botthom of one of thim boghoules."

And Mrs. Kilfoyle heroically hustled her Thady into the house as she saw him on the brink of beginning loudly to relate his encounter with the strange man, and desired him to whisht and stay where he was in a manner so sternly repressive that he actually remained there as if he had been a pebble dropped into a pool, and not, as usual, a cork to bob up again immediately.

Then Mrs. M'Gurk made a bold stroke, designed to shake off the hampering presence of the professionals, and enable Ody's amateur services to be utilised while there was yet time.

"I declare," she said, "now that I think of it, I seen a feller crossin' the ridge along there a while ago, like as if he was comin' from Sallinbeg ways, and accordin' to the apparence of him I wouldn't won'er if he *was* a one of thim tinker crathurs—carryin' a big clump of cans he was, at any rate—I noticed the shine of thim. And he couldn't ha' got any great way yet to spake of, supposin' there was anybody lookin' to folly after him."

But Constable Black crushed her hopes as he replied, "Ah, it's nobody comin' *from* Sallinbeg that we've anything to say to. There's after bein' a robbery last night down below at Jerry Dunne's—a shawl as good as new took, that his wife's ragin' over frantic, along wid a sight of fowl and other things. And the Tinkers that was settled this long while in the boreen at the back of his haggard is quit out of it afore daylight this mornin', every rogue of them. So we'd have more than a notion where the property's went to if we could tell the road they've took. We thought like enough some of them might ha' come this way."

Now Mr. Jerry Dunne was not a popular person in Lisconnel, where he has even become, as we have seen, proverbial for what we call "ould naygurliness." So there was a general tendency to say, "The divil's cure to him," and listen complacently to any details their visitors could impart. For in his private capacity a policeman, provided that he be otherwise "a dacint lad," which, to do him justice, is commonly the case, may join, with a few unobtrusive restrictions, in our neighbourly gossips; the rule, in fact, being—Free admission except on business.

Only Mrs. Kilfoyle was so much cast down by her misfortune that she could not raise herself to the level of an interest in the affairs of her thrifty suitor, and the babble of voices relating and commenting sounded as meaningless as the patter of the drops which jumped like little fishes in the large puddle at their feet. It had spread considerably before Constable Black said to his comrade—

"Well, Daly, we'd better be steppin' home wid ourselves as wise as we come, as the man said when he'd axed his road of the ould black horse in the dark lane. There's no good goin' further, for the whole gang of them's scattered over the counthry agin now like a seedin' thistle in a high win'."

"Ay bedad," said Constable Daly, "and be the same token, this win' ud skin a tanned elephant. It's on'y bogged and drenched we'd git. Look at what's comin' up over there. That rain's snow on the hills, every could drop of it; I seen Ben Bawn this mornin' as white as the top of a musharoon, and it's thickenin' wid sleet here this minute, and so it is."

The landscape did indeed frown upon further explorations. In quarters where the rain had abated it seemed as if the mists had curdled on the breath of the bitter air, and they lay floating in long white bars and reefs low on the track of their own shadow, which threw down upon the sombre bogland deeper stains of gloom. Here and there one caught on the crest of some grey-bouldered knoll, and was teazed into fleecy threads that trailed melting instead of tangling. But towards the north the horizon was all blank, with one vast, smooth slant of slate colour, like a pent-house roof, which had a sliding motion onwards.

Ody Rafferty pointed to it and said, "Troth, it's teemin' powerful this instiant up there in the mountains. 'Twill be much if you land home afore it's atop of you; for 'twould be the most I could do myself."

And as the constables departed hastily, most people forgot the stolen cloak for a while to wonder whether their friends would escape being entirely drownded on the way back from the fair.

Mrs. Kilfoyle, however, still stood in deep dejection at her door, and said, "Och, but she was the great fool to go let the likes of him set fut widin her house."

To console her Mrs. O'Driscoll said, "Ah, sure, sorra a fool were you, woman dear; how would you know the villiny of him? And if you'd turned the man away widout givin' him e'er a bit, it's bad you'd be thinkin' of it all the day after."

And to improve the occasion for her juniors, old Mrs. Keogh added, "Ay, and morebetoken you'd ha' been committin' a sin."

But Mrs. Kilfoyle replied with much candour, "'Deed, then, I'd a dale liefer be after committin' a sin, or a dozen sins, than to have me poor mother's good cloak thieved away on me, and walkin' wild about the world."

As it happened the fate of Mrs. Kilfoyle's cloak was very different from her forecast. But I do not think that a knowledge of it would have been consolatory to her by any means. If she had heard of it, she would probably have said, "The cross of Christ upon us. God be good to the misfort'nit crathur." For she was not of at all an implacable temper, and would, under the circumstances, have condoned even the injury that obliged her to appear at Mass with a flannel petticoat over her head until the end of her days. Yet she did hold the Tinkers in a perhaps somewhat too unqualified reprobation. For there are tinkers and tinkers. Some of them, indeed, are stout and sturdy thieves, veritable birds of prey, whose rapacity is continually questing for plunder. But some of them have merely the magpies' and jackdaws' thievish propensity for picking up what lies temptingly in their way. And some few are so honest that they pass by as harmlessly as a wedge of high-flying wild duck. And I have heard it said that to places like Lisconnel their pickings and stealings have at worst never been so serious a matter as those of another flock, finer of feather, but not less predacious in their habits, who roosted, for the most part, a long way off, and made their collections by deputy.

CHAPTER IV

A GOOD TURN

ALONG the road to Sallinbeg little seemed to be abroad besides foul weather, but there was a great deal of that. The gusts that came flapping wide-winged over the bog met the wayfarer with a furious hurtle and grapple, as if for want of better sport they had concentrated all their forces upon his sole repulse; and the drops they dashed into his blinded eyes and against his benumbed hands were as icy as they could be without ceasing to be wet. Their combined assaults were calculated feelingly to persuade a man of his uninfluential position in the scheme of things—his voice in this matter was so tyrannically howled down—or, if of less philosophic mind, to bring home to him the special disadvantages of going half-starved and clad in threadbare tatters. This was the plight of Thady Quinlan as, leaving Lisconnel, soon lapt out of sight behind him amid the grey web of the rain-mists, he tramped haltingly away, with Mrs. Kilfoyle's cloak bundled under his arm, and the dread of pursuit on his mind, and in his heart a great remorse, the object of which you are perhaps guessing wrongly. But he had also a hope and a purpose, and is therefore not wholly to be pitied, although the one did wane until the other looked impossible, as mile after mile unrolled its drenched and dreary length without bringing him apparently nearer to his goal.

All the while, however, he was slowly gaining upon a traveller, who had taken the same road a few hours earlier, hopelessly and aimlessly, and even more inadequately equipped than he. It was his sister Judy Quinlan, from whom he had parted on the worst of terms about three o'clock that morning. The fact is that the Tinkers' raid upon Jerry Dunne's premises, although carried out with unusual success, had led, not at all unusually, to complications when it was time to divide the spoil. Over Mrs. Dunne's second-best shawl it was that the difficulty arose. Mrs. Dunne, despite her husband's thrifty turn, owned many shawls, few of them inferior enough to be worn at all frequently, and she had pinned on this one three times only during the half-dozen years of her proprietresship. So it was certainly bitter bad luck that she should by chance have worn it to Confession on Friday, and got it soaked coming home, and hung it up in the passage by the back door to dry slowly, "instead of to be all cockled into gathers wid the heat of the fire blazin' on it, you stookawn," as she explained with exasperation to Ellen Roe, her servant-girl, who had officiously suggested the kitchen hearth. For this precaution proved tragically self-defeating, and put its object into the very hands of Thady Quinlan and Joe Smith, when, under cover of the wild, wet night, they forced the feeble lock, and made a clean sweep of all portable property that lay within easy reach. The shawl formed the most valuable prize. It was very admirable, indeed, being of a dappled fawn colour, with an arabesque border of shaded chocolate and amber; but in the eyes of its new owners its greatest charm was its weight and thickness. Judy Quinlan declared, pinching a fold fondly between a finger and thumb, that just the feel of it done your heart good. Her own shawl was really only a ragged cotton table-cover, and had, as she often remarked, "no more warmth in it than an ould dish-clout." I should observe, to make the situation clear, that the Tinkers' confraternity at this time consisted of Thady Quinlan and his sister Judy, and their married sister Maggie Smith, with her husband, and his brother, and his father, and three or four children. Hence it is obvious that in any dispute which might arise between Judy and Maggie, the latter was likely to have numbers preponderantly upon her side. And this was what now actually took place, the place being the driest end of the un-roofed cabin in Dunne's boreen, where the Tinkers had for some time past made their camp.

The screed of thatch still adhering to the wall sheltered their fire of purloined sods, and it burned steadily and strongly between the blasts which made its red flame duck and sweel, and sent the white ash-flakes fluttering. So there was light enough to show how covetous gleams from the sisters' eyes flashed together on the shawl, of which each held a corner. And no great wisdom was needed to forecast a storm. Mrs. Smith's shawl was undeniably better than Judy's by many degrees; but she had not the magnanimity to consider this, even so far as to propose that Judy should at any rate enjoy the reversion of her own. On the contrary, she had rapidly planned its division between her two little ragged girls. Judy, for her part, had set her heart desperately upon the acquisition, and she deemed it her best policy to say in a tone studiously matter-of-course:

"Faix, now, it's glad enough I'll be to get shut of this ould wad that's on me. Every breath of win' goes thro' it as ready as if it was a crevice in a wall, fit to freeze you into mortar."

A very vain device, for her sister promptly rejoined with a sarcastic laugh and a tightened grip: "Musha moyah, how bad you are entirely. Don't you wish you may?" which intimated plainly that the shawl was not to be had uncontested.

At this crisis Judy had fully expected to be backed up by Thady; but he naturally taking a more dispassionate view of the matter, recognised with reluctance the futility of pitting himself singly against three opponents, two of them better men than he, who was "no great things at all, let alone havin' one knee quare." Therefore he turned his back upon the controversy, and feigned unconsciousness of it, instead of bouncing up and saying with appropriate action, "And I'd like to know who at all's got a better right to it than herself has?"

His defection aggrieved her so bitterly, that the fiercest of her wrath turned upon him; and after a wrangle wherein all the parties concerned had made liberal use of those "aculeate and proper" words against which the wary Bacon warns his quarrelling readers, she flounced away into the darkness of the small hours of the stormy December morning, loudly avowing her determination never to see a sight of the ugly, dirty, mane-spirited poltroon, or open her lips to him as long as she had an eye or a tongue in her head. Jeering laughter followed her exit on a skirl of sleet-fledged wind.

She seethed over her anger for many a long mile, to such fierceness was its flame fed by disappointment and more potent jealousy. For had not Thady, the only person she cared much about in all the world, turned against her and sided with Maggie, "who was always a greedy grabbin' little toad ever since she stood the height of a creepy stool?" It was an hour or so before daybreak when she sat down to rest under an immense bulging boulder that loomed dimly on her beside the road a little way beyond Lisconnel. Then she began to look backwards and forwards. Far back to the time when her father kept a little shop in Bantry, before he was stone broke one bad year and took to carrying the remnant of his stock-in-trade about in a basket as a higgler, which eventually led other members of his family to wander, less reputably, for their livelihoods. She remembered that even in those days Thady was always her ally, and had lamed himself for life by a fall on the road when running to rescue her from the Hutchinsons' wicked mastiff, who had knocked her down near their gate, and was standing over her with a growl and a grin of which she still sometimes dreamed. And again she remembered how once she had been laid up for a long while with the fever, and had crept out of the Union infirmary to find that her relations, supposing her dead, had all "tuk off wid thimselves to the States," and was keening like one demented over her desertion outside McNeight's public, when what should come familiarly round the corner but Thady himself, who had stopped behind, foregoing his assisted passage, because the divil a fut of him would stir out of it so long as there might be e'er a chance at all of Judy coming back. Whereupon it recurred vividly to her mind how she had just called him, among other things, "a great dirty, good-for-nothin' hulk of a poltroon," and had expressed a hope that she might never again see sign nor sight of any such a hijjis baste hobblin' anywheres on her road; to which he had rejoined that she might go to blazes and welcome for anythin' *he* had to say agin it, and that bedad a crosser-tempered ould weasel of a wizened-up ould witch wouldn't be apt to land there in a hurry. At last, being very tired, she escaped for a while from these fluctuations of wrath and ruth into a nook of sleep, but the bitter cold routed her out of it soon after sunrise, and she took the road again, cramped and numbed, in the teeth of the gusty showers that were still stalking over the bogland.

As she went, the hills beyond Sallinbeg rose up frowning before her through rifts in the cold white fleece trailed and knotted about their front of harsh purple gloom, on which the streaks and patches of ravines and fences and fields, with here and there a cabin gleaming, began by degrees to be traced dimly as if a fragment of the countryside were reflected on a dark thunder-cloud. But she was now thinking more about her journey's end than about anything she saw on the way thither—the bleak many-windowed workhouse at Moynalone that she well knew must be presently her fate. Since she had thrown herself on her own resources, three ha'pence was all she could command for ransom from the durance into which self-preservation assuredly would not forbear to betray her. Experience gave a dreary definiteness to anticipation. Once again she would morning by morning awaken in the grim whitewashed ward to all the old hardness and roughness of existence with a tyrannous restraint and monotony superadded. She said to herself, it is true, that she might as well be in one place as another, since she would not have Thady to go along with anymore—the black-hearted, thievin' miscreant—and if she had as much wit in her as an ould water-rat, she'd just creep away into some dry ditch, and be done with the whole of it. Still, as she did come short of that wisdom, the alternative continued to lie across her path, a murky shadow, which she could by no means evade nor disperse.

The invisible sun was low when Judy came to a place where the road forks, sending one branch to creep across the level bogland towards Sallinbeg, and one to climb up among the first tilted slopes of the mountains. Here the Rosbride river comes jostling its way down a rocky ravine spanned at the mouth by a bridge, past which the swift, brown stream darts along in a more spacious and smoother channel, bound for Rosbride Bay. Judy stood for a while and looked down over the parapet at the swirls of creamy foam that swept under the arch. Then she took out of her pocket a battered-looking heel of a loaf, and began to munch it. But before she had half finished it, she tossed the crust away into the river, being too heartsick to go on eating once the rage of hunger was subdued. She wished sincerely that she dared fling herself after it, but she was far too much cowed by cold and weariness to muster the courage for such a resolve. Perhaps there was not under Irish skies that December day, a more miserable woman than Judy Quinlan as she stood all alone in the world on Rosbride bridge, while a black mountain rampart lifted itself slowly against the shrouded west, and the dusk thickened on the long, shelterless road, whence eager blasts whistled a summons to her, nearer and nearer, till they fluttered her rags, and keened about her ears, and chilled her to the bone.

Suddenly something heavy and soft seemed to grasp her by the shoulders, and thence fall around her in long, wide folds, covering her from head to foot, much as if a small tent had been blown down on her. Of course she screamed shrilly, and almost in the same breath she saw that Thady was at her elbow. He had for some little time been stalking her warily, with the great coat expanded ready to throw over her, and having done so, was now holding it on with a rough hug. The joy with which he had at last caught sight of the forlorn, bedraggled figure had overflowed irrepressibly into this joke, and its successful accomplishment put the finishing touch to his happiness. As for Judy, if the sun had leaped up again in a fiery flurry, till the hills and the plain and the river were all flooded with flushed light, gleaming and glowing, it would have but dimly symbolised the transfiguration of her world. In the twinkling of an eye her stark despair was changed into rapturous relief, a miracle which just at first made the marvellous cloak seem almost a matter of course. Any good thing might naturally be expected to befall her since Thady was not estranged and lost to her after all. "Whethen now, and is it yourself come streelin' along?" she said. "You tuk your time, bedad. I'm here this half-hour."

"Sure, I stopped till I would get a thrifle of things together," said Thady. "And what d'you call that for an ould flitterjig?"

"It's not too bad," said Judy, stroking down

the cape with caressing fingers. "A grand weight there's in it, to be sure. But where at all did you come by it? You're not after gettin' it off of thim thievin' rapscallions of Smiths, anyway?"

"Thim or the likes of thim—sure not at all," said Thady, loftily. "'Twas in a house away down below there at Lisconnel. A young woman bid me step in to ait a pitaty, and, tellin' you the truth, I'd no fancy to be delayin', for I'd a mistrust in me mind that the pólis was follyin'. The notion I had was to ax her had she seen you goin' by, on'y I wasn't wishful to be lettin' on I was anythin' to you, in case they come along. So I thought she might be chance pass the remark herself. But out she ran, and the first thing I noticed was this consarn lyin' convanient to me hand in the windy. And wid that I whipped it up and made off. For anythin' I could tell, I might ha' met me fine gintleman full tilt at the door; and begorrah, it's as heavy to carry as a pair of fat geese. Howane'er, I knew it's distressed you were entirely for the want of such a thing, and bejabers, you've got it now."

"Troth have I," said Judy, delightedly groping her way about her new garment. "Rael dacint it was of you to be bringin' it to me, for perished and lost I did be, and that's no lie. Och but it's the grand one. Look at the hood there is to it. Sure it's as good as a little house of your own. You might be out under buckets of wet in it, and ne'er a tint you'd git whatever."

"Ay, or, for that matter, takin' a rowl through the river there, and sorra the harm it 'ud do you wid that on," said Thady, with pride. "But we'd better be quittin' out o' this," he added, with a shrug and a shiver, "for the win's tarrible, and there's a shower comin' up on us yonder as thick as thatch. I was thinkin' you'd maybe had thrampin' enough for this day. 'Twill be as dark prisintly as the inside of a cow, and we'd see daylight agin before we come to Moynalone. So we might put the night over under th'ould bridge. There's a good dry strip along the one side of it, and the way the rain's dhrivin' we'd git a grand shelter."

Judy readily agreed, and they descended the little stony footpath which led down to the river. Beneath the arch, where Thady's booted steps reverberated hollowly, they found, as he had said, a broadish strip of dry ground, for the bridge had allowed the stream ample measure in its stride. The little platform was bordered by a scattering of stones and boulders, amongst which the shallow water gurgled. It seemed to Thady and Judy that their quarters would be very tolerable; but they soon made a discovery which promised luxury indeed. This was a dead branch, which lay at one end of the arch, having evidently been floated down the current, and perhaps hauled out of the water by some thrifty body, who, however, had made no further use of it. Long ago that must have been, for it was dried and bleached till it glimmered through the dusk like an intricate white skeleton. Better fuel no one could desire. Thady made for it at once with knife and matchbox, and in a few minutes crackling flames were crunching up the twigs and gnawing at a log. The red light washed flickering over the wet walls, and was caught on the glancing of the water as it fled by, rapid and dark. Blue smoke trailed up lazily against the frame of the arch, blurring gleams of tossed foam as it melted out into the mist.

But a fire naturally suggested food, and Judy said ruefully, after feeling in her empty pocket: "It's starved wid the hunger you'll be, Thady, and the sorra a taste of anythin' have I in the world. 'Deed now, if I'd on'y known the way it 'ud be, and I passin' thim houses below in the boreen a while ago! I seen where there was a big cake of griddle-bread coolin' itself, laned agin the windy-ledge, and man nor mortal near it. I might ha raiched it down as aisy as puttin' me fut to the ground. But sure I was that knocked about wid one thing and another, I thought I wouldn't be bothered wid it, so I just left it where it was, I did so—may God forgive me," she said, with unfeigned contrition.

Thady, however, did not seem to share in her regrets. He was lifting his cluster of cans off his shoulders, and extracting from one of them a bundle tied up in a red handkerchief. "Is it starved you'd have us?" he said as he untied the first corner. "Starved! How are you?" And he continued to repeat: "Is it starvin' she said?" while he was undoing the several knots. When they were all unfastened, the handkerchief was seen to hold a number of eggs and a fair supply of broken bread. Thady might well scout the possibility of famishing. "That's somethin' like," he said, as he saw Judy surveying his stores, "and I've a shillin' somewheres besides."

"Glory be!" said Judy, looking as if she could scarcely realise a world with which they were so much beforehand.

"And we'll be givin' them a boil in a one of the little saucepans," said Thady. "Raw eggs do be ugly could brashes, and we've plinty of wather handy—lashins and lavins of dhrink runnin' on tap there, so to spake."

Supper was accordingly prepared on these simple lines with much success. They boiled many eggs and ate them, using their scraps of bread for plates—an expedient not unknown at far earlier banquets—and they scooped up water to drink out of the palms of their hands—also in an old-fashioned manner. But when they had finished Thady gave a comparatively modern touch to the entertainment by lighting his pipe. He occupied the nearest place to the fire, in consideration for the scarecrow-like raggedness of his garments, which now began to weigh upon Judy's mind amid the comfort of her magnificent wrap.

"Froze stiff you'll be in thim ould tatters, man alive," she said despondently. "Sure, you might as well be slingin' yourself round wid the ould wisps of spiders' webs up over your head for any substance there is in thim. I won'er, now, could I conthrive to reive the top-cape off of this. 'Twould be as good that way as a cloak apiece for the two of us."

Thady, however, said decidedly: "Blathers, not *at all*. Is it destroyin' it you'd be after? I'm plinty warm enough." And he rolled the big red handkerchief which had held the eggs into many folds about his neck, tucking it down under his coat-collar all round. "There was a surprisin' hate in it," he said.

By this time the dusk far and near had gloomed into darkness—the black beetle had scared away the grey moth. As Thady and Judy sat with their backs to the curving wall, they caught only fitful glimpses of the opposite one when any long-fronded flickers of the fire-light waved across and touched it. More often they fell short, and made quivering circles shine where they struck the broken water in the mid-stream. Without, beyond either arch, nothing was distinguishable except glimmers of white foam shaken and tossing. On the left, looking up the river, it seemed as if many spectral hands, borne nearer and nearer, came waving and beckoning out of the night, to pass by and away down the river, still beckoning and waving, carried further and further, on into the night again. Every now and then a waft of the wind sighed in on them along with the river, puffing about the flame and smoke, and blowing ice-cold in their faces. When it had passed Thady always inquired: "Is it warm at all, Jude?" and she always answered, drawing "its" folds together with ostentatious satisfaction: "Och scaldin'."

But between whiles there was little conversation to interrupt the monologue of the river, which seemed to find itself many voices under the bridge. The one unceasing rustle of the main stream was frayed along its margin into a myriad finer noises of murmuring and plashing, as the massed foliage on a bough dwindles at its edges into more delicate traceries of distinct sprays and leaves. Round some stones the water whispered mysteriously, coiling in and out of gurgling recesses, and against others it broke with a clear chiming tinkle as if elfin anvils rang; here it droned on with a bee's hum soft and steady, and here it chuckled and chirped, bubbling up in sudden little rapids and cascades. At Judy's feet was a thin flat stone, which rested loosely on the top of another, and flap-flapped, bobbing up and down as the ripple rose and fell. Sitting idle in the firelight, warmed and fed to unwonted contentment, Judy watched it half drowsily for a while. Presently she said:

"That's the very way the lid of our ould kettle

would be goin' at home when it was on the boil, and me poor mother 'ud bid us keep an eye on it—like enough to keep us out of divilmint. Och, but that was a cosy little room of a could night. D'you mind it, Thady?"

"Ay, sure," said Thady, "but it's one while ago."

"It is that. A matter of thirty year and more, anyway, since we owned the little shop. Sure now I remimber the day they shut it up, and put us out of it, as plain as if it was on'y this mornin'. Grand we that was childer thought it, because of somebody givin' us the ind of an ould jar of sweets out of the windy to pacify us. Bedad the fightin' we had over it was fit to ha' raised the town. But I grabbed meself a biggish lump of peppermint twist, and would be slinkin' behind me mother to finish it, and she talkin' at the door to ould Mrs. McClenaghan, and I heard her sayin' her heart was broke. So I got wond'rin' to myself if the raison was maybe that we'd ate it all on her. Och, but it's the quare foolishness people does be remimberin'!"

"Belike the raison of that is because it's as plinty as anythin' else wid thim," said Thady, cynically, "or maybe a trifle plintier."

"Sure we was on'y brats thim times," said Judy, apologetically. "For anythin' we could tell we might as well be streelin' about under the width of the sky like a string of wild duck, as stoppin' at home wid a roof over our misfort'nit heads. Ould Mrs. McClenaghan next door had a cloak the same pattern as this," Judy continued, selecting her memories with better judgment. "But 'twas all tatters at the bottom, not worth a bawbee to mine."

And Thady said with interest: "Had she now?"

"And as for me ould shawl," Judy went on, "it's been a scandal and a caution this last three or four year; droppin' in bits it is, and small blame to it. I wish I'd a penny for every mile I've tramped in it. Do you remimber the joke me mother had about it's bein' a conthráry thing that people thravellin' 'ud always begin a mile at the wrong ind? She'd be talkin' that way to hearten up me father; but as often as not he'd on'y let a roar at her to whisht, he was that discouraged. 'Twas a great wish he had, poor man, to git her back settled in a little place of her own before he was took. But 'twas in the big barracks of a Union at Monaghan——"

"Well, it's all one to the two of thim now anyway," said Thady, finding that Judy's reminiscences of their family history did not tend to enliven his meditations over his pipe.

"Ah sure, everythin' will be all one to the whole of us, plase God, one of these days," said Judy, who in her present mood could not easily have realised the keen contentions and scorching jealousies of the night before; "and when we get done with the thrampin', 'twill make little enough differ whether it's one mile we wint or twinty hunderd. On'y I'd liefer than a good dale thim two had had better luck wid it all. Cruel put about they were many a time, and wantin' the bit to keep the life in thim, and it just fretted out of thim in the ind I'm thinkin'. The thought of it comes agin a body when one's sittin' warm and snug," Judy said, gazing remorsefully round her shadowy, gusty lodging, and then into the flames, lighting up a bare earth-patch, and down at the dark folds that fell about her as she crouched on it. She seemed sunk into a reverie. But after a while she looked up and said without apparent relevance: "Heaven be her bed this night, the cratur. Thady, you heathen, we'd a right to be sayin' the Rosary before we git too stupid altogether. The eyes of you are droppin' into your head wid sleep this minnit."

"And me just after lightin' me pipe," remonstrated Thady.

"Ah thin, hurry up and finish it," said Judy, betraying by this injunction an invincible ignorance touching a man's sentiments towards his last screw of tobacco, "or else I'll be off sound. It's the fine warmth makes me sleepy. Sure wid this on me sorra a breath of could gits next or nigh me to be keepin' me awake."

"Och thin, wait till it's out," said Thady.

"I will so," said Judy. "Sling another stick on the fire, lad, the way you won't be perished sittin' there in thim woful ould rags. I've plinty of prayers I might be sayin' till you're ready."

But in a little while, Thady, lingering over his pipe, became aware, somewhat to his relief, that she had gone fast asleep, muffled up to the chin in her cloak, with her head leaning back against the stone wall. He sat and looked at her for some moments with an expression partly complacent and partly compunctious. "Bedad now the crathur was bein' perished alive before I brought that to her," he said to himself. "Very apt she was to be gettin' her death. 'Twas great luck I had entirely to pick it up. It's the hard life the likes of her has whatever thrampin' around. Ay, glory be to God, 'twas the best good turn iver I done her."

Just at the time when Thady the Tinker was making these reflections while the firelight flickered and the waters fleeted under Rosbride bridge, some mile or so higher up the stream, where the long mountain slopes are folded closer and steeper about it, a great turmoil had arisen in a deep hollow among walls of the bare rock. Down one face of these, a huge glistering slab, the river had for certain thousands of years been taking a foamy leap; but to-night it happened that the rains, beating for many days on the mountains, had eaten away the clay setting which cemented a ponderous lump of rock into a niche immediately over the fall, and the mass had now crashed down into the channel on the very verge, blocking all the waterway. This, however, was a door hard to keep shut, when every affluent rill and runnel out on the broad mountain shoulders went darting swift and white, so that every minute swelled the forces gathering pent in the barred passage. As the bridled torrent seethed and climbed, hissing, behind that barrier, the great stone tottered and swayed, and before the first foam-crest could overpeer it, yielded to the weight of waters leaned against it, and rocks and flood, thunderously roaring, rushed down together.

The sound of it, dulled into a moan, came through Rosbride bridge, and Thady, who had grown very drowsy, thought to himself that the wind was getting up, and that they couldn't have done better than stop where they were, instead of to be setting off tramping on such a dirty wild night. God knew where they might have got to.

The flood that broke away, with wave tumbled over wave, out of the whirling pool, had not far to race down its stony stairs before it reached a place with a turbulent floor, where the white mouths of other two streams foamed into it through rock-rifts, loud-throated on either hand. Thenceforward the water which had threaded the large boulders in heavy strands coiled like monstrous braids of snaky locks, rose up and drew together above their tallest heads into a single obliterating fold, as it slid on smoothly with only now and then a quiver puckering its surface, as if it had rolled over some live creature that writhed. Its mounded solidity made its rapid motion look strange and terrible. Where circles of thin froth swam round on it slowly, it was as black and white as a bit of the bog in a snowstorm or under a drift of summer daisies. At the turn of the ravine's last winding above the bridge, it plucked away as it passed a small company of fir-trees, that long had dropped their cones and needles into the river from a coign of vantage on a jutting crag, and a minute after, anybody who had looked up from beneath the arch would have seen the glimmering points of foam extinguished like lights, further and nearer, lost amid the shadowy onsweeping of something that set all the darkness astir as if it were one vast wing unfurling. And then for a moment, in the narrow space lit by the fading fire, he would have known that he was cut off from the world by chaos, which poised towards him a formless surging front, and stooped and fell. But as it happened nobody was keeping a watch there.

What wakened Thady was the clang of his cluster of tinware, which the wave dashed against the wall behind him. But before he knew this, it had gathered him up and swung him across with it over to the other side of the arch. There he caught hold of a twisted ivy-tod and a bough of mountain-ash, whence he dropped on the bank, and crawled up it out of reach, commenting in forcible language upon the occurrence, by which he was still astoundedly bewildered.

Judy, who was aroused in like manner, had her chance too. For a branch of the same tree crooked a friendly arm towards her as she was borne past, and she would have grasped it only that the weight of her heavy cloth cloak dragged her down. So that instead of returning to dry land for many a long day's tramp, she went out to sea in company with sundry wrenched-off boughs, and mats of heather, and bundles of withered bracken, and other such waifs and strays, none of which were ever again heard tidings of any more than they were inquired after in the lonely places they had left. Only for some stormy days the wrecked and sodden banks of the Rosbride river were haunted by a forlorn-looking object of a lame tramp, who sought vainly what his despair hoped to find. As he roamed about in it, he had just one spell of consolation, which he was often muttering over to himself. It was something he called, "The best turn, anyway, I iver done the crathur in her life.' Little enough, God knows, little enough, but the best good turn."

CHAPTER V

FORECASTS

WHEN Mrs. Joyce used in her last days to predict regretfully that her youngest daughter would never marry, she said a bold word, for at this time still Theresa's years fell short of twenty, and she was generally recognised as the prettiest girl to be seen at Mass in the small, ugly chapel down beyant near Ballybrosna. Some people, it is true, said that she was "just a fairy of a crathur, and too little for anythin'," and she was, no doubt, diminutive in size. Nor had she any brilliancy of colouring to make amends in a humming-bird's fashion for the insignificance of her proportions, resembling rather, with her dark eyes and hair, one of those filmy white blossoms which look the paler and frailer for their knots of ebon stamens, or the delicate moth who shows fine black pencillings among his pearly down. Still, nobody denied that she had "an uncommon purty face of her own," and the neighbours, moreover, always found her "plisant and frindly and gay enough," when they found her at all. But they remarked among themselves that one seldom seen e'er a sight of Therasa Joyce these times anywheres about. They supposed she was took up wid lookin' after her mother, who wasn't gettin' her health over well this good while back. I think myself that Theresa's invisibility could be only in part accounted for thus, as the explanation does not cover the fact that to slip the wrong side of the dyke, or turn aside among screening hillocks and hollows when she noticed the approach of her acquaintances, was the course she always adopted if she could achieve it without hurting anybody's feelings. Theresa much disliked doing this, as a rule, though she broke it on one occasion in a way that surprised and puzzled those who knew her best.

But whether Mrs. Joyce forecast the future rightly or wrongly, she had certainly an erroneous impression on her mind when, as often happened, she wound up her disconsolate musings by saying resentfully, "And the back of me hand to some I could name." If she had proceeded to do so, she would probably have mentioned persons who had done nothing to bring about the result she was deploring, and she never thought of connecting it with the events which had accompanied Ody Rafferty's flitting from the Three Mile Farm more than a twelvemonth before Denis O'Meara came to the place.

Until Ody took up his abode at Lisconnel he had always lived with his father, who farmed a remote bit of land out towards Lough Glenglas. It was a holding which had been wrested from the grip of a surrounding bog by earlier generations of Raffertys, who were a strenuous race; but in Ody's father's time their energies had taken a turn not conducive to reclamation, or even to the maintenance of what was already won. All Ody's many elder brethren—sisters there were none— had run wild, and ended by running it so far afield that the narrow, whitewashed house, lonesome and bleak, saw them no more. Its mistress also died, failing, perhaps, other means of exit—running wild being in her case impracticable—and finding life impossibly dreary without Ned, the least-good-for of her sons; and the household was thus reduced to old Michael Rafferty, and his aunt, and little Ody. These domestic changes, in conjunction with other untoward chances, sadly hindered farming operations, and nature made prompt use of the pause. Season by season the patch of tilled ground seemed to shrink at the wish of the greedy black land that girdled it about. The outlying fields grew first garish with golden ragweed and scarlet poppies, and then dull green again with the brown-knotted rushes and sombre sedge, and all other marsh growths, until the re-annexation was complete, and they once more were homogeneous part and parcel of the conquering bog. Old Michael used to trudge heavily round his dwindling territories, which were haunted by memories of better days. There had been a time when they had actually "kep' a pair of plough-horses." I believe that he would have fretted his heart out much sooner than he did if it had not been for Ody, his only remaining son, "whose aquils," his aunt Moggy sometimes remarked rather bitterly, "he consaited you wouldn't find plintier in the world than an apple sittin' on a sloe-bush." As the boy grew up the old man's pride and pleasure in him were tempered by apprehensions lest he should "take off wid himself like the other lads." However, Ody never did this nor anything worse than wax somewhat over-confident and self-opiniated; and a year or so before his father's death he became associated with Felix O'Beirne in the management of an illicit still off away in the bog, which gave him an object in life, and had a sobering and settling effect upon him.

He was not more than twenty when his father suddenly died one early spring morning, and he found himself left responsible for a few acres well cropped with weeds, and sundry arrears of rent to be extracted from their produce. Whereupon he resolved to abandon the struggle, and set up on a less ambitious footing in one of the cabins at Lisconnel. So he got ready for the move by selling off his little bit of live stock, all except Rory, the old black pony, who had a very large head and a white face like a grotesque mask, and with whom he would not have parted on the most tempting terms. As for his great-aunt Moggy, when she heard of this arrangement, she resigned herself to her fate, which was obviously the Union away at Moynalone. What else should become of her, since she was past field-work, and nobody could expect Ody now to be bothered with keeping her idle, and he with scarce a penny to his name after settling with Mr. Nugent. "Ody," she reflected, "didn't mind a thraneen what way he had things in the house, and didn't care to be keepin' fowls, so what good 'ud he get out of her at all?" Moggy was a dull and rather cross-tempered old person, who had grown up in souring shade, and never had a life of her own to live, nor yet a faculty for slipping smoothly into other people's. Her slight intercourse with Ody had hitherto chiefly consisted of quarrels. In fact, only the day before his father's death, they had fallen out abusively about the broiling of some bacon, and this seemed to make her destination all the more inevitable. Therefore Moggy likewise set about her few dismal preparations, oppressed by a stunned sense that the black hour she had been dreading most of her life was now just going to strike.

On the morning of the day Ody was to flit she held a sort of carouse at her solitary breakfast over the remnant of a pound of tea which she had saved after the wake. Tea was ten prices fifty years ago, and a very rare luxury at the Three Mile Farm. As she poured it strong and black out of the badly broken teapot, the whole one being packed up, she thought that was the last time she'd ever have the chance again in this world to be wetting herself a cup of tea, and she thickened it recklessly with lumps of damp brown sugar, and swung it round in her cracked saucer to cool, and tried hard to enjoy it. She was still lingering over it when Ody came into the kitchen, which caused her, poor soul, instinctively to thrust away the betraying teapot out of sight on the black hob.

"What way was you intindin' to go, then, aunt?" said Ody.

"To Moynalone?" she said, turning to face her future with a deep sinking of heart. "Sure, I suppose it's trampin' over I'll be."

"And I won'er how long you think to be doin' it," said Ody—"a matter of ten mile?"

"Where's the hurry at all, supposin'?" said his aunt, desperately.

"Blathers!" said Ody, "there's room in the cart waitin' ready. You'd be better bundlin' yourself into it than to be sittin' here all the mornin' delayin' us."

"'Deed, then, beggars drive as chape as they walk," she said, "and I might as well be gettin' the lift as far as you can take me."

The old white-faced pony preferred to pace slowly on the long bog-road, and, as Ody always respected his whims, the journey barely ended with the March daylight. The old, sad-visaged woman sat all the while under her muffling shawl in silent apathy undisturbed, and as during the latter stages of the drive a blinking drowsiness co-operated with her want of interest in the scenes through which she jogged, she naturally looked around her in bewilderment when roused by the jerk of the stopping cart. She expected to find herself in the streets of Moynalone, drawn up, probably, at the door of the big Union workhouse. But, instead of its long rows of casements staring down blankly on her, she saw only the one mole's-eye window of a tiny whitewashed cabin peering at her from beneath its thatched eaves, and all about it the great lonely bog spreading away with never a trace of any town.

"Och, wirrasthrew, man, what are you after doin' on me?" she said, beginning to bewail herself querulously. "Sure you haven't brought me to any place at all. Every hour of the black night it'ill be afore ever I'll get there now, and the Union'ill be shut, and what's to become of me then I dunno. You'd a right to ha' tould me——"

"Blathers!" said her nephew, "git down out of that wid your yawpin'. D'you want the folk here to think you're a sackful of ould hins? And go in and be seein' after a bit of fire; it's late enough to be sure. What fool's talk have you about the Union, and bad luck to it? You'll find the things for the supper in the inside of the ould churn. Union, moyah!"

And old Moggy, alighting with cramped limbs, entered her home at Lisconnel, feeling blissfully as if she had been *unpacked* out of a most horrible nightmare.

Ody was probably actuated by several unassorted motives in dealing thus with his superfluous old great-aunt. Pride and pity and perversity and generosity—all had, no doubt, some influence upon his conduct, while long use and wont had unawares given her the same sort of hold upon his affections that was possessed in a much higher degree by Rory, the pony, whose humours were of course easier to put up with than human foibles. But the old woman measured his magnanimity by the immensity of the benefit which it had conferred upon her, and with a strong revulsion of feeling she formed an opinion of his virtues and talents as exalted quite as that which she had often secretly jibed at in his father. Accordingly she sang his praises unweariedly among their new neighbours, and, as Ody was vain enough not to dislike the echoes which reached him, he soon began to look upon her with more complacency, so that they agreed much better than heretofore. She found no small solace, too, after her long cronyless isolation up at the Three Mile Farm, in the company of Mrs. Joyce, and Mrs. Keogh, and the other Lisconnel dames. In short, a kind of Indian summer of content seemed to be setting in for her. Moggy's mind, however, was of the self-tormenting type, and soon devised means of marring it. They took the form of apprehensions that Ody would presently get married, and that thereupon "the wife would put her out of it." If she had only known, Ody was at this time, as for many years ensuing, far too much taken up with himself, and Rory, and "the little consarn away in the bog," to entertain any such project; but as it was she felt that the event, with all its direful consequences, perpetually hung over her, and might at any moment bring her new prosperity to a miserable end. Her impending great-niece-in-law was a vaguely appalling spectre, who threatened to take the roof from over her head, and the bit out of her mouth, and turn her adrift to founder hopelessly on the workhouse doorsteps. But it was not until more than a year after their settlement at Lisconnel that she endued her bogey with one definite form, by making up her mind that Ody "was thinkin' of Theresa Joyce."

Her reason was that she had one fine evening seen him carrying Theresa's water-pail for her down the hill, an ordinary act of courtesy enough, but the sight of which suddenly darkened the world before her foolish old eyes more dismally than if the golden fleece of the summer sunset had been smothered under the blackest pall ever woven in cloud-looms. "Fine colloguin' they're havin' together," she said to herself as she watched them and their long shadows down the slope, "and he sloppin' the half of it over the edge instead of mindin' what he's doin'. It's throwin' me out on the side of the road she'll be." In reality Theresa was wondering why there would be, a quare black sidimint like, in the water on some days and not on others; and Ody was explaining the phenomenon confidently and erroneously on an extemporised theory of his own. But to old Moggy's fears it seemed quite possible that they might be fixing the wedding-day. For Theresa Joyce herself she had no manner of misliking at all, considering her to be "a very dacint plisant-spoken little girl," but Mrs. Ody Rafferty seemed none the less certain to evict her without remorse. And Ody's aunt retired to rest that night in a despondent mood.

It was just about this time that Denis O'Meara came to stay at Lisconnel on sick leave. The O'Mearas lived in one of the three cabins which used to stand near the O'Beirne's forge, but which the great Famine and Fever year left tenantless for ever after. Their household consisted of the two infirm old people with their melancholy middle-aged son Tim, and their sickly grandson, little Joe Egan, who was Denis's cousin. Now Denis had been wounded in a battle somewhere out in India, and had been promoted sergeant—"and he but a young boyo so to spake"—and owned four medals, and stood six foot three in his stockings, and was as fine a figure of a man as you could wish to see, let alone his gorgeous scarlet uniform, which was a sight to behold; so if he was not a hero, get me one, as we say in Lisconnel. But Lisconnel was quite satisfied with him in that worshipful character, and found it very easy to adopt the appropriate attitude towards him. For Denis was good-natured and cheerful and never conceited at all, nor vain when there was anything more to the purpose for him to be; qualities which have an irresistible fascination in distinguished personages and make their followers' duty a pleasure. It was wonderful how his sojourn enlivened everybody, even his mournful little old grandmother, whose gratification expressed itself chiefly in regrets that his poor father and mother had not lived to see the illigant man he'd grown. When she said this to the younger matrons of Lisconnel, they thought that the crathurs' fate was commiserable indeed, and earnestly hoped that they themselves would be spared, plase God, to witness the splendid careers that lay before their own Denises at present playing among the puddles. But the older ones had to content themselves with the knowledge that if they had only just so happened to get the same chances, their own lads would have done the very same things; a fact which seemed to give them a sort of hypothetical proprietorship in Denis's glory. His presence brightened up society as a tall poppy brightens up all a sombre potato-plot, and his conversation brought strange lands and extraordinary events within one remove—a single pair of eyes and ears—of everybody's experience. For many years after "the summer we had Denis O'Meara up here" made a vivid time-mark in our annals; and I fancy that the stories of some of his exploits, with their outlines looming large through a mythical mistiness, still float in our atmospere. There is at least one legend relating how a soldier out in the East cut off a mad elephant's head at a stroke of his sabre, with the hero of which Denis O'Meara could probably be identified. Altogether he was so exceptionally brilliant a figure both in himself and in his fortunes, that the interest which he excited had no element of envy in it, as might have been the case had emulation seemed less utterly beyond everybody's reach.

Next to his cousin, Joe Egan, a stunted, starved-looking sprissawn of a lad, perhaps the most appreciative of his admirers was big Hugh McInerney, whom people were apt to call an omadhawn. He also was, comparatively speaking, a stranger at Lisconnel, having come there only that spring to give John O'Driscoll a hand with the building of his mud cabin, after which he stayed about doing what odd jobs offered at that slack season of the year. Now and then he tramped on distillery business for Felix O'Beirne, and generally acquitted himself in a manner which appeared worthy of contempt to young Ody Rafferty, who was his companion on these expeditions. Ody expressed his opinion in unqualified terms, saying, "Sure it 'ud disgust you to see him moonin' along like an ould donkey strayed out of a fair." But his senior partner, rather to his annoyance, persisted in replying, "But, mind you, the chap's no fool." He had nobody belonging to him at Ballybrosna, whence he came, and some people said that he had been a workhouse child.

At the time of Denis O'Meara's arrival, he was darning the widow Joyce's thatch for her, and "not killin' himself ever the job," as people said, when they reckoned how many days he had been visible crawling about on the top of her little house, a conspicuous position in which he looked, Mrs. Con Ryan remarked, "a quarer great gawk than he did on dry lan'." He was occupied thus on the first afternoon that Denis walked up there with some of the other lads, and while they talked to Mrs. Joyce and Theresa underneath, the thatcher took a leisurely and critical survey of the scarlet and golden newcomer, from his wonderfully polished boots to his sleek dark head and fierce moustache. The verdict he pronounced to himself with unfeigned satisfaction was, "Grandeur's no name for him." Hugh himself, of large and lumbering frame, had a shag of reddish flaxen hair, which made thatch-like eaves above his small, light-blue eyes and high burnt-brick-coloured cheek-bones. He wore whitey-brown rags. After the rest had gone on and in, he slithered down to the ground and told Theresa, who was still standing by the door, that she didn't look the size of a bit of a lady-bird beside the soldier fellow. If anybody else had made this personal remark, Theresa might have been a little hurt by it, as she wished herself of more imposing stature; but sure nobody minded poor Hugh McInerney; at any rate she said, "Aye, he's a terrible big man, isn't he? Apt to knock the head off himself he'd be if he was offerin' to come in at our door."

However, on the very next day Denis contrived to accomplish that feat without any such accident when he called in at the Joyces' to ask was his grandmother there—which she was not, nor indeed likely to be. Failing to find the old woman, he postponed his quest for the present and stayed talking to Theresa, who, as it happened, was at home; and then he stopped again outside to help Hugh McInerney by handing him up some rolls of green-sodded scraws and slippery bundles of rushes. His long reach made him serviceable here, though his left arm was still partially disabled by the sabre-cut that had invalided him. The gleam of the red coat at the Joyces' door had apparently as fascinating an effect upon Lisconnel as if the place had been inhabited by a population that bellowed and gobbled its greetings instead of saying, "How's yourself, lad?" and "It's a grand day, thank God," as it came sauntering up dispersedly from various quarters. Before many minutes had passed quite a numerous group were collected, for in these long midsummer days there is little to be done up here except save the turf, a business which fine weather makes short work of. In the weeks before the potato-digging, employment becomes as scarce as the pitaties themselves, and the hours hang limp and flaccid between the meals which punctuate them with a plateful of coarse-grained gruel. Therefore to Christy Sheridan and Terence Kilfoyle, with half a dozen of their neighbours, the sight of their distinguished visitor was an oasis in a very arid desert, and they made towards it thirstily.

By and by the group drifted away from the road before the Joyces' house into the rough sward behind it; rather literally drifted, as the cause of the move was the wind, a strong soft west wind which had been blowing over the bog all the morning in great wide gusts. They seemed to lean hard against whatever they met, and made standing still an effort, and devastated conversation by carrying off important fragments of it uncaught, no matter how loudly one bawled. But the big boulders and furze-clumps strewn about in a slight depression close by offered seats and shelter opportunely; so amongst them presently appeared Denis O'Meara's scarlet tunic, and Theresa Joyce's brown-striped shawl, and Mrs. Ryan's white-frilled flapping cap, which she said was bein' fluttered to destruction off her ould head, and Hugh McInerney's many-rifted caubeen, for he declared that until the flurry of the blast went down a bit you might as well be lettin' on to thatch the sails whirlin' of a win'mill. And the rest of the company following suit might be described in terms of their attire as for the most part sad-coloured and dilapidated. It was just such a gathering as may be sitting to sun themselves at Lisconnel this day—if it happens to be a fine summer one—but with a touch of brilliance, both for eye and ear, added by the young soldier's presence. They had, however, but fitful gleams to bask in, for the sky was all feathered over with little silver-white plumes, which the wind kept ruffling by so fast that the light flickered in and out continually, as if it had come through a canopy of large slowly waving leaves. Still, they gossiped beneath it with much satisfaction, and catechised Denis about his adventures, and told him all the news of the countryside; and there seemed to be no particular reason why they should not go on doing so indefinitely. What in the end broke up the assembly was a slight mishap that befell Theresa Joyce.

It cannot be denied that Theresa was rather vain about her long black hair, which she had only of late begun to put up in thick silken coils. Her mother said you had to take your two hands to a one of them, like as if you were twisting a big *suggawn* (hay-rope); and they looked almost too heavy for her small head, no matter how closely they were wound about it. A rippling wave, moreover, ran through these tresses, which were exceedingly soft and fine; so her vanity was perhaps excusable. At any rate, it led her to fashion herself a small knot of cherry-coloured ribbon made of a bit that had trimmed the sleeve of her mother's purple merino gown. It was a *very* small knot, because most of the bit had got mildewed lying up, before Theresa grew to concern herself about such things. But it looked as bright in her hair as a ruddy berry on a dark foliaged creeper, and she wore it with a pleasure, which was destined to be brief. For as she sat knitting with the quietly creeping fingers of an expert in that art, a vagrant gust maliciously whisked off her little gawd, and tossing it contumeliously on the ground, as if it were not worth carrying, began to puff it along, skimming over the heather and tussocks. Denis O'Meara all but rescued it for her, only that Hugh McInerney—the omadhawn—starting forward at the same time, blundered up against him, and tumbled with him into a furze-bush. And before they picked themselves up, the cherry-coloured knot had met its fate in the shape of the Ryans' black and white kid. She was tethered close by, and had been apparently absorbed in scratching her forehead with her left hind foot in a way that said much for the limberness of her youthful joints. But as the bit of ribbon flirted past her she made a rapid snatch, and swallowed it at a gulp. Mrs. Ryan stood dismayed at possible serious consequences to the kid, and Theresa at the certain loss of her scrap of finery; and everybody else was saying to Hugh McInerney: "Och, you great omadhawn, why couldn't you keep yourself aisy? He had it safe enough on'y for you gettin' under his feet"—everybody, that is, except Denis O'Meara, who said: "Sure now the both of us wasn't mindin' rightly where we was chargin' to; and the raison of that belike was the nayther of us thinkin' so much of what we was runnin' after, as of who we was runnin' for—and small blame to us bedad."

But Hugh's self-esteem was not restored by the good-natured excuse. He said: "Truth it is, I'd a right to ha' sted quiet.. For the on'y notion I had was puttin' meself for'ard to be gettin' a hould of it before any of the others." And he walked off crestfallen to resume his perch on the thatch.

As for Theresa, she ignored Denis's pretty speech, and said 'deed now she remembered her mother had bid her step up and see what way Ody Rafferty's aunt was that morning. And she, too, withdrew from the group to make this visit of inquiry.

As she passed on her way under the place

where Hugh was thatching, he dropped a small handful of rushes on her head to call her attention, and when she looked up she saw his red-brick-hued face in a wild tow-coloured halo peering down at her from over the eaves. "I am sorry I lost it on you," he said.

"Ah, no matter about it; and it wasn't your fau't more than another's," said Theresa.

"You'd ha' had it now," said Hugh, "if it wasn't for the little goat gettin' the chance to ait it while himself was tumblin' over me. But I'd as lief have your hair the way it is now. It is the blackest ever I seen. One might think you'd gathered it out of the middles of them red poppies there. Stick a couple of them in it, if you want anythin'; but to my mind it's better widout. On'y if you've the fancy to be tyin' the bit of red string through it, I'm sorry it was ate."

Hugh's head drew back, and disappeared from her view; but next moment she heard him say mournfully: "What am I after doin'? Puttin' me fut that far down a houle it's caught fast between a couple of rafters. Firrm it is, begorrah. If I don't mind what I'm at, it's pullin' the half of their house down, and wranchin' me ankle I'll be before I free meself." And she saw him struggling cautiously on the roof all the while she was ascending the slope to Ody Rafferty's door, within which his aunt was at present a prisoner.

A reluctant and repining one she was, having been seized with a bad attack of lumbago at a time when she felt particularly anxious to keep a vigilant eye upon what occurred in her neighbourhood, instead of being left dependent upon hearsay for a knowledge of anything happening outside her four draughty walls. Many a care-infested hour she fretted away between them. For how could she tell with what insidious steps the calamity to ensue from Ody's courtship of Theresa Joyce might all the while be stealing on her? She dared not confide her fears to any neighbour, nor would she have put much faith in the report of observation unwhetted thereby; and she lived in daily dread of hearing the news announced as no mere conjecture or rumour, but a very hard fact. As the days wore on the idea took possession of her more and more completely, but she could only wreak her helpless ill-humour by doing foolish and futile things, such as dilating to Ody upon the imprudence of getting married, and the undesirable qualities of black-looking slips of colleens—a simple and ingenious expedient for putting him out of conceit with all and any of them; while she assumed towards Theresa a demeanor so glum and repellent that the girl could not attribute it entirely to the irritability caused by rheumatic twinges, and from one of her charitably intentioned visits returned with a disconcerted expression, and a resolve, which she kept, to pay no more. But in fact Ody was during these weeks even more than usually engrossed by the affairs of the inobtrusive little manufactory, which he and Felix O'Beirne superintended away in a retired part of the bog; and not they alone, but Lisconnel collectively, had been going through some excitement on this account. This was occasioned by the livelier interest which the police had recently manifested in that branch of home industry, stimulated by admonitions from their authorities to the effect that the hunting down of illicit stills, and confiscation of the produce, might with advantage be carried on more energetically. Hence had resulted several appearances in Lisconnel of the constabulary from Ballybrosna and other stations, and when these occurred Ody was in his element of wiles and stratagems. More than once he enjoyed the moment of their visitors' departure on a wild-goose chase, " consaitin' they've got us be the hind leg this time for sartin;" and long did he chuckle over the evening when they came and "sat discoorsin' as plisint and aisy as a rabbit in its houle," by a hearth where there was "enough of the stuff to float the lot of them lyin' widin six inches of their shiny brogues." It was, however, thought expedient to guard against a repetition of this perilous entertainment, and the contraband crocks were transferred to a still more secluded hiding-place in the queer tiny sod-and-stone shanty with [which] Hugh McInerney, who had displayed unexpected strategical ability and presence of mind under late emergencies, now knocked up for himself in a hollow behind the hill. So old Moggy's fears might have been better employed. Then about this time, too, a thrill was caused by the mysterious horseman, who visited the O'Beirnes' forge one night, and got old Felix to break open for him an immensely strong, small iron box which he carried. The same box being found next morning lying empty in the little Lisconnel stream, beside which the horse, "a grand big roan," was quietly grazing, while his rider was nowhere, nor was ever after anywhere, to be seen; an incident which gave scope for infinite speculation at Lisconnel.

All these things happened before Ody's aunt

got about again. By that time it was well on in August, and the season having been hot and dry, Lisconnel's oat-patches were already reflecting as if in a mirror, tarnished somewhat and rusted, the broad golden blaze that had looked down on them so steadily, and people had begun to think about reaping. The Ryans' field, indeed, was so ripe by the day of Ballybrosna Big Fair, that Paddy Ryan commissioned Hugh McInerney to bring him back a reaping-hook from it. Hugh was going to attend it on business of his own, and Ody Rafferty had some bulkier commissions to execute in behalf of his neighbours. But he encountered some difficulties in getting under way, due to the inopportune devices of old Rory, whom he proposed to bring with him. Ody had been careful not to put on his best clothes until he had caught the beast, because, as he remarked, " He well knew the crathur 'ud be off wid himself hidin' in the unhandiest place the divil 'ud put in his mind, if he noticed e'er a dacint stitch on him." Yet despite this precaution, when his master went to look for him after breakfast, no black pony was in sight.

"And he that'll be foosterin' everywhere under your feet other whiles, he's that fond of company," said Ody's aunt, who hobbled out of doors for the first time to assist in the search. "Belike he's seen you rubbin' up your brogues, and be raison of that he's took off wid himself. Bedad, now the big ould head of him is as full of desate as it can hould."

"He's a notorious schemer, God forgive him," Ody said, rather sadly, for it went against the grain with him to admit defects in Rory.

But his scheming bade fair to prove successful, as Ody after long hunting stood baffled at the door, with his expedition seemingly frustrated, when Hugh McInerney passing by reported that he "was after seein' the baste lanin' gathered up close agin the back of the big stone above there, wid a continted grin on the ould gob of him that 'ud frighten you wid the villiny was in it." Whereupon the two young men went to dislodge him from his fool's paradise, and the three started together without further delay.

Till a short way down the road they met old Felix O'Beirne, and with him Denis O'Meara, at whose heels followed Joe Egan, ragged and small, his habit being to dog his splendid cousin so persistently that old Mrs. Byers next door said she wondered "the young chap didn't of an odd while take him be the two shoulders and sling him over the dyke."

"So you're off to the fair," said old O'Beirne. "And is it sellin' the pony you'd be at last? Sure, now, he'll be the pick of the market, that's sartin."

"Ah, they'll niver give me me price for him, the naygurs," said Ody.

"Our Captin-Commandin' here had a right to take him off of you for a throoper," said old O'Beirne, "and, faix, there wouldn't be his aquil in the len'th and breadth of the army. What 'ud you offer for him, lad? Look at the size of the head he has on him, and the onnathural white face of him that's fit to scare a rigimint before it, if there was nothin' else."

"Is it broke bankrupt you'd have me then?" said Denis, "settin' up to be buyin' meself mounts of that expinsive discripshin?"

"Musha, good gracious, man, promise him the first thruppinny-bit you meet floatin' down the river on a grindstone, and you'll be buyin' every hair in his tail," said the old man. "But come along and don't be delayin' thim. They're goin' after fairin's for their sweethearts, the way you'd be yourself if you worn't too great a naygur. Or, maybe, there isn't anythin' good enough for her to be had in Ballybrosna—is that the raison of it?"

Little Joe was beginning to say in a resentful shout: "Naygur yourself—he and I are goin' to get——" But Denis pulled him on jocularly by the collar, and the parties went their several ways.

Ody then said: "Sweethearts is it? He's the quare ould man for talkin'. Glory be to the great goodness, I'm throubled wid ne'er a one. 'Here's out of it,' sez I. 'Onnathural,' sez he, musha cock him up, and himself shoein' ould garrons all the days of his life. Hi along, Rory, jewel!"

But Hugh said, meditatively, and more than half to himself, which was rather a habit of his: "Well, now, for the matter of the fairin', it's just the best len'th of ribbon I can get thim to give me for a shillin'. Yella it's to be. I wasn't long aither plannin' a way to find out the colour she'd like. Sure, I gave her a bunch of flowers wid poppies in it, and daisies, and furze-blossom, and foxglove, and forgit-me-not, and midowsweet, and sez I to her, which of thim was the finest coloured. And, sez she, the furze-blossom was, be raison of it bein' the bright gould all over, that the others had mostly only a spark of somewheres inside. So it's to be yella. Tellin' you the truth, I'd liefer she wouldn't be wearin' e'er such a thing at all, anyways not in her hair, that's a sight purtier just in the big black twists. But, sure, it's the fancy she has, and more-betoken, I think bad of me lettin' the little goat swally the weeny bit she had on her. Ay bedad, I'd a right to be bringin' it to her; and, at all evints, I'd be doin' a foolish thing to come home widout it, and me not gettin' the bit of fat bacon these six weeks next Saturday to make up the price. I won'er now what len'th they'd give you for one shillin'?"

But Ody, who had not been listening, only said, oracularly: "Och! that's accordin'," which did not materially assist Hugh's speculations.

Yellow ribbons were not plentiful at Ballybrosna fair, and Hugh McInerney had to ask for them vainly at several stalls before he came to an old-clothes cart, where the proprietress, being hot and cross, took him aback by replying: "And who ever heard tell of sellin' ribbons be the len'th, you quare-lookin' stookawn?"

"Sure it's meself couldn't say but you might; I niver had any call to be buyin' such a thing before. But a bit that one shillin' 'ud be the price of is what I'm wishful to be gettin', if it was yella—and beggin' your pardon, ma'am," Hugh answered with a glib meekness, which mollified the old woman as much as his not undesigned mention of his shilling.

So she said, "'Deed, now, I believe I've a splindid yella bit somewheres, a trifle creased in the folds, that I could make you a prisint of for a shillin'." And she rummaged, and unrolled before him interminable coils of vivid dandelion-hued ribbon. "The grand colour of it couldn't be bet," she said, "in Ireland. You could see it a mile off, and you wouldn't get the match of it in Dublin under half-a-crown. If she wouldn't be plased wid that, you've got an odd one to satisfy."

Ody with Rory came by as she was wrapping it up in paper, and Hugh, pointing to his purchase with a melancholy air, said, in an aggrieved tone: " It's a *terrible* quantity they're about givin' me—yards and yards—enough to rope round a hay-stack; and it's an ojis colour. Troth, now, if she takes the notion to be stickin' the whole of it on top of the little black head of her, it's an objec' she'll make of herself, she will so. It's a pity. I'd liefer there hadn't been the half of it."

"What for then are you gettin' more than enough of whatever it is?" Ody asked not unreasonably. "Supposin' you wanted any such thrash at all at all."

"Ah, sure, I settled in me own mind to be spendin' me shillin' on it, and that's the way it is," Hugh said resignedly. "Maybe she'll have more wit, the bit of a crathur; she might never put it on. So now I've on'y to see after Paddy Ryan's rapin'-hook, and then I'm done. And is it carryin' them two bags all the way home you'd be? Sure there's plinty of room for them on the baste."

"Ay, is there?" said Ody. "But the fac' is Rory's in none too good a temper this minyit, goodness help him, and he'll be apt to thravel more contint, the crathur, if he sees he's not the on'y body wid a loadin'."

"Rax me over the one of them," said Hugh, "I've nought barrin' the bit of ribbon, and the rapin'-hook 'ill be nothin' to me at all."

And in this way they plodded back to Lisconnel.

CHAPTER VI

A FAIRING

UP at Lisconnel, meanwhile, as the idle hours loitered by, Ody Rafferty's aunt grew tired of her solitary housekeeping, and late in the afternoon she made her way down as far as the Joyces'. Here a number of the neighbours were sitting about in almost the same place where Theresa had sustained the loss of her cherry-coloured knot. But to-day there were no rough breezes stirring to bring about such disasters by their unmannerly pranks. The sun-steeped air was so still that the thick bushes stood as steady as the boulders, and even the rushes nodded slightly and stiffly. As the old woman hobbled down the slope she saw Denis O'Meara's scarlet uniform gleaming martially against a background of dark broom and hoary rock. Its wearer was, however, very peacefully employed in pulling the silky floss off the heads of the bog-cotton, which lay in a great heap before him on a flat-topped boulder, with a big bunch of many-hued wild flowers beside it. Theresa Joyce, who sat opposite to him, was pulling bog-cotton too, though less diligently, for it might have been noticed that she often looked off her work, and towards the scrap of road that lay within her ken. Joe Egan was at his cousin's elbow, and a few other lads and lasses made a rough circle. But old Mrs. Joyce, and old Mrs. Ryan, and old Paddy Ryan, and old Felix O'Beirne had established themselves on a low grassy bank at a little distance. It was kept so closely cropped by the Ryans' goat that its dandelions grew dwarfed and stalkless, and were set flat in the fine sward like mock suns. All this day the real sun had shone on it so strongly that the air was aromatic with the odour of its dim-blossomed herbs, and to touch it was like laying your hand on the warm side of some sleek-coated beast. Old Paddy said you might think you were sitting on the back of an ould cow, but his wife rejoined that "you'd have to go far enough from Lisconnel, worse luck, before you'd get the chance of doin' such a thing." And she shook her head over the reflection so regretfully that a matter-of-fact person might have inferred her to have been formerly much in the habit of enjoying seats on the backs of cows.

These elders, from where they sat, commanded a comprehensive view of the crops of Lisconnel, its potatoes and oats, green and gold, meshed in their grey stone fences, and flecked with obstructive boulders and laboured cairns. In the middle of the Ryans' neighbouring field there is a block of quartzite, as big as a small turf-stack, which gleamed exceedingly white from amongst the deep muffling greenery of the potato-plants. Mrs. Joyce had been praising their thriving aspect to old Paddy, who, however, was disposed to express a gloomy view of them.

"It's too rank they're growin' altogether," he said; "ne'er a big crop you'll get under that heigth of haulms. 'Heavy thatchin' and light liftin',' as the sayin' is."

To Felix O'Beirne the smooth leafy surface recalled a far-off incident of the War, when the dense foliage of a certain potato-field had permitted the execution of a curious military manœuvre. It was one of old O'Beirne's favourite stories, and he often related it at full length, but to-day it was cut short by the arrival of Ody Rafferty's aunt, whom Mrs. Joyce and Mrs. Ryan were prompt to greet, making room for her between them on the bank with an alacrity which somehow conveyed an impression of uneasiness lest she should establish herself elsewhere.

Presently she said: "And what at all is Theresa busy wid over yonder—and young O'Meara? Is it bogberries they're after pullin'?"

Mrs. Joyce said: "No, ma'am, it isn't bog-berries;" and left further explanations to Mrs. Ryan, with the air of one who refrains from self-glorification, but counts upon its being done for her, more gracefully, by deputy.

"Sure wasn't he out on the bog the len'th of the day, since early this mornin', he and little Joe, gadrin' her the bog-cotton?" said Mrs. Ryan. "The full of a pitaty-creel he brought her. They have it there in a hape."

"'Twas because he heard her sayin' last night she wished she had a good bit of it to stuff the pillow she's makin' me," put in Mrs. Joyce. "Off he went after it the first thing this mornin'."

"Whethen now, is that the way of the win'?" said Ody Rafferty's aunt, with a pleased smile, striking out unfamiliar paths among her wrinkles. "Troth, but I'm rael glad to hear it. Bedad, it's a grand thing for little Theresa."

"He's a very dacint poor lad," Mrs. Joyce said, looking over with pride at the handsome young sergeant, and thinking that Ody Rafferty's aunt must have some good nature in her after all, since she was so evidently glad of their good luck.

"'Deed but there's not a finer young man in the kingdom of Connaught this day," said Mrs. Ryan, who could, of course, be frankly laudatory. "And wid everybody's good word, high and low, and drawin' grand pay, and the colonel in his rigimint ready to do a turn for him any time, and a rael steady kind-hearted lad to the back of that. But sure he's after as nice a little girl as he'd ha' found anywheres, wid all his thravellin', and as good as gould. He'll be very apt to be spakin' out to her prisintly, for it's gettin' near his lave's ind, and what for would they be waitin'? But to my mind it's as good as made up after what he's done to-day."

In a little while after this Ody Rafferty's aunt slipped away, and set off hobbling along the road towards Duffclane. She wanted to intercept her grand-nephew on his way home and tell him this news. For all day she had been haunted by an apprehension that Ody meant to return with a fairing for Theresa, the presentation of which

might bring about a crisis in his courtship very
disastrous from her own point of view. Old
Moggy surveyed her world rather steadily at all
times from that particular outlook, finding in her
solitary superfluousness little to deflect her gaze.
The disappointment which, on her own theory,
these tidings would bring to Ody did not do so
now, and she put her best foot foremost, animated
by the pleasure of telling some new thing, one,
moreover, that threw a reassuring light upon her
situation. With even her amended opinion of the
lad she could hardly imagine that he would have a
chance against magnificent Denis O'Meara, whom
nobody would have ever expected to look for a
wife in poor little Lisconnel—but you never could
tell, and she felt that it still behoved her to be on
her guard against all possible perils. Therefore
she at present thought it expedient to waylay
Ody, and let him know that if he had any notion
of Theresa Joyce, he was a day after the fair.

Hobbling on bent and breathless, wrapped in
her rusty black shawl, with her shadow flitting far
out over the level bog amid the slanted beams,
she looked a not inappropriate messenger of woe,
symbolically impotent and insignificant; a little
dark speck in the wide westering light; a feeble

stir of life creeping on the verge of a vast silent solitude; and full, withal, of baseless fears and futile plots, concerning the withered shred of existence that remained to her. She was just in the nick of time, she said to herself, when she saw the trio presently coming over the top of the hill. Ody was pointing out conciliatingly to the morose Rory how they'd be at home now nearly in the time he'd be waggin' his tail; and Hugh McInerney was resolving that he would go on straight to his own place, and defer the presentation of the ugly yellow ribbon until to-morrow. All three were hot and fagged and dusty.

"Well, lad, and what's the best good news wid you?" Ody's aunt said to him, as they met.

"Little enough," said Ody.

"And you comin' out of a fair?" she said. "Bedad now, we make a better offer at it ourselves up here for the matter of news."

"What's that at all?" said Ody.

"Sure amn't I just after hearin' tell of a grand weddin' there's goin' to be prisintly?" said his aunt, "and that doesn't happen every day of the year."

"Och, a weddin'," said Ody. "I was thinkin' maybe there was somethin' quare at our little place beyant yonder. But as long as it's nothin' worser than weddin's you're hearin' tell of, I'm contint, if you listened the two ears off your head."

"It's Denis O'Meara and Theresa Joyce has made a match of it," said his aunt, conscious that she was slightly overstating facts; "settled up it is on'y this evenin'. And the weddin's bound to be before his lave's out—so there's for you."

"Sure good luck to the both of thim," said Ody, "Theresa Joyce is a plisant little bein', I'll say that for her, and divil a bit of harm there is in O'Meara aither. A fine chap he is for a sodger; not that they're any great things as far as I can see—just pólis a thrifle smartened up."

Ody's thoughts were for the moment running on the police, a couple of whom he had lately espied at a short distance coming across the bog.

"Well, if you wanted to see the two of thim," said his aunt, raising her voice as he began to drive Rory on, "there they are, just at the back of her place, sortin' the stuff he's after gettin' her on the bog. He brought her the full of the pitaty-creel. Her mother's as plased over it as anythin', and sot up too, aye is she bedad."

The old woman was for the time being almost

as much disappointed as relieved by the equanimity with which Ody had received her tidings; yet if she had but known, they had not failed to produce a strong sensation. Only she never thought of considering how they might affect that quare big gawk Hugh McInerney. What did occur to her in his connection as he begun to trudge alongside her after the pony, was that "he was as ugly as if he had been bespoke." For Hugh's long tramp under the sultry sun had scorched him a deeper and more uniform red brick than usual, and his shock of tow-coloured hair jutting from beneath an unnoticeable round cap, looked more than ever like thatch over his blinking blue eyes. When they had gone a few yards in silence he suddenly said musingly—

"I dunno why he wouldn't have as good a right to be bringin' her anythin' she had a fancy for off the bog in a pitaty-creel, as me to be buyin' her len'ths of hijis-coloured ribbons to make a show of herself wid. But all the same, I'd as lief he'd let it alone. For some raison or other I've the wish in me mind I was slingin' the whole of it into one of thim bog-houles out there—and that 'ud be no thing to go do on her. . . . And that was a quare story the ould woman had about thim gettin' married. Somebody was apt to be makin' a fool of her. Who was it would be tellin' her I won'er?"

But old Moggy partly overheard and said: "Thim that knew what they was talkin' about, supposin' it's any affair of yours."

So he did the rest of his meditating inaudibly. He said to himself that he was steppin' home straight—continuing the while to walk in quite the opposite direction—and that he wouldn't be goin' to the Joyces' place to-night at all; what 'ud bring him there, and it gettin' so late? But of course he went there, as surely as a swimming bubble goes over the cataract's smooth lip, or a fascinated little bird down the snake's throat. For the sensation which he had begun to experience, and which was a strong one, and strange to him, was nothing less than jealousy. He was jealous of that pitaty-creel.

When he came to the place Ody's aunt had told of, he found a group of young Joyces and Ryans and others gathered among the boulders and bushes in a circle of which the heap of bog-cotton formed the centre; and a glance having showed him that it included Denis and Theresa, he sat down facing them, and said to himself:

"If I'd known, now, it was bog-cotton she was wantin', I could ha' been gadrin' her plinty last night after I come home. There's a gran' big moon these times, wid lashin's and lavin's of light to be gettin' thim kind of glimmerin' things by. I seen a black place below between the sthrame of wather and the roadside all waved over white wid it, like as if it was a fall of snow thryin' could it flutter off away wid itself agin out of the world. I'd have got her enough to fill a six-fut sack. What for didn't the crathur tell me?"

Pursuing these and other such reflections Hugh's attention, which at all times had a long tether, strayed far afield. He did not hear Denis O'Meara inquire of him twice whether Ody Rafferty had got his fine price for the old pony; not yet Peter Ryan rejoin after an interval that he supposed it was such a big one, anyway, Hugh McInerney couldn't get it out of his mouth—that was sizable enough. No doubt it was this symptom of absentmindedness that emboldened Thady Joyce to set about twitching out of Hugh's pocket the flimsy paper parcel seen protruding from it, a feat which he achieved undetected, while his surrounding accomplices nudged one another and whispered: "Och he has it now—whoo-oo he'll do it."

Thady conveyed what he had filched to Molly and Nelly Ryan, who manipulated it for some time amid much giggling; and then Nelly, with dexterous audacity pinned their handiwork on to the cap of her neighbour Denis O'Meara, who sat all unawares. Thus it came to pass that when Hugh was at last roused to a vague sense of tittering all round him, which reached him much as the clacking chirp of sparrows gets meaninglessly into our frayed morning dreams, and looking up out of his reverie, stared about him for an explanation, the first thing his eyes lit on was Denis's smart cap surmounted by a mass of gaudy yellow ribbon in immense bows and loops and streamers, flapping and waggling absurdly at every movement made by their unsuspecting wearer. And the spectacle caught his breath, and dazzled his sight with a sudden scorching blast of wrath. For it seemed to him that Denis was not making merely a mock of him and his fairing, which he thought intrinsically of small amount, but through it of Theresa herself and her foolish little fancies. And there sat Theresa looking on, with a quick pink flush, and shining eyes, and a quiver about her mouth. The next moment Hugh had hurled at the bedizened cap what he happened to be holding in his hand. And this was Paddy Ryan's new reaping-hook.

Thereupon followed a terrible confusion and clamour, which seemed to fill at a sweep all the spacious drowsy light of the sunsetting. For the missile had gone surely to its mark, and had not simply knocked off Denis's cap, but made a shocking gash in his temple, so that there were only too sufficient reasons for the rising shrieks of "Holy Virgin, he's murdhered—he's kilt!" Amid all the turmoil, with Denis fallen on the ground, and Hugh standing staring, and everybody else rushing through other like crows in a storm, one person alone appeared to act with a definite purpose, and that was little Joe Egan. The event had made him like one possessed with rage and despair. To Joe, weakly and timorous and not over-wise, his valiant, handsome, good-natured soldier cousin had come as the most splendid apparition that had shined upon him in the dim course of his fifteen years; and he had spent the past three months in adoring it very devoutly. So that now to see him laid low suddenly in this savage fashion was a sight that might well cause a burning thirst for vengeance upon the miscreant who had dealt the stroke. Joe generally had to get his revenges wreaked by deputy; and now, as he darted away, his intention was to find the pólis somewhere, and bring them to take up "that great bastely murdherin' divil, Hugh McInerney," and if by any means possible get him hung. He attained his object sooner than might have been expected, as not far down the road a pair of constables were run into by a small tatterdemalion figure, who, choking and stammering and writhing in an ague fit of fury, proceeded to inform them that "Big Hugh McInerney was just after murdherin' Denis O'Meara up above there—takin' the head off him wid a rapin'-hook," and, further, that "if they looked in the dirty thief's little place at the fut of the hill, they'd find that every other stone in the walls of it was nothin' else but a crock of poteen."

This was the cause of the police's prompt arrival on the scene, where nobody resented Joe's action. Denis's injury, though so grave, happily did not seem to be mortal, in fact, on this occasion young Dan O'Beirne, albeit scarcely more than a spalpeen, displayed a handiness and resource about bandaging and other remedies, which foreshadowed his future reputation throughout the district for knowledgableness in surgery and medicine. Hugh McInerney was, of course, at once arrested, without any resistance on his part, or any sympathy from the indignant neighbours. He appeared to be what old Will Sheridan termed, "fallen into a serious consternation," and was heard to make only one remark. It was when people were saying that Theresa Joyce had took a wakeness, and her brothers had carried her indoors. "Och, the crathur," he said, "and it might aisy have hit her, very aisy. Miself's the quare divil."

Once the police and their prisoner had gone, Denis having been brought into the Ryans' house, a deep and melancholy hush settled down upon Lisconnel, as if a murky wing had flapped out its brief flare of excitement. The whole thing had happened so quickly that the rich light from the west was still bronzing the edges of the flat-ledged furze boughs, and rosing their white stems, when the little hollow behind the Joyces' house rested quiet and deserted, with no traces left of the company lately there assembled, except a litter of silky white bog-cotton tufts, soon to be swept away by the breeze, and the unchancy yellow ribbon, which had been torn out of Denis's cap, and lay coiling among the rough grass, whence, as the dusk thickened, it glinted like the wraith of a lost sunbeam or a ray from an evil star.

But that night fell very dark, with a moon so closely veiled that the flaggers and bulrushes waving their swords and spears fast by, dwindled into mere rustlings and murmurs—the air was full of them. At the dimmest hour anybody who had stolen out of a neighbouring door, and passed between the faintly glimmering white boulders, as if in search of something lost there, might have seemed only one of the whispering shadows. And these might have begun to say, "Sorra aught can I do at all, at all. And ne'er a soul is there to spake a word—all of thim agin him, and it no fau't of his, when he would be torminted that way. They'd no call to go play such a thrick on him, and he didn't mane it a' purpose, I very well know; but the other chap was intindin' to annoy him, sittin' there wid a great ugly grin on his face. I wish he'd never come next or nigh Lisconnel." But be that as it may, when the next morning's light twinkled among the dewy blades, the yellow ribbon had disappeared.

After this the days seemed to drag heavily at Lisconnel, where a dulness and flatness had come over society. Dr. Hamilton had carried off Denis O'Meara to Ballybrosna, and there was nothing to fill up the blank he left except speculations about his chances of recovery, and censures upon Hugh McInerney, monotonously unanimous. In his favour, indeed, no one seemingly had a word to say. People declared that "they'd never have thought he'd take and do such a thing, for though he might ha' been a quare sort of bosthoon, he was always dacint and paiceable." But cancelled praise is the bitterest of blame; and they added that "it was rael outrageous of him to go do murdher on the likes of Denis O'Meara, and no credit to Lisconnel for it to be happenin' him there. Iligant charácters it 'ud be givin' them if he wint back to the rigimint wid his eyes slashed out of his head, as much as to say he hadn't a fair chance among us unless he'd come wid his side-arms."

The neighbours were of opinion, too, that "it was no wonder little Theresa Joyce had got a bit moped and quiet, after her sweetheart bein' as good as destroyed before her eyes, and it hard to say if she'd ever see a sight of him again."

"It was a misfort'nit thing," Mrs. Con Ryan remarked one day, when the subject was under discussion, "that young O'Meara hadn't actually spoke out before it happint thim. 'Twould ha' made her a dale aisier in her mind now, I wouldn't won'er. Because the way the matter stands, he might take up wid some diff'rint notion, and just be off wid himself like a cloud blown out of the sky, and she couldn't be sayin' a word, if she was ever so sure of what he was intindin'."

Young Mrs. Keogh, to whom she made the observation, refused to entertain this view, and replied, "Sorra a fear is there of that. It was aisy to see he'd ha' gone to the Well of the World's End after her, let alone steppin' up from the Town, if he's spared to get his health. Ay, he'll be comin' back for her one of these fine days, sure enough, plase God."

But the fulfilment of her confident prediction looked several degrees more doubtful in the light of one of the two pieces of news which Mrs. Carbery, accompanied by her daughter Rose, conveyed to the Joyces' on a bright September morning a short while after. Her son had come home with it from the Town too late the night before. One of them was that Hugh McInerney, who had been awaiting the assizes in Moynalone Jail, had died of the fever there on last Friday. There was nothing very surprising in this event, as Hugh's open-air life could have but ill acclimatised him to the atmosphere of the unclean little jail; and it was not likely to be very deeply deplored at Lisconnel, where he had not been known long, nor, as we have seen, much to his advantage.

As Mrs. Carbery sat in the three-cornered armchair, with the sun-dazzle off a burnished mug on the dresser shimmering into her eyes, and making her blink quaintly, she said, with rather severe solemnity, that "she hoped the young fellow had had time to repint of his sins, or else it was very apt to be a bad look-out for him, and he after comin' widin a shavin' of takin' another man's life no time at all ago, so to spake—ne'er a chance but it would be clear in everybody's recollection."

Mrs. Joyce, however, said: "Ah, sure maybe the crathur wasn't intindin' any such great harm all the while, God be good to him. And, anyway, where he's gone he'll find plinty ready to be spakin' up for him, and puttin' the best face they can on the matter."

"Ay will he," said old Biddy Ryan, who was calling too, "and bedad it's one great differ there is, be all accounts, between that place and this. For here if a misfort'nit body does aught amiss, the first notion the rest of us have, God forgive us, is to be axin' what worser he was manin', like as if it was some manner of riddle, that there's bound to be an answer to, if one could find it."

"'Deed, and I dunno if they haven't very far to look, ma'am," said Mrs. Carbery, with dignity, "when a chap does his endeavours to take the head off another man wid a rapin'-hook, ma'am."

"And *I* dunno, ma'am, for that matter," said old Biddy, also with dignity, "if it's any such a great dale better to have one's mind took up wid invintin' other people's bad intintions than if it was wid one's own."

"Ah, well! I wouldn't be thinkin' too bad of poor Hugh McInerney, at all events," said Mrs. Joyce. "'Twas maybe a sort of accident, for he seemed a dacint crathur afore that. Och now, to think it's on'y a few odd weeks since he was creepin' about over our heads up there, mendin' th' ould thatch! You'd whiles hear him hummin' away, talkin' to himself like some sort of big bee —and in his grave to-day! But isn't it a lucky thing that he's lavin' nobody belongin' to him to be breakin' their hearts frettin' after him? Theresa, child dear, you've ne'er a stim of light to be workin' in, sittin' there in the corner."

But Theresa said she had light enough to blind

her, and was only winding a skein, and could see better to do that in the dark. So Mrs. Carbery passed on to her second piece of news, which, though less tragical than the first, was not likely to sound very cheerfully in the ears of some among her audience. It ran that her son Ned was "after seein' Denis O'Meara down beyant, and that he was doin' finely, next door to himself again: and that the people in the Town did be sayin' he was coortin' Mary Anne Neligan, the people's daughter that he was lodgin' wid—a terrible fortin she was said to have—and that he'd be very apt to be takin' her along wid him prisintly when his lave was up." Mrs. Carbery supposed they were none of them ever likely to see him again up at Lisconnel. And the rest of the neighbours, having heard her tale, supposed so likewise, and said among themselves that Theresa Joyce was to be pitied.

Yet not many days after this, while the early autumn weather was still soft-aired and mellow-lighted over our blue-misted bogland, where the leaves and berries were brightening, and even the little frosty-grey cups on the lichened boulders getting a scarlet thread at the rim, on one clear, dew-dashed morning, who but Denis O'Meara himself should come stepping into Lisconnel? The neighbours who saw him go by were glad to notice that he looked as well as ever he did in his life, and he greeted them all blithely though briefly, eluding every attempt to entangle him in conversation, and making very straight for the Widow Joyce's house, which was by these same observers considered to betoken a healthy frame of mind.

Only Mrs. Joyce and Mrs. Kilfoyle were in the little brown room when he arrived, but they gave him a cordial welcome, and he took a seat from which he could keep a watch on the door while they talked about different things. One of these, naturally, was the melancholy end of Denis's assailant—poor Hugh McInerney—and Mrs. Joyce said it was little enough they'd have thought a while ago that it would be Denis who'd come back. "But indeed," she said, "if anythin' had took you, we'd ha' been in no hurry ever to set eyes on the other unlucky bosthoon."

Denis said: "Faith, ma'am, I'd give six months' pay the thing had never happint. Divil a bit of harm I believe there was in poor McInerney; and I spoke to Dr. Hamilton to spake to Mr. Nugent and the other magistrates for him; but they said, after what me cousin Joe let out about the poteen at his place, the pólis would be wishful to keep him convanient to thim for a while; and to be sure, they kep' him too long altogether. I know, ma'am, young Rafferty and the rest had his shanty pulled down before the pólis come up next day; but they thought they'd git somethin' out of him. The little jackass ought to ha' held his tongue. It was a pity, bedad. Hard lines it is on a man to be losin' his life, you may say, along wid his temper, just be raison of a bit of a joke."

Still as he looked out into the sunshine he could not help thinking that he would have had a greater loss of his life than poor Hugh McInerney, who, it was evident, would always have met with a cold reception from everybody at the Joyces'. Then he said to Mrs. Joyce: "And how's Theresa, ma'am?"

Mrs. Joyce was in the middle of replying that she was grandly, and had just run over to Mrs. Keogh on a message, when Theresa herself came in.

Denis jumped up quickly, saying: "Ah, Theresa, it's a great while since I've seen you."

But Theresa only lifted her head without turning it, and walked straight on as if nobody had accosted her.

"Arrah, now, Theresa darlint, don't you see Denis O'Meara?" said her mother, puzzled and rather dismayed.

And then Theresa did turn and look at him. "Yis, I see him," she said—and, indeed, she might as easily have overlooked the red flame in a lantern as the tall scarlet lancer in her mother's little misty-cornered room. "I see him," she said, "and I hate the sight of him." And thereupon she turned again, and walked out of the door, leaving a dead silence behind her.

This was one of the very few harsh sayings that Theresa Joyce has uttered in the course of her long life, and it came like a shock upon her hearers.

Mrs. Joyce at last said blankly: "What at all has took the child?"

And Bessie Kilfoyle said to Denis, who stood dumbfounded: "But indeed now, you may be sure there's not a many up here, at any rate, who do that."

But he replied: "If *she* does, it's many enough for me, Mrs. Kilfoyle. And I won't stop here to be drivin' her out of the house. So I'll say goodbye to yous kindly, for I'll be off now to Dublin to-morra or next day."

"And in coorse," Mrs. Joyce remarked ruefully, after he had departed, retreading his steps through the bright fresh morning with so crestfallen a mien that all the neighbours knew things had not run smoothly, "you couldn't raisonably expec' him to stay here to be hated the sight of. And indeed, what wid one thing and another, it's none too good thratement the poor lad's got up at Lisconnel, more's the pity."

Theresa herself never had any explanation to offer of "why she would be that cross wid poor Denis O'Meara." Her mother accounted for it by pique at the Carberys' ill-timed gossip about his imaginary courtship of Mary Anne Neligan; and Mrs. Kilfoyle was for a while inclined to the same opinion, until one day by chance she espied in the little old tin box which contained Theresa's treasures, a roll of bright yellow ribbon wrapped up very carefully; and thenceforward she silently ceased to hope that things might all come right yet, if Denis O'Meara came back again on leave.

So, although Mrs. Joyce may have drawn wrong inferences, the results were much as she had foreseen. Theresa never married, and when her mother died she went to live with her brother

Mick at Laraghmena, where she is living still, notwithstanding that it is so long since all this happened—since the fine summer when Denis O'Meara was at Lisconnel, and Hugh McInerney, who luckily left nobody to be breaking their hearts fretting after him, died in Moynalone Jail.

The yellow ribbon lies safely in her box, and with it a grimy bit of paper, brought to her one day by a trusty hand, to which Hugh found out a way of committing it "before he was took bad entirely." Theresa herself has never deciphered its wild scrawls, being an unlettered person, but its bearer read it over to her until she knew it by heart every word. "For your own self the yella ribin is," the letter ran, "but don't be wearin' it unless you like it. And I'm sorry the man got hit; but I do be dhramin' most nights that it's you I'm after rapin' the little black head off of; and I'd liefer lose me life than think I'd be after hurtin' a hair of it. But the Divil was busy wid me that evenin'. And I'm very apt never to get the chance to set fut again out on the big bog. It 'ud do me heart good to see the sun goin' down in it a great way off, for this is a quare small place. It's a long while. But sure, to the end of all the days of me life," it said to her, like an echo beaten back from the walls of the great abysm, "it's of yourself I'll be thinkin' off away in contintmint at Lisconnel."

CHAPTER VII

MR. POLYMATHERS

IT was to an accidental circumstance that Lisconnel owed the prolonged sojourn there of perhaps the most distinguished scholar who has ever visited us. For when he arrived at O'Beirne's forge one misty June evening, the night's lodging only was all he asked or desired. But in those times, now some fifty years since, we had "a terrible dale of sickness about in the country," and next morning the stranger was down with the fever, which, although so mild a case that even Bridget O'Beirne never gave him over more than twice in the same day, brought his journey perforce to a halt. At the beginning he was very loth to believe that he must relinquish his intention of reaching Dublin by a certain date—the first Monday in July; however, having once recognised the impossibility of doing so, he showed no haste to quit his quarters, and his stay with the

O'Beirnes lengthened into months as the summer slipped away. At this time the forge was owned by Felix O'Beirne, blacksmith, shebeener, and ex-whiteboy, and with him lived his orphan grandsons, Daniel and Nicholas, his very old, ancient mother, who still drew enjoyment in whiffs through the stem of her black dudeen, and his elderly sister, Bridget, who had taken little pleasure in anything since the redcoats shot her sweetheart in the War. The missing third generation was represented occasionally when Mrs. Dooley, Felix's married daughter, came on a visit. It was conjectured among them that "the fancy the ould gintleman had for larnin' all manner to young Nicholas continted him to stop." And this may have had something to do with it, though less, probably, than the vaguer fact that he from the first "took kindly" to the O'Beirnes, and they to him. His appearance puzzled them a little. He was of a massive, large-boned frame, such as nature seems to design for rough uses; but, as Felix remarked, "you could aisy tell be ivery finger and thumb on him that hard work wasn't the handle he'd took a hould of the world by." He wore a very long, grey frieze coat, and a chimney-pot hat so old and tall that it looked as if it must have grown slowly to its great height. When he took it off he uncovered a shock of soft white hair, like the wig of a seeded groundsel, about a face which was furrowed and wrinkled ruggedly enough, in a different pattern somehow from what is commonly seen at Lisconnel, where sun and wind have a large share in the process. His baggage consisted of two bundles, very unequal in size and weight. The contents of the smaller one were mainly a shirt and three socks, knotted loosely in a blue cotton handkerchief; the other was done up carefully in sacking, and he liked to have it under his eye.

Of course the O'Beirnes' visitor was often talked about among the groups gathered of an evening, much as they are nowadays, for gossip and poteen within the broad-leaved forge doors, through which on dark nights the fire still blinks as far across the bog as the amber of the sunset, or the rising glow of the golden harvest moon. Even from Felix's first report it appeared that the stranger was no ordinary person.

"Won'erful fine discoorse he has out of him, anyway," he told the neighbours a few nights after the arrival; "ivery now and agin he'll out wid a word as grand like and big as his Riverence at Mass—goodness forgive me for sayin' so. Sometimes we've been hardset to tell what he's drivin' at. But that's the way it is wid thim words that has a power of manin' in thim. They're apt to bother you a bit when you're used to spakin plain."

"Belike it's the fever in his head sets him talkin' oddly," said young Barney Corcoran. "I mind me brother Joe when he was bad wid it would be ravin' wild. Sorra the sinsible word there was out of him for the best part of a week."

This way of accounting for his guest's fine language rather affronted Felix, and he consequently said, "Musha now, was there not? And how long might yourself be under that descripshin of fever?"

"Ah sure, what 'ud we do at all if poor Barney was took that way?" said Peter Keogh, "and nobody able to tell was it ravin' he was, or settin' up to be talkin' raisonable for any differ they could see."

Barney cleared his throat disconcertedly, and the old man, recalling his responsibilities as a host, and perhaps not admiring his sarcasm thus elaborated, said conciliatingly, "Och, he'll do right enough if he niver raves any worse than Mr.

Polymathers. All that ails him is that we want to git a bit used to his manner of spakin'."

"Polymathers?" said Peter.

"To be sure, Polymathers. Did you say it any better than I?"

"Well, I nivir heard tell of anybody called that way before. It's a quare she-he soundin' sort of name," said Peter.

"Faix, then, there may be plinty quarer in it, we niver heard tell of, if that was all," said Felix. "Anyhow, it's his name, and his people's afore him. Himself tould me his father was the ouldest of all the Polymatherses there was in the counthry he came out of—somewheres down south, I think he said—and the head of the whole of thim forby."

"Ay, he did so," said Dan. "Sez you to him, there was a dale of water run down hill since the time there was O'Beirnes blacksmiths in this part of the counthry; and your father was a one, sez you. And sez he to you, he couldn't be any manner of manes purtind to be the aquil to what *his* father was. And sez you to him, what was he? And sez he, it was one of the Polymatherses he was, and well known for his larnin' through the len'th and breadth of the county Sligo. And a name it was, he sez, any man might be proud of ownin'."

"Be jabers, himself has the great consait of it, at all ivents," said Peter. "But he might find people could be tellin' him there's Keoghs as good as any Polymatherses iver was in it—ivery hair."

The stranger's patronymic having thus been ascertained, it was desirable to fix his calling, and, despite his disclaimer of inherited erudition, several circumstances bespoke him a schoolmaster, even before the question seemed settled by the first act of his convalescence being an inquiry into the amount of book-learning which Dan and Nicholas had amassed during their sixteen and fourteen years. This was not large, though as much as could be expected, considering that in all Lisconnel there were not just then, I believe, more than four volumes, one of which being merely the index to a non-existent *Encyclopædia*, can scarcely rank as literature. The boys themselves, and their grandfather, were deeply interested in the examination, and very anxious that it should have a creditable result. For learning and the learned have at all times been held in profound respect among us away on our bogland, where the devotion to something afar springs perhaps the more abundantly because so many things are remote. On this occasion Mr. Polymathers opened his most sizable bundle, and it was seen to be filled with books, not fewer, doubtless, than a score, in leather bindings, ragged and battered, and brownly time-stained all over their margins, as if the river of years had for them run no metaphor, but a russet bog-stream. They comprised *Homer*, *Virgil*, *Livy*, and other ancients; likewise two Latin lexicons, which looked extravagant until you observed how each did but supplement the other's deficiencies, and this so imperfectly that their owner was still liable to search in vain for words between Mo and Na.

These, however, were evidently not the most prized portion of Mr. Polymathers's library, though he displayed them with some complacency, reading out here and there a sonorous "furrin" phrase, at which his audience said, "More power," and "Your sowl to glory," and the like. It was when he handled the shabbiest of the volumes, with broken backs and edges all curling tatters, that his touch grew caressing. The lookers-on, contrariwise, thought but poorly of them because they set up, seemingly, to be illustrated works, and their pictures, mostly of uninteresting round and three-cornered objects, struck Lisconnel art critics as very feeble efforts. To be sure Mr. Polymathers called them *dygrims*, but that was no help to the overtaxed imagination. Only young Nicholas O'Beirne listened intently to the explanation which he gave of one of them. Nicholas was a long, thin lad, with melancholy grey eyes and a square forehead, whose capacity his grandfather had held in some esteem, since it had been discovered, years ago, that "the spalpeen could make out an account for four sets of shoes, and half a stone of three-inch holdfasts, and a dozen of staples, and two gallon of the crathur, and allow for a hundredweight of ould iron, all in his head, and right to a farthin'." Now the melancholy eyes darkened and brightened with excitement as Mr. Polymathers discoursed of right lines and angles and circles, and expounded the mysterious signification of certain Ah Bay Says. And he had thenceforward an unweariable pupil in Nicholas, companied, albeit with less ardent zeal, and at a slower rate of progress, by his elder brother, Dan.

More general interest, however, continued to be taken in the stranger's classical attainments.

Everybody—the O'Beirnes themselves, their neighbours in the cabin-row close by, now long since an untraceable ruin, and the people of Lisconnel proper, a couple of miles further on—felt uplifted by the residence among them of a man, who they boasted would talk Latin to you as soon as look at you. But as we never enjoy our own happiness fully until it has been looked at through other men's envious eyes, they could not here remain content with simply possessing this privilege, or even with dilating upon it to their less favoured friends down below and down beyant. They longed to make a parade of it, to give a demonstration of it. And the method of doing so which they came to consider most desirable was the bringing about of a conversation in Latin between Mr. Polymathers and Father Rooney, the Parish Priest. For if that took place they could easily imagine his Reverence riding home to report in the Town what a wonderful great scholar entirely they had stopping above at Lisconnel. Moreover, the conversation itself would be a rael fine thing to have the hearing of. Terence Kilfoyle, for instance, said that it would be as good as a Play, which, as he had never seen one, was to entertain unbounded expectations.

And at last, after they had wished the wish for some weeks, a prospect of its fulfilment came into sight together with Father Rooney's cream-coloured pony jogging along through the light of a fiery-zoned July sunset, in which Mr. Polymathers was basking by the O'Beirnes' door. In those days his Reverence was a youngish man, ruddy, and of a cheerful countenance, a substantial load for his sturdy nag, and altogether, in his glossy black cloth, a figure very different from their gaunt, sad-visaged, shaggily-garbed old guest. He was at the time of Father Rooney's approach seated on a two-legged, three-legged stool, propped precariously against the ray-rosed cabin wall, and was teaching Dan and Nicholas the twelfth proposition of the second book of Euclid. Dan had not yet grasped it, but it all lay as clear as a sunbeam athwart Nicholas's brain, and he was fidgeting like an impatient horse at the slowness of his fellow.

Several of the neighbours chanced to be about, for the forge saw a good deal of company in those long empty days before the potato-digging could begin. They all drew together into a small crowd, and closed in step by step to watch the first meeting between these two notable persons, much admiring the deftness with which old O'Beirne secured it by pronouncing one of the pony's shoes in need of tightening, and the felicitous opening he made by assuring his Reverence that "divil a bit need he be mindin' the delay, because Mr. Polymathers there had enough *furrin languages* to keep thim all divarted, if the baste owned as many feet as a forty-legs, wid the shoes droppin' off ivery pair of thim. That was to say, in coorse, supposin' he got the chance of convarsin' a bit wid somebody aquil to answerin' him back iligant, the way there wasn't e'er a one of thim could make an offer at doin' no more than thim little weevils of chirpin' chuckens."

Yet the interview turned out disappointingly after all. If such a thing had not been, of course, exceedingly improbable, one might have fancied that each scholar stood in awe of the other's reputation, they steered so clear of all recondite subjects; keeping to the merest commonplaces about rain and potatoes and turf—which anybody else could have discussed quite as knowledgably. In vain, whenever there was a promising pause would the bystanders nudge one another, whispering, hopefully, "Whist, boys—they'll be sayin' somethin' now." Only the plainest English followed, and at last, when Father Rooney rode on, his parting joke, which referred to the difficulty his pony would now find in the way of becoming a barefooted pilgrim, left for a wonder solemnly irresponsive faces behind it.

Michael Ryan said, with a touch of resentment, "Ah, well, one couldn't maybe expec' it of thim to be throublin' thimselves talkin' fine for the pack of us, as ignorant as dirt, in the middle of th'ould bog."

And his wife said, "'Deed, now, I wouldn't won'er meself if the raison was his Riverence 'ud think bad of usin' his Latin words for anythin' else on'y prayers and such. It might be somethin' the same as if he went and took his grand vistments to go dig pitaties in; and that 'ud be a great sin, God knows."

But old Felix, who was, as we have seen, a rather touchy person, construed this suggestion into an implied censure on his own wishes in the matter, and he said, huffily—

"Sorra the talk of sin I see in it at all, ma'am. 'Tis a dale liker they just couldn't get out wid it convanient offhand. The same way that I'd aisy enough bate out a shoe on me anvil there, when it's bothered I'd be if you axed me to make a one promiscuous here of a suddint on the roadside."

Mr. Polymathers himself meanwhile was perhaps dimly conscious that he had disappointed hopes, and failed to rise duly to the occasion; and this may have been why he slipped indoors, and fetched out a small book he had never produced before, bound in a dingy greenish blue, with a white paper label.

"D'you know what that is, sir?" he questioned, rhetorically, handing it to Felix O'Beirne. "It's the Calendar, let me tell you, of the College of the Holy and Undivided Trinity, *juxta* Dublin. There's a print of the Front of the Buildings attached to the fly-leaf. I'm after pickin' it up this spring at Moynalone. 'Twas new the year before last, and comprises a dale of information relative to terms, examinations, fees, and so forth."

"Begor, then, it looks to be a wide house," said Felix, confining himself to the picture as a comprehensible point. "It's apt to be an oncommon fine place, sir, I should suppose."

"You may say that, me man," said Mr. Polymathers, emphatically. "Not its match in the kingdom of Ireland. The home of literature and the haunt of science. And it's there I'll be, plase God, next October."

"Musha, and will you be thravellin' that far—to Dublin?" said Felix.

"Ay will I, and would have gone last month on'y for the fever delayin' me till after the mid-summer entrance. Me savin's amount to somethin' over thirty pound, so I may venture on the step, and prisint meself at the Michaelmas term. In short," said Mr. Polymathers, re-poising himself upon his rickety stool, "I might describe myself as an unmatriculated candidate undergraduate of the University of Dublin."

"And what at all now would that be, sir, if I might be axin'?" said Felix, humbly, after the awe-stricken pause which followed Mr. Polymathers's proclamation of his style and title.

"It's a necessary preliminary," said Mr. Polymathers, "to proceeding to the Degree of *Baccalaureatus in Artibus*, or *In Artibus Baccalaureatus*—the *ordo verborum* is, I take it, immaterial, to judge by the transposition of initials in the case of——."

"Faix, but it's the fine Latin you can be discoorsin' now, and his Riverence half-ways home," said Felix reproachfully.

Mr. Polymathers, glancing round a circle of deeply impressed faces, felt that his prestige was restored, and even began to enjoy a foretaste of the triumph, which had been one part of his dream through the long laborious years. But he was puzzled how to bring the full grandeur of his design clearly before this uninstructed audience, and after reflecting for a while in quest of concise yet adequate definitions, he launched out into an eloquent description of the ceremonial observed in conferring degrees at Dublin University. It may be surmised that many of the details were due to his own fondly brooding fancy. For not only did the highest learning in the land crowd the Hall in their academic robes, but the Lord Lieutenant himself took a prominent part in the proceedings, which were enlivened by military music and thunderous salutes. Mr. Polymathers nearly toppled off his tricky stool more than once without noticing it in his excitement as he rehearsed these splendid scenes, declaiming with great unction the formulas long since learned by all his heart, especially *Ego, auctoritate mihi concessa*, and the rest, until he came to his peroration: "And all this pomp and ceremony, mind yous, to the honour and glory of science and fine scholarship. It's a grand occasion, lads; it's an object any man might be proud to give——" Here he pulled himself up, warned by an unusually violent lurch, that his theme was running away with him. But having by no means worked off his enthusiasm, he expended some of it, as a schoolboy might have done, in throwing a small bit of turf at a stately white hen, who just then sailed across the dark doorway, like a little frigate under the most crowded canvas. She immediately took flight with floundering screeches, which drowned what the old man was muttering to himself. However, it was only "*Admitto te—admitto te.*"

After these revelations Mr. Polymathers was looked up to more than ever, as one not only endowed with rare gifts, but destined by their means to scale heights of hardly realisable exaltation. "Be all accounts there was no knowin' what he mightn't rise to be at Dublin College," the neighbours said. They also often remarked that it was "a surprisin' thing to see a great scholar like him spendin' his time over taichin' thim two young O'Beirnes." If the speaker happened to be afflicted with a twinge of envy about those educational advantages, he was apt to say "thim two young bosthoons" or "gomerals." But Dan and Nicholas were not, in fact, any such thing. Nicholas, indeed, quickly proved himself possessed of what Mr. Polymathers called "a downright astonishin' facility at the mathematics," far outstripping Dan, not quite to Dan's satisfaction, as he had always enjoyed the pre-eminence conferred by superior physical strength and a practical turn of mind. So well pleased was the old man with his eager pupil that he would have liked to do his teaching, "nothing for reward," but his host's hospitality, and his own ambition, would not permit this. Now and then he rather puzzled Nicholas by an apologetic tone in answering questions about his University career. And once at the end of a lesson he said, as if to himself: "May goodness forgive me if I'm takin' what he'd have done better with. But sure he's young—he's plenty of chances yet." However, as the time for his departure drew on, all his misgivings, if such he had, seemed to vanish away, and his thoughts became very apt to journey off blissfully to Dublin in the middle of the most interesting problems. Nicholas had to wait till they came back.

Mr. Polymathers left Lisconnel on a fine

autumn morning, when the air was so still that the flashing and twinkling of the many dewdrops seemed to make quite a stir in it. The sky was as clear as any one of them, and in the golden light the wavering columns of blue smoke rose with curves softly transparent. He started with a buoyant step, as well he might, since he was setting out on the enterprise into which he had put all the spirit of his youth. He felt some regret at parting from his Lisconnel friends, but his plans and prospects were naturally very preoccupying, whereas they had the ampler leisure of the left-behind to deplore his flitting, which seemed likely enough to be for good. Nearly four years, he had explained, must elapse before the crowning height of the B. A. Degree could be won, and it was only just possible that he might manage to tramp back on a visit meanwhile, during some Long Vacation. This doubtful chance was cold comfort for that ardent scholar Nicholas O'Beirne, who grieved more than anybody else. Most ruefully did he help Dan to carry the candidate undergraduate's library as far as the Town; nor could he take more than a downcast pleasure in Mr. Polymathers's farewell gift to him of the raggedest *Euclid.* And as he stood watching the car out of sight, his eyes were as wistful as if a door briefly opened on glimpses of radiant vistas had been inexorably barred in his face.

Yet after all Mr. Polymathers's absence was not to be measured by years or months. One evening on the threshold of December, Lisconnel was lying roofed over by a massy livid-black cloud, which came lumbering up and up interminably, and which the weatherwise estimated to contain as much snow as would smother the width of the world. The north wind moaned and keened dismally under the toil of wafting on this portentous load, and its breath was bitingly sharp, so that when the lads came in from the forge, their grandfather said, "Ah, Dan, shut over the door, for there's a blast sweepin' through it 'ud freeze ten rigiments as stiff as staties." We usually take a large view of things at Lisconnel. Dan went to carry out this order, but instead of doing so he suddenly shouted: "Murdher alive! Here's Mr. Polymathers."

Through the grey gloaming came a Mr. Polymathers, very different from what he had been on that brilliant, hopeful morning only a few weeks ago, when he had stepped lightly, and held his head up as if he were looking a friendly fortune in the face. Now his feet stumbled and dragged as he fared slowly against the wind's blustering, with his eyes on the ground, and his movements seemingly guided more by the weight of the bundle he carried than by his own will. Before he came within even loud shouting distance, everybody felt a presentiment of disaster; but he had not spoken a word to justify or discredit it by the time he got indoors.

"Musha, and so it's yourself, sir," old Felix then repeated, in a congratulatory tone. "Ah, but it's a hardy evenin', and it's perished you are, sir. Come in be the fire."

"Ay, I'm back," Mr. Polymathers said slowly, after a hesitating pause, as if the remark had been interpreted to him by some second person, "I was bringin' the books, thinkin' the lad might use them—he's young enough. But I'm not come to stop on you," he added, speaking faster, "on'y just for this night. Early to-morra I must be off to Ardnacreagh, and try for the taichin' there again. 'Twas on'y on account of bringin' the books I came this way. I'll be on the road quite early."

His insistence on this point made, somehow,

a very melancholy impression on Felix; but he replied jovially: "Is it to-morra? Bedad then, sir, don't you wish you may slip off on us that soon, and we after gettin' a hould of you agin? What fools we are. Not if you was as slithery, ivery inch of you, as a wather-eel."

The wraith of a relieved smile at this came over Mr. Polymathers's face; still it looked so grey and withered, and his eyes were so sunken, and his large, bony hands so shaky, that all with one consent refrained from questions which they were agog to ask; and when Mrs. Keogh by and by dropped in, and being an inquisitive and not very quick-witted person, said, "Saints among us—it's Mr. Polymathers. And how's yourself, sir? And are you bringing home the grand Degree?" though they all listened eagerly for the reply, they wished she had held her tongue.

"The divil a Degree, ma'am," said Mr. Polymathers, "and niver will."

There was a short silence, and then he turned round on his stool—it was the same from which he had made his boast in the summer sunset, but Dan had meanwhile mended its broken leg with the handle of a worn-bladed spade. "I've given up," he said to them. "I no longer entertain the project of becomin' a graduate, or for the matter of that an undergraduate of Dublin University; and if I'd done right, I'd niver have taken up such an idea. I've put it out of me head. But it's been in me mind a great while—a terrible long while."

"Look you here, Mr. Polymathers, sir, are you after gittin' any bad thratment from any people up in thim places?" said Felix, who always liked better to lay a grievance on some human and possibly breakable head than to believe it the work of the vengeance-baffling demon bad-luck.

"Not at all, not at all," said Mr. Polymathers, when the question reached him. "I've nothin' to complain of. They're very respectable people in Dublin, and it's a fine city. But me head's a bit giddy yet wid the drivin' they have in the streets, that makes one stupid. I mind there was a car tatterin' along, and I cróssin' over the College Green, had me down on the stones, on'y a dacint lad gript a hould of me, and whirled me inside the College gates. There I was before I rightly knew anythin' had happened me, and I after spendin' the best part of me life gettin' to it. 'Twasn't the way I thought it 'ud be. . . . But the College is as grand as any notion I had of it; on'y since I've seen it, 'tis like a drame to me that ever I set fut in it, just a sort of drame.... Great ancient places the squares are; I walked round the whole of them before I found the Hall. A couple of chaps in uniform like came axin' me me business, but I tould them fast enough that I was a candidate—ah, goodness help me.... And the Hall's a spacious and splendid apartment. On'y it was strange, now, to see it full of nothin' but young fellows, scarce oulder than the two lads there. I might, sure enough, have known the way it 'ud be, if I'd come to considher, but somehow it seemed to put me out, as if I'd no call to be there at all. There was one of them began pricin' me ould hat, and another of them tripped him up against a black marble construction with a pair of angels atop of it, that there is on the wall—sure they were just spalpeens. But I'll give you me word, when they called me up to the examiner's table, there was a young gintleman sittin' at it in his black gown and his cap wid the tassel—bound to be one of the College Fellows, and ivery sort of a fine scholar—and for all the age there was on him he might ha' been me son or me grandson.

"So he handed me over a little black *Virgil* wid the page opened where I was to exhibit me acquaintance wid the text. It was merely a bit of an oration of Queen Dido's that I've known ivery line of these forty years as well as I know me own name, and better. And what came over me is more than I can tell, but the minute I took the book in me hand, it seemed to me as if ivery atom of sinse and manin' slipped out of the words, or out of me head—I couldn't say which, and I just stood starin' at them and starin', till iverythin' else got whirlin' round about me, fit to shake the panes out of the big windows, and the pictures off the walls. . . . Belike himself persaived I was flusthered, for, 'Take your time,' sez he; and after a while they stood steady enough. But, the Lord be good to me—sorra a syllable of the sinse come back. And be that I well knew it was all up wid me; and I was thinkin' me father's son had no business to be standin' there makin' a show of meself in the middle of Trinity College. So the lad in the cap said again, 'Take your time, sir, take your time.' But I said to him, 'God help me, sir, I've taken very nigh all I'll get, for I declare to you, lad, I'm over seventy years of age. But as for your time, sir,' I said, 'I'll be wastin' no more of it.' And wid that I put down the book, and out I wint. I mind the sun in the square nearly dazzled the eyes out of me fool's head. I niver seen it blazin' brighter—and there was a big bell somewhere boomin' away, as if they'd set the heart of the world tollin'; it's ringin' in me ears yet. . . . And a couple of days after that I quit out of Dublin, and I've been trampin' back to this counthry, takin' me time, as he said—there's no hurry now about anythin'. So that was the ind of me University Degree."

"I just wish I could git discoorsin' wid that young feller," said old Felix, vindictively, "himself and his tassel in his cap."

"Sure, man, 'twas no fault of his," said Mr. Polymathers, "and I can live widout a Degree, if that's all. Me betters did before me. To tell you the truth, I've thought often enough as I was comin' along now, that I dunno how at all I'd have had the face to meet me poor father one of these days, and I cocked up with a *Baccalaureatus in Artibus*, and he wid not so much as a dacint stone over his grave to commemorate his name, that was the most illusthrious Polymath in the county Sligo, wid more larnin' in the tip of his ear than ever I got into me ould skull. Never a hap'orth of good was I at anythin' except the trifle of mathematics, but he was as great at the Classics. . . . I used to humbug meself somewhiles lettin' on I hankered after it because it would ha' gratified him maybe to hear of the event. But little I ever done to plase him, God forgive me. Let alone goin' and makin' an ould fool of meself up at Trinity College. . . . 'Twas a terrible upset to him when I turned again the Priesthood, after he had the money saved up for the seminary and all. Words about it we had, and the ind of it was he put it all into me brother Ned's little farm. Ned had no more fancy for larnin' than the bastes of the field. A trifle of it would ha' come in very handy sometimes for buyin' me books; howane'er it was not to be. . . . And the books there—I on'y brought them along to lave wid you for the youngest lad—ay, Nicholas. He has a head on his shoulders for the mathematics, I can tell you; he might do something yet, if he got his chances. They're no use to me now, and I'd as lief be shut of the sight of them. And to-morra I'll be off to Ardnacreagh."

So the gaunt old man talked on, groping his way out of hesitating pauses, and straying into dreamy meditations, as if he sometimes forgot his story, and sometimes its hearers. They did not know what a life-wreck it outlined, but they saw and surmised enough to make them think of him as "the crathur," and speak to him with more deference than if he had returned in a radiant glow of success, symbolised as some of them had anticipated, by scarlet robes as splendid, at least, as Father Rooney's at High Mass. And Felix O'Beirne took occasion of a madly skirling gust to say, "Listen now to that, sir, and don't be talkin' wild of thravellin' off to-morra. If I might be sayin' so, you'd a dale better stay quiet where you are this minyit. And as for taichin', sure it's proud and thankful the two boyos 'ud be for e'er a bit more. There's Nicholas mopin' about like an ould hin that's lost her chuckens iver since you quit."

Mr. Polymathers did stop quiet—very quiet—but he taught the boys no more. In fact, he did nothing except sit all day staring into the fire, as if he had lost something in it. Once after Nicholas had sat looking very hard at him for a long time with the ragged *Euclid* ostentatiously open at a crux, he seemed to rouse up, and putting out a hand for the book, began an explanation. But it died away unfinished in an aimless muttering, which both shocked and saddened Nicholas, and the experiment was not repeated. Then towards Christmas time all the neighbours were saying that Mr. Polymathers was greatly failed to what he had been. And Bridget O'Beirne reported that you might as well be argufyin' wid a scutty wren to swally down the full of the ducks' dish as persuadin' him to take a raisonable bite and sup. Dr. Hamilton from the Dispensary, who was consulted on the case, "consaited," Bridget told inquirers, "that he might be after gettin' a sort of stroke like unbeknownst;" but her own opinion was that "he had, so to spake, lost the knot off his thread, and 'twould be much if he didn't slip away out of it on them, afore they seen e'er another green laif on the bushes."

It was, at any rate, more than happened. One snowy afternoon, when he had been busy for some time "scrawmin' a manner of letter," which related, he said, to the disposition of his property, Mr. Polymathers grew so much worse that Dan and Nicholas ran off for the Doctor and the Priest, and before their arrival could possibly be expected, it became evident that he could not wait to receive them. Bridget O'Beirne, deploring the hap by his bed in the small room off the kitchen, thought a few minutes before he went that she heard him murmuring something coherent, and she called to little Rosy Corcoran,

"Child alive—me head's bothered—come in here and listen, can you make out at all what he's sayin'?"

Rosy came reluctantly and listened. "I think," she whispered, "it's some sort of prayers like what his Riverence sez."

"Ah, then, glory be to God for that itself," said Bridget, "there might be a good chance for him after all."

But she had been misinformed. The words Mr. Polymathers was muttering over and over to himself were: *Admitto te—admitto te.*

CHAPTER VIII

HONORIS CAUSÂ

THE evening of the day after Mr. Polymathers died was a very wild black-and-white one out of doors all round Lisconnel, yet, notwithstanding the flakes in the air and under foot, the O'Beirnes had received some company. Not at a wake, however; the purpose of their assembly was to discuss a serious business matter, upon which old Felix O'Beirne wished for friendly counsel. Hence his contemporary, old Paddy Ryan, had prodded little round craters in the snow with his thick stick all along the good step of bleak road which lay between his house and the forge, and with him had come on the same errand Terence Kilfoyle, who, although of so much junior standing, was esteemed as a man of notably shrewd sense and judgment. But then neither he nor the neighbours knew how often he took and gave Bessie Kilfoyle's advice. These two were present by express invitation, but another pair of guests, the Dooleys, would never have been asked for the sake of their opinion, which they were indeed encouraged to keep to themselves, and appeared at this domestic crisis merely by virtue of family ties. Old Felix had always thought little of his daughter Maggie's mental powers, and less ever since her marriage with Peter Dooley, who kept a shop in the Town, and could be described as " an ould gombeen man," if one wished to regard him from an unfavourable point of view, which his father-in-law not uncommonly did. He had been heard to say of Peter that "the chap was that smooth-spoken you might think he was after swallyin' a one of his own graisy dipts, on'y he'd liefer be chaitin' some poor body over the sellin' of it"—a perhaps not inexcusable preference. As for Peter, he contemplated humanity with a jovial cynicism, and rather enjoyed the society of the old blacksmith, despite the gruff sarcasms which sometimes made their womenkind turn the conversation apprehensively. *He* had been heard to say of Felix that " It was aisy work runnin' down other people's business, and small blame to th' ould man if he had a fancy for a light job now and agin, when he would be tired poundin' th' ould iron at a profit you couldn't see to pick up widout a strong pair of spectacles." Proximity had brought to the consultation Mrs. Carbery and Tim O'Meara from adjacent doors; and they, with old ancient Mrs. O'Beirne and her daughter and the two lads, formed quite a large party about the fire. The business to be brought before them was Mr. Polymathers's Will.

Now, lest it should be thought that unseemly haste was displayed in attending to this affair while Mr. Polymathers still lay in the little next room, I must explain that for special reasons the nature of the funeral arrangements depended upon the result of the conference; and how deeply important such a point would be considered at Lisconnel I need remind no one who has occasionally been perplexed by our propensity for the pinching and scraping which takes toll of a life-long penury, that a brief show of pomp may invest the last scene of all. This propensity is not seldom misconstrued into the outcome of a mere personal vanity, whereas it has its root in the worthier sentiment of veneration for our Kind. Ould Pat Murphy, who has subsisted all his life upon an insufficiency of pitaties, and inhabited a largish sty, never loses the sense that he owes something better to himself in his character of a human being, and he takes painful steps to ensure the ultimate discharge of the debt. One of these days he who has hitherto come and gone in un-imposing guise shall be borne, on wheels if possible—but here I mention grandeur never even dreamed of up at remote Lisconnel—in unwonted state, certain to draw the gaze of every passer-by. But as if with a fine touch of courtesy, he so times his assertion of dignity that none of his fellows shall thereby be abashed nor envy-bitten. No ragged wayfarer shall wish to change places with him as he passes solemnly along, nor grudge him the unshared splendour of his sombre equipage; not even if it display the crowning glory of woolly black plumes to waggle over his head. Accordingly, when Pat has died on his humble bed, which is as likely as not just earth tempered with straw, under his rifted thatch, through which he may perhaps see the stars glimmer with nothing except the smoke-haze and gathering mists between, he is conveyed thence with whatever pomp and circumstance his savings permit, and all his neighbours feel that the right thing has been done.

It is true that Mr. Polymathers had given no sign of any such sentiment. When discreetly sounded on the subject during his last days, he had replied: "Ah! man, it's very immaterial," in a tone of indifference as unmistakable as the phrase was ambiguous. And from this fact, coupled with his written instructions, it might, one would have thought, safely have been inferred that he desired no costly magnificence at his obsequies. Yet the point was obscured in his late host's mind by a thick cloud of doubts and scruples.

Mr. Polymathers had died surprisingly rich, not less than twenty-five pounds, seven shillings and threepence having been counted awestrickenly out of his leathern pouch. The ground rents of all Lisconnel did not reach to such a figure. It had been larger still before his disastrous expedition to the University; but it had never undergone any diminution so long as he abode under Felix O'Beirne's roof. On the first Saturday after his convalescence he had inquired, pouch in hand: "And what might be the amount of me pecuniary debt to you, sir?" And old O'Beirne had replied: "And you spendin' your time puttin' the heighth of larnin' into the two lads' heads! Bedad, sir, it's debt the other way round, supposin' there was to be any talk about it." The same little scene, dwindled at last into a mere form and ceremony, had taken place on every succeeding Saturday. . Not that Mr. Polymathers did not feel he had grounds for more than merely formal demur. But he was then facing the steep hill of his ambition, and had sometimes to stoop as he climbed.

But now, when he had turned back baffled, and all his climbing was done, old Felix had no engrossing object to blunt a sense of many scruples that must be removed before he himself or his family could with honour derive profit from the event; as they would do if Mr. Polymathers's instructions were carried out. For by that document, which he had finished drawing up only just in time, all his property was left unreservedly to Nicholas O'Beirne, with the injunction that as little of it as possible might be expended upon "the burying." Of course it was an extraordinary thing that such a piece of good fortune should befall, such a number of pounds accrue to, anybody at all; but apart from this there seemed to be nothing very strange in the bequest. Everybody knew that Mr. Polymathers had entertained "a great opinion entirely" of Nicholas' abilities. Time and again he had said that the lad would be heard of in the world if he got his chance of some good teaching. And he once more expressed the same conviction, only at fuller length and in finer language, in the composition which had been the last effort of his wearied brain. "It would give me," he wrote, "the utmost satisfaction to think that the legacy may eventually smooth his path to the attainment of those University distinctions which have eluded my own grasp." And almost his latest moment of consciousness had been pervaded by a faint thrill of pleased pride at the turn of the sentence as he read it over. This high style was not, however, maintained throughout, and the purport could not be misunderstood. Furthermore, everybody knew that he had said he had not a relation belonging to him in this world; and that being so, it was natural enough for him to make a promising and favorite pupil his heir. At first sight, therefore, no difficulties presented themselves; but old Felix slept upon the matter, and by morning grave doubts had risen in his mind. The gist of them was that "If they took and grabbed the ould gintleman's bit of money, and he after dyin' all his lone up among them there, wid ne'er a one of his own folks near him to see he had his rights, it might look ugly enough agin them, and set some people passin' remarks he'd be long sorry to have made on him, or any of his name;" and that for the precluding of such animadversions it might behove them to provide "a buryin'" not merely decent but "very respectable whatever," and to expend the remainder of Mr. Polymathers's personality upon a headstone for his grave, and Masses for his soul. To set against these apprehensions were Mr. Polymathers's wishes and Nicholas's interests; and the longer the old man balanced them in his mind, the more perplexing became their tremulous poise. So at last, goaded by the urgent necessity for a prompt decision, he turned to seek it among his neighbours. He could not forbear a hope that their voices might be convincingly in favour of giving Nicholas his chances; still his strongest feeling was that it would be a relief to get the matter settled one way or the other.

Very different in its degree of intensity was the interest with which his grandson Nicholas looked forward to the issue. The question to be decided seemed to him of almost as vital importance as if it were: Whether or no the sun should rise again next morning. For him at least, it depended upon that whether his world should loom back again in a dreary blankness, or waken lit with new and wondrous gleams. Nicholas's thirst for knowledge and love of learning were much more essentially part and parcel of him than his hands and eyes, and had so far found little except dreams and desires to thrive upon. Even before the memorable summer evening when the gaunt old man in the curious big hat had asked for the night's lodging, which lengthened into a season's sojourn, he had often wandered among visions of places where there were as many books as anybody could read—a dozen maybe—and some people in it with a power of book-learning—as much perhaps as his Reverence or the Doctor—only neither priest nor quality, but just neighbours whom he could question about anything that came into his head, as he used to question his grandfather, and Paddy Ryan, and Terence Kilfoyle, until he got tired of being asked, in reply: "Musha good gracious, and who could be tellin' you that?" an answer which had repeatedly left him a discouraged atom of bewilderment, symbolically environed by our wide-spreading bog. Since Mr. Polymathers's visit, these visions had grown clearer, but not under any rays of hope. His initiation into the elements of mathematics had pointed out the road along which he should travel, but had simultaneously revealed all its obstacles, insurmountable for him solitary and unequipped. In those days his mind was constantly fumbling at some insoluble problem with the sense of frustration that one has who gropes vainly in the dark, well knowing how a single unattainable match-flare would put what he is seeking into his hands. And no brighter prospect seemed to lie before him anywhere in his future.

So when he suddenly learned that Mr. Polymathers had left all his money—sums and sums—to be spent on "getting schooling for Nicholas O'Beirne;" and when the sums and sums were actually counted out on the table, he felt as if a door into enchanted regions had majestically opened in a blank wall. That night he went to bed in a state of joyous excitement, only dashed by some pangs of self-reproach for being unable to feel more sorrow at the flickering out of his poor old teacher's dim life. He had to frame excuses for himself by recollecting how his great-aunt Bridget had said, "Ah, sure the crathur's better off, God knows. What else 'ud he do, and the heart of him broke, but quit out of it, if he got the chance? Ay, bedad, some people have the quare good luck."

And when he got up with his happiness still fresh and strange in the morning, there was his grandfather declaring "he didn't know if they'd have a right to touch the bit of money at all; it might be no thing to go do; schoolin' or no schoolin', he wouldn't be givin' people any call to say the O'Beirnes were after playin' a dirty thrick." At this Nicholas's experience was like that of a desert traveller who should see a mirage of palms and pools grow swiftly before his delighted eyes into a substantial oasis, and then anon, or ever he could approach it, shimmer back, with all its sheen and shade, into mocking illusion again. For thus did it fare with his hopes as his grandfather talked of renouncing Mr. Polymathers's bequest. Moreover, the grounds which the old man alleged forbade his grandson, lothfully though he listened, to utter a word of protest, and even made him half ashamed of his vehement longing to do so. Nicholas had been an O'Beirne for but fourteen years, yet he had already entered upon his inheritance of family pride. Only he could not bring himself to believe that the honour of his house called for so prodigious a sacrifice; and he could have urged a dozen arguments against it, if some other person had been the legatee. As it was, all that delicacy would permit him to do for himself was to give piteously inadequate expression to his sentiments in casual remarks about the grandeur of getting a bit of learning, and the difficulty of understanding some things out of one's own head. Altogether that day was the longest and the most anxious that he had ever spent.

Dan also, though his fortunes were not involved to the same extent as his younger brother's, was not easy in his mind. All day he had been thinking rather badly of himself, and suspecting that other people thought worse of him than he deserved, and the reflection was depressing and irritating. The news of the legacy certainly had not given him unmixed pleasure, as he felt that it ought to have done; but at the same time he was aware that he neither grudged nor envied Nicholas his good fortune, and that this unamiable frame of mind would nevertheless probably be ascribed to him, if he betrayed any dissatisfaction or disapproval. The truth was that he could not help feeling some mortification at the way in which both Mr. Polymathers and his grandfather assumed the forge to be his destiny and portion in life. Dan did not by any means despise it: he took an interest in the work, and a pride in the fact that farmers sent their horses thither from beyond the Town, so well reputed was old Felix O'Beirne's shoeing. But it did not follow that he wanted to be a blacksmith all his days. Even if he had done so, he was sixteen, and consequently of an age to resent any prescribed calling, especially since he knew that the selection here had been made as the result of an unfavourable comparison of his abilities with those of another person. "Dan is no fool, mind you," Mr. Polymathers had said once. "But for intellect you need never name him on the same day of the month as Nicholas," a verdict which fell with a slight shock upon Dan, accustomed to the precedence given by two years' seniority, superior strength, and a more practical turn of mind. What was far more serious, however, Dan secretly cherished an ambition of his own. It took the form of thinking that it would be a wonderfully fine thing if he could ever get to learn the doctoring, and be able to drive about on a car like Dr. Hamilton, with a name and a remedy for everybody's ailment. A particularly fine thing it seemed to understand the construction of bones and joints, a knowledge which would put it in his power to prevent people from coming to such grief as, for instance, poor Matt Haloran down at Duffclane, who must limp on a crooked leg to the end of his days, because the man who pulled in his dislocated ankle for him had made a botch of it, through not knowing rightly what he was about. Dan had been much impressed, too, by several cases where a few drops of brown stuff out of a bottle had put people to sleep when various aches and pains had long hindered them from closing an eye, a result which the neighbours were occasionally disposed to view with mistrust, as rather probably wrought through the agency of "some quare ould pishtrogues (charms)," but which to Dan's mind proved the possession of a skill as enviable as it was beneficent. Beside it hammering out horseshoes appeared a tedious and aimless pursuit, and he sometimes thumped away in a very vague dream of one of these days finding himself more congenially employed. Now, however, it was perfectly clear to him that if Nicholas "took off wid himself to get scholarship," his own portion must be to stick to the anvil. For otherwise supposing his grandfather got past his work, or anything else happened him, there would be nobody left to look after Dan's great-aunt, who was not very old, and his great-grandmother, who was such a wonderful age entirely that no one could say how much longer she mighn't live. Even the wildest of dreams are not quite easy to scare away, and it was this chiefly that marred his content with Mr. Polymathers's testamentary dispositions. Still, when he heard his grandfather's doubts, and saw his brother's downcast looks, he became almost as anxious as Nicholas himself that the neighbours might talk away the old man's scruples and allow the will to stand.

Thus there were many eager hopes and fears lodged that evening in the O'Beirnes' living-room, which was all throbbing with fire-light, as the neighbours began to drop in talking out of the dark. People are apt to speak loudly when they get their breath after a battle with snowy blasts; and the sound of voices came strangely into the stillness close by, where there was only a cold glimmer of candle-light, and nobody conversing, unless we count old Bridget O'Beirne, who had slipped in to repeat a few prayers, and say to herself with a sort of grudging wistfulness that everybody else was getting away. Then she came back to her world again, and mended the crumbling red-hot bank with sods out of her apron, and shovelled up the snow-balls shaken off their visitors' clogged brogues, that they might not melt into mud patches on the floor.

To Dan and Nicholas, looking on from opposite corners, it seemed a long while before anything to the purpose was said. Everybody had to comment upon the snow, and Paddy Ryan's remark was that "if it kep' on at it that-a-way, they'd be hard enough set to get through the dhrifts be the day of the buryin'." This caused Mrs. Carbery to remember how she "had been at a one up in the County Cavan, where the gate into the buryin'-ground was all blocked up, so that the whole of them had to lep over what would be be rights a ten-fut wall. And if they did, the half of them plumped up to their necks in a soft place on the other side, and came as near losin' their lives as could be thought. Bedad now, they were comical to behould, goodness forgive her for sayin' so, all bawlin' and flounderin' about like a flock of sheep stuck in a bog, on'y it was a white bog and black sheep, as she minded Tom Ennis, that was a quare codger, sayin' at the time." And this again started old O'Beirne upon reminiscences of remarkable buryings which had come under his own observation.

"Comical it may have been," he said, "but I'll bet you me best brogues ne'er a one of yous ever witnessed a quarer buryin' than a one I seen down in the south some ould ages ago, when I was a slip of a lad. But I'll maybe ha' tould you the story, ma'am—about the flood in the Tullaroe River?"

"Was that the time it riz up suddint and dhrownded the crathur that was diggin' the grave?" said Mrs. Carbery.

"Sure not at all: that happint up at Lough Gortragh, and this I'm talkin' about was in the Tullaroe River, a dale souther of the Lough. Outrageous it does be in the wet saisons. So one harvest day, when it was flowin' over all before it, there was a walkin' funeral about crossin' at the ford. The way of it was, they were after hangin' a lad up at the jail. In those days it's very ready they were wid the hangin,' and in a hurry over it too sometimes. Howane'er the frinds of this lad had got lave to be buryin' him dacint after he would be hanged; and me poor father, and meself, and plinty of other people were follyin'. Till they come to the ford, and when they seen the manner the wather was runnin' wild, the bearers had a notion to be turnin' back; but they made up their minds, and on they wint. And as sure as they did, one of the lads must needs slip his fut, and they right in the middle of the river, and down wid the whole lot of thim, like a stook of oats in a gale of win'; 'twas twinty wonders e'er a man of thim ever got his feet under him agin. Faix, now the yell every sowl let you might ha' heard anywheres at all; for some of thim was thinkin' the misfort'nit body was apt to be swep' away and mortally dhrowned to the back of bein' hung; and some of thim wasn't thinkin' any such a thing. But as for the coffin, I'll give you me word if it didn't take and set off wid itself floatin' away bobbin' along atop of the wather as light now, as if it was a lafe dhropped down from the boughs archin' over our heads—and wasn't that cur'ous enough? And as quare as anythin' it was to behould the people all peltin' along be the two wet banks of the river as hard as they could dhrive, and thrippin' theirselves up over the roots of the trees, and slitherin' into the pools, wid the coffin just skimmin' and swimmin' away down the sthrame ahead of them, as aisy and plisant as if it was a bit of a pookawn. You might ha' sworn there was ne'er a nothin' in it, to look at it. And he they were after hangin' a fine big man, 'ud weigh every ounce of fourteen stone. I tould you it was a quare thing. So where it would be sailin' to nobody could say; very belike out into the bay below. But sure when it come where the river runs past th' ould church, the strong current that was racin' under it just gave a sort of lap round wid it, and washed it clane up on the flat stones at the gate goin' into the buryin'-ground, and left it lyin' there, same as if the lads had set it down off their shoulders. Bedad now it was a very lucky thing it so happint there was none of the pólis or red coats about, be raison of their gettin' notice the buryin' was somewhere else—oncommon lucky."

"It's as quare as the rest of it," said Peter Dooley, who had heard the story before, "that nobody among them had had the wit to put a few brickbats in it, or some good big lumps of heavy stones. Stones is plinty, and chape enough."

"They're things you haven't the sellin' of then, I'll go bail," said old Felix. He spoke in resentment of the interruption, but Mr. Dooley took the speech as a flattering tribute to his business capacity, and acknowledged it with a good-humoured smirk.

So Bridget might have spared herself the uneasiness which made her say hurriedly to her brother: "If you was lookin' for Mr. Polymathers's bit of writin', Felix, I left it lyin' convanient to you under the plate there on the table."

"Oh, ay, bedad, that's what's been botherin' me," said the old man, reachin' for it, "I dunno rightly what to say to it. But sure any of yous that like can be readin' it, and see what he sez for yourselves."

Reading was not a question simply of liking with all members of the company; but everybody could hold the paper and look wise, and if he were none the more so afterwards, that may have been only because he knew the contents of it beforehand. When it was Peter Dooley's turn he examined the signature closely, and said, "But what name's this he's put to it? 'John Campion' I see, but divil a sign of any Polymathers."

"Ah, that was another thing was botherin' me, too," said old O'Beirne, rather dejectedly, "a little while ago, when Dr. Hamilton was comin' to see him. For th' ould gintleman tould him Campion was his name; and it appairs Polymathers is some discripshin of thrade, and not rightly called to anybody at all. So I was thinkin' he was maybe annoyed wid our callin' him out of his name all the while; but he said all that ailed it was it was a dale too good for him; and better plased he seemed we would keep on wid it. Oh ay, 'John Campion's' right enough."

"I niver heard of any such a thrade as polymatherin'," said his son-in-law; "would it be anythin' in the pedlarin' line?"

"Is it pedlarin'?" said old O'Beirne, "and he that took up wid larnin' and litherature he couldn't ha' tould you the price of a pinny loaf. Faix, man, if I was Maggie I'd just put a good dab of strong glue in your place behind the counter down-below, and stick you standing steady in it, for buyin' and sellin's all the notion you have in your head here or there. Pedlarin', sez he."

"Well, at all events," said Peter Dooley, unperturbed, "he's got together a dacint little fortin one way or the other. Maybe he didn't come by it any worser; but sure that's no great odds now. And plain enough he sez the young chap there's to have it—that's all the one thing wid yourself. But, anyhow, I dunno who could aisy conthrive to be takin' it off you, and he lavin' no one belongin' to him. You have it safe enough. Grab all you can, and keep a hould of it when you've got it, sez I. But you're safe enough, no fear."

Nicholas, watching his grandfather's face from his corner, would have given ten years of his life to throttle his uncle's reassuring speech midway.

"There's no mistake, I should say, about what he was intendin'," said Terence Kilfoyle, in whose hands the paper was by this time; "and who'd be apt to know better than himself what he had in his mind so long as he was right in his head."

"And if he wasn't, it's little likely he'd be to ha' got that written. Hard enough work it is, accordin' to what I can see, even when a body has all his wits to the fore," said old Paddy Ryan, whose acquaintances did as a rule get more out of breath over a letter than over a wrestling match or the recapture of an active pig.

"Mad people do be surprisin' cute some whiles, mind you," said Mrs. Carbery. "There was a deminted body used to be up at our place—Daft Jimmy they called him—and if you axed him the time of day he'd tell you to the minyit, exacter than any clock that ever sthruck, and he belike not widin a mile of e'er a one."

"It seems a sight of money to be layin' out on larnin'," pursued old Paddy; "I dunno where you'd be gettin' the vally of it that-a-way, onless he was larnin' everythin' twyste over, same as you put two coats of whitewash on a wall if you're after mixin' a drop more than you want. You might do it then."

His friends' arguments and illustrations had apparently a depressing effect upon old Felix, and he said with impatience, "Weary on it, man-alive! Sure there's no doubt about what he was manin', at all at all. The question is, have we any call to be takin' him at his word, and spendin' it away from aught 'ud do him a benefit—the buryin' and Masses and such?"

"That might be a diff'rint thing," said Mrs. Carbery.

"I'd scarce think it," said Terence Kilfoyle, "considherin' he'll say no more to make it so. The job's out of his hand, and 'ill stay the way he left it."

"He might ha' changed his mind afore now, for anythin' we can tell," said Mrs. Carbery.

"'Deed, then, he might so, the poor man, Heaven be his bed," said Mrs. Dooley.

"You could ax the priest about it," Tim O'Meara said diffidently, out of the melancholy muteness which it was his habit to maintain.

"That's as much as to say it should go for Masses," said old Felix, clutching at any shred of definite opinion, "for it's on'y in the nathur of things his Riverence 'ud be recommindin' thim."

But Tim shrank away from the shadow of responsibility, protesting, "Och, not at all, not at all. I wasn't as much as sayin' anythin'."

The old man tossed up his chin disgustedly, and meditated gloomily during a brief pause.

"There's no denyin'," he said then, "that poor Mr. Polymathers had a won'erful great opinion of himself over there." He nodded towards Nicholas's corner, and used this periphrasis with a sense that he had taken a precaution against perilously arousing the boy's vanity. "Times and agin last summer he was sayin' to me the lad 'ud do credit to us yet if he had his chances. A pity it 'ud be, he said, if he didn't iver git to school, or maybe College itself. And gave him his books and all. But sure, I dunno would that make it look any the better for us if we was to be grabbin' his bit of money, and we the on'y people he had to see he got fairity after he was gone. Ne'er a word have I agin schoolin' and College if there would be no doubtin' over the matter; but there's some things you can't stand too clear of, like the heels of a kickin' horse. It might have a square, bad apparance, rael mane; and long sorry I'd be for that. What 'ud you say, now?"

He looked slowly round the flickering room, but met with no response from old or young; all silent, from his mother, asleep in her elbow-chair by the hearth, to his grandson Nicholas, very wide awake, in a nook beyond her. Then his eyes travelled across to the opposite corner, and as they lit there upon his other grandson, he specialised his question into, "What 'ud *you* say, Dan?"

Dan, thus abruptly called upon, was intensely conscious that two eyes shining out of the shadow over against him had fixed him with an unwavering gaze. And it is hard to say how he would have answered their urging if at the same moment Mr. Dooley at his elbow had not been loudly whispering to Mrs. Dooley—

"Colleges? Sure that's just talk he has be way of an excuse for keepin' it. A great notion he has of spendin' it on Colleges. He knows better, bedad."

Mr. Dooley, who was rather like several sorts of rodent animals in the face, wore a smile at his own penetration.

"I dunno but it might look ugly," Dan suddenly said.

He was staring straight before him, yet he knew somehow, as if by a sixth sense, that the shining eyes opposite ceased their watch with an angry flash; and he had scarcely spoken before he would have given anything to call back his irrevocable speech.

His grandfather's puzzled will closed on the opinion with a vice-like grip, as if at a touch given to a powerful spring. Indecision was with him an unwonted mood, from which it was an irresistible relief to escape, even at some cost. And nobody who knew him could suppose that his mind, once made up, would alter.

"Begorrah, Dan, I believe it's true for you," he said. "'Twould be no thing to go do, and divil a bit of me 'ill do it. Whatever's over from the buryin' and bit of a grave-stone may go for Masses; sorra a penny of it a one of the O'Beirnes 'ill touch."

So Nicholas lost his chances, which seems a pity when one considers how, for the sake of bringing them to him, old Mr. Polymathers, dazed and enfeebled and hope-bereft, came tramping on that long, long journey, day after weary day, under the scowling wintry sky, and against the ruffling blasts, back again across the breadth of Ireland. The road was all strewn for him with the wreckage of his shattered dream, and the one gleam of consolation that lighted him on the way had been the thought that his savings might now give a help to the lad up at Lisconnel. This had often been in his mind when he set off, shivering in the bleak morning, and when he stopped to shift his over-heavy bundle, and when he roused himself painfully from the bewildering lethargies that fell upon him. But he had reckoned without the pride of the O'Beirnes.

It was a pity, too, that the affair should have led to an estrangement between the two brothers, which set in as tacitly as a black frost, for neither of them ever said a word to the other about Dan's intervention. This silence left him in the thorny grip of misgivings as to the motives with which Nicholas might be charging him. That he had done it on purpose to spoil Nicholas's chances out of spite was one of these. And although Dan knew very well that he had spoken from an altogether different impulse, he was conscious of having had feelings which seemed to give him a cruelly clear insight into the possible workings of

Nicholas's mind. "Consaitin' that it was because I was invyin' him, that's what he's thinkin' agin me," he said to himself as the days went by, and he perceived, or fancied, that Nicholas in his disconsolate moping about had no other aim than to keep away from wherever Dan might be.

But Dan's unhappiness took an acuter phase in a fortnight or so, when Nicholas began to resume his mathematical studies. There lies just opposite the O'Beirnes' front door a low turf bank, gently sloping, and mostly clothed with short, fine grass, but liable to be cut into brown squares, if sods are wanted for roofing a shed, or for spreading a green layer of scraws under new thatch. This had been done on a rather large scale in the past autumn, and the boys had been in the habit of utilising the smooth, bare patches as tablets whereon to trace with pointed sticks, or any handy implements borrowed from the forge, the figures and diagrams occurring in Mr. Polymathers's scientific lectures. Nicholas now, albeit he had buried both teacher and hope, began once more to draw his circles and triangles and polygons on the soft mould, as it grew damply and darkly through the wearing snow coverlid. Sometimes in the excitement of demonstrating involved relations between AB's and BC's he would for a while forget his disappointment almost as completely as he did the wet-winged winds that had been flapping and wheeling about the house ever since the thaw set in. His obliviousness could not, however, ensure him against the effects of cold shower-baths, and before long his geometrical drawing was done to the accompaniment of a hollow-sounding cough, which made Dan remember a time some years ago when Nicholas had been so seriously ill with pleurisy that voices had said at their door, "Ah, the crathur, he'll scarce last the night. Dr. Hamilton has no opinion of him at all. 'Deed, now, his poor grandfather's to be pitied, losin' such a fine young lad." And he also remembered having occasionally heard his great-aunt say that Nicholas took after his poor mother, and would never comb a grey head. Now, therefore, the figure of Nicholas sitting out on the bank in a vibrating mist of rain, with his feet in a puddle, and his hair flickering in damp strands about his thin face, became for Dan an ominous and saddening spectacle.

But while he was ruefully contemplating it one day, a happy idea struck him. He would get Nicholas some clean white paper to draw his *dygrims* on. "And then belike he'd be contint to sit in be the fire, instead of to be catchin' his death scrawmin' out there in the mud under teems of rain." Grand writing-paper was to be had at Isaac Tarpey's, down in Ballybrosna, and Dan at this time happened to be in possession of a whole shilling, which he dedicated more than willingly to the purchase.

Isaac Tarpey presided over the Ballybrosna Post-office, which was in some respects a singularly complete establishment, as not only was the raw material for a letter kept in stock there, but the letter itself could, for a consideration, be written on the premises by the postmaster in person. It is true that Isaac did not supply more than the barest necessaries of scribes, the bread and water, so to speak, of stationery, the very plainest pens and paper and ink. He kept his ink in a single moderate-sized jar, out of which he measured penn'orths and ha'p'orths into the various receptacles brought by customers who came to demand "a sup" or "a drain." On these sales his profits were certainly enormous, not less than cent. per cent., but then the consumption of that article was extremely small in Ballybrosna. It took a long while to reach the sediment at the bottom of the jar, and Isaac's letter-writing, done at the rate of thruppence a-piece, probably was a more lucrative branch of his business, though the correspondence of the Town was not large enough to put his services in frequent requisition. Partly on this account, and partly because he was by nature a strong conservative, Mr. Tarpey set his face sternly against the spread of education. He was distressed by the appearance of any symptoms of it among the neighbouring youth, even when it took the form of an inquiry for his limp paper and skewer-like pens. In fact, the diffusion of penmanship was what he most seriously deprecated and discountenanced. "The Lord knows," his main argument ran, "the foolery them spalpeens 'ill be gabbin' permiscuis would sicken you, widout givin' them the chance to be sittin' down aisy and invintin' it." His wife once suggested that "the crathurs might be more sinsible like, when they were takin' time to considher themselves." But Isaac said, "Pigs may fly."

At the time when Dan came for his paper the office was occupied by Norah Fottrell, engaged in dictating a letter to her sweetheart, Stevie Flynn, away in Manchester. The composition still looked discouragingly brief, despite Isaac's big, flourishing hand, yet Norah's ideas had already run so short that she was staring in quest of more up among the cobwebby rafters over her head.

"You might say," she said, after a pause, "that I hope he's gettin' his health where he is."

"I've said that twyste before," Isaac objected severely.

"Och, murdher, have you?" said Norah, reverting to the rafters with a distracted gaze.

"Couldn't you tell him the price your father got for the last baste he sould?" said Isaac.

"Bedad, I might so," said Norah; "'twas on'y thirty shillin', but it 'ud take up a good bit of room. And look-a, Mr. Tarpey, couldn't we lave the rest of the page clane? As like as not the bosthoon wouldn't be botherin' his head spellin' out the half of it."

The adoption of this course expedited Norah's love-letter to a happy close. But when Dan took her place at the counter Isaac assured him, not without satisfaction, that "they were cliver and clane run out of all their writin' paper, barrin' it might be a sort of butt-ind of loose sheets left litterin' at the bottom of the drawer, and they that thick wid dust you could be plantin' pitaties in them, forby gettin' mildewed lyin' up in the damp so long."

It was not so much compunction at Dan's disappointed countenance as an irresistible hankering after a good bargain that ultimately led the postmaster to sweep this uninviting remnant together, and fix upon it the price of sixpence. The charge was exorbitant, considering the small quantity and damaged state of the goods, yet Dan carried off his little packet quite contentedly, announcing that he would step over again for another sixpenn'orth next week, when, as Isaac reluctantly admitted, a fresh supply of stationery would have arrived.

As Dan left the office he passed an unknown gentleman, tall, with a shrewd sallow face, dark, peaked beard, and alert grey eyes, who had been leaning against the door while the bargain was struck. The stranger was Mr. Alfred B. Willett, of New York, a wealthy engineer, who on his way home from Europe had been visiting his friend Dr. Hamilton of Ballybrosna. His curiosity now was roused by Dan's evident eagerness to acquire materials for the drawing of diagrams, the pursuit striking him as so strangely incongruous with the aspect of the brown-faced stalwart ragged youth, that he stepped inside when the place was empty to make inquiries on the subject. The postmaster's information was to the effect that "the O'Beirnes above at the forge had always had the name of bein' very dacint respectable people up to then, and he'd never before seen any of the young ones settin' themselves up to be askin' after such things. He hoped it mightn't be a sign that the old man was goin' foolish, and lettin' the lads get past his control. But sure enough we must all of us put up wid growin' good for nothin' sometime, unless we happint to ha' never been worth anythin' to begin wid. And he wished he had a penny ped him for every one of that sort he'd met in the coorse of his life."

This cynical disquisition was not very enlightening. However next week when Dan slipped over again for his second sixpenn'orth, Mr. Willett it chanced was there too, having called to report on the excessive thickness and other undesirable peculiarities of some ink lately supplied to him. It had been, in fact, composed of "the sidimint" artfully diluted with a drop of vinegar; but Isaac Tarpey said it was "thick wid the stren'th was in it," and set about uncorking his fresh jar with an affronted air, when his customer persisted in pointing out that its adhesive properties were less valuable in ink than in glue. Meanwhile Mr. Willett fell into a conversation with Dan, which ended in his engaging the lad to accompany him as guide on a shooting expedition next day. The arrangement turned out satisfactorily, and was repeated more than once, with the consequence that Dan and the stranger talked about many things in the course of several long tramps, until one evening the latter, sitting on a stone wall after a steep pull uphill, made Dan an offer which caused the most familiar objects to seem unreal, because a marvellous dream was coming true among them. For Mr. Willett proposed to take Dan home with him, and have him taught whatever he most wished to learn. "You're a smart lad, Dan," he said, "and I reckon you'll make more of that in the States than in this country."

"Ah! the doctorin'," said Dan, turning as red as the young sorrel leaves, and letting his darling wish slip out in his surprise as involuntarily as he would have blinked at a flash of lightning. But next moment he remembered Nicholas, and fell silent; Nicholas, who had not looked him in the face since that snowy evening weeks ago. The dream seemed to stop coming true.

"There's no need to make up your mind in a hurry," said Mr. Willett, "you can be thinking it over between this and Monday."

Dan did think it over deeply that night and the next day and the day after. He thought how fine, if rather fearful, it would be to go on such a journey; and what a splendid thing to learn the doctoring business, and some day come home again able to cure everybody of anything that ailed them. "For out in the States, like enough, they had all manner of contrivances the people over here had never taught Dr. Hamilton," whose skill was occasionally baffled. He imagined the neighbours' surprise when he came driving up on his car; if possible he would be driving a little blue-roan mare like Farmer Finucane's Rosemary, with whom he had made friends in the course of many shoeings. He thought he would be sorry to miss seeing them all for so long; and yet it would certainly be very pleasant, in a way, to get to a place where things were a bit different sometimes, not like here where when you were getting up in the morning you knew what was bound to be happening all day just as well as you did when you were going to bed that night. And next he thought that such days would be coming to Nicholas, while he himself was away seeing and learning "all manner of everything;" and that if he had held his tongue that time, maybe Nicholas would have got his chance with Mr. Polymathers's money, instead of its all being spent away on nothing. And he thought that it wasn't his fault, for what else could he say when he was asked all of a minute, except the first thing that came into his head? And he wondered how it would be if anything happened to his grandfather. Nicholas wasn't over-strong, and too young altogether besides. And then he thought again that Mr. Willett was cleverer than anybody he had ever seen, and more good-natured; it was a pleasure to go about with him; and people were great fools to give up their chances. Maybe Nicholas might get another some day. And maybe Mr. Polymathers had been mistaken in thinking that he was the one best worth teaching.

All these things Dan thought, and the result of his cogitations was that on the Monday he stole a sheaf of Nicholas's most complicated cobweb-like diagrams from their hiding-place in the wall, and brought them with him when he went by appointment to meet his patron off beyond Knockfinny. And when Mr. Willett said to him: "Well, Dan, what about the States and the doctoring?" he replied inconsequently by holding out the sheets of paper with the explanation: "It's me brother, Nicholas, sir, does be doin' them mostly out of his own head."

Mr. Willett looked at them for some minutes with interested ejaculations. "Upon my word," he then said, "if these were done out of his own head, he must have about as much mathematics located in it by nature as a spider."

"Aren't they good for anythin' at all then, sir?" said Dan, not knowing exactly what he hoped and feared.

"Good? They're astonishing," said Mr. Willett. He asked some questions about Nicholas's age, schooling, and so forth; after which he said: "You must take me to see this brother of yours, Dan. I expect he'll have got to come right along with us."

But Dan stared round and round the spacious brown-purple floor they were standing on, and after a far-off flight of wild fowl, and up at the sky, where the clouds travel without let or hindrance, before he answered hesitatingly: "The two of us couldn't ever both go, sir. How could we be lavin' the forge and all on me ould grandfather? And Nicholas never makes any great hand of the work."

"Ah! is that the way the land lies?" said Mr. Willett, as if half impatient, and half amused, but not best pleased. He looked hard at Dan, and thought he saw how matters stood, "You've no mind to leave the old grandfather and the rest of the concern, but you think it would be more in the other lad's line."

As a matter of fact Dan was at that particular moment feeling strongly how easily he could have reconciled himself to the separation, and how entirely it would be the making of him to do so. But he did not gainsay Mr. Willett's statement. To himself he said, "He's a right to have his chances; and the one of us is bound to stop in it"—a mode of expressing his sentiments which showed that he had much need of culture; and aloud: "Nicholas always had a powerful wish to be gettin' some larnin'; and I'm a fool to him at the geomethry anyway."

The upshot of it all was that when some six weeks later Mr. Alfred B. Willett sailed for New York, Nicholas O'Beirne accompanied him, and

Dan O'Beirne remained at Lisconnel. It was on a gleamful April day that they set out, with soft gusts roaming all around, as if they had come from very far off, and were eagerly exploring the strange places, and many light clouds flitting by swiftly above, as if they had a long journey before them, and were in a joyous flurry over it. Dan spent the slow-paced hours in the forge, where he hammered loud and long, and seldom looked across the threshold. The pleasantest thought in his mind was the remembrance of a short conversation which he had had with Nicholas while they were tying up Mr. Polymathers's old books at the kitchen-door just as the grey chink in the east filled with rose-light, and the earliest breeze came over the bog waving the withered grasses. Dan had said to Nicholas: "Sure I wouldn't be grudgin' you e'er a bit of good luck, lad." And Nicholas had replied: "And never did."

After Nicholas's departure many days bad and good rose on Lisconnel, but few of them brought any tidings of the absent. Letters passed now and then, laggard and uninstructive as such letters must be, and they grew rarer and briefer as time went on. Perhaps a dozen years had gone by, when Dan one day received simultaneously an American newspaper and a parcel. The newspaper was marked with large blue chalk crosses at a paragraph which related how the degree of D.Sc. had been conferred *Honoris Causâ* upon Mr. Nicholas O'Beirne by the University of Sarabraxville. And in the parcel, more astonishing still, was a brown-covered book, lettered on the back: *A Treatise on Conic Sections, by Nicholas O'Beirne.* By this time Dan had been left alone at the forge; but he was courting Mary Ryan, Mick Ryan's daughter, so he naturally conveyed to her this remarkable news. It produced a profound impression. Old Paddy her grandfather was with difficulty brought to realise the fact that "they were after makin' a doctor of young Nicholas O'Beirne, him that went out to the States the year before the Famine." And when he had got the idea into his head, it seemed to act like a swivel-joint, and set him nodding to the tune of: "Well tub-be sure; glory be to God; young Nicholas O'Beirne."

"I wish to goodness he'd come over and cure Mick, poor man," said Mick's wife. "For he hasn't been worth pickin' up off the road ever since he was bad with the fever last year, and he might as well be dhrinkin' so much ditch-wather as the ould stuff Dr. Carson's givin' him."

"Ah but it's not the medical doctorin' Nicholas has gone to," said Dan, the shadow of a shadow crossing his face, "there'd be diff'rint letters for that." And he proceeded to read out the report of the degree conferred *honoris causâ* upon the distinguished young Irishman, Mr. Nicholas O'Beirne, whose recent contributions to the study of the higher mathematics had roused so much interest in scientific circles.

"Ay, true for you, Dan," said Mary; "you don't hear them callin' Dr. Carson an Honory-causy."

Dan's shred of Latin had grown rustier than the oldest iron in his stock, but was not yet utterly worn away. "The manin' of that," he explained, "would be, *be raison of honour*, and I should suppose, they've gave it to him for the sake of what all he's after doin'."

"Bedad then, Dan," said Mrs. Mick, "some one had a right to be givin' you an Honory-causy yourself, considherin' the cure you're after makin' on Mr. Finucane's ould mare, and everybody of the opinion she'd never stand on four feet again to the ages' ind."

"Och blathers, ma'am," Dan said, modestly,

"sure anybody wid the sight of their eyes might aisy enough ha' seen what ailed the crathur. That was no great comether. And look at what Nicholas is after doin'; he's wrote a book, no less."

The "Treatise on Conic Sections" created an even stronger sensation than the news of the honorary degree, especially among those who had letters enough to spell out the familiar name on the title-page. Dan's Mary was not one of these scholars, but she found another page to admire, saying that the circles "drew in and out of aich other like a lot of soap-bubbles, had an oncommon tasty look, and so had all them weeny corners, wid the long bames between, the moral of a chain-harrow, you couldn't mistake it. Sure it's proud of it anybody might be."

Probably Nicholas was very proud of this first heir of his invention, diagrams, and all. Whether it ever had any successors seems doubtful; certainly none of them arrived at his old home. But his Treatise is still safely stowed away there in a corner of the dresser. Most likely it is the only copy of "O'Beirne on Conic Sections" existing in Ireland; and who would expect to find it lodged in a smoke-stained cabin on the wild bogland between Duffclane and Lisconnel?

CHAPTER IX

BOYS' WAGES

ONE leaden-roofed morning in the winter after his brother Nicholas had gone to the States, young Dan O'Beirne was in rather low spirits, and rather out of humour. It was not unnatural that such a mood should occasionally overtake him, since he had reached apparently a straight and monotonous tract of road, which would have looked interminable to the eyes of seventeen had not his household companions been now all declining folk, whose presence brought under his constant obversation the last stages of "a long journey in December gone." Half a century or so of smithy work, even with some unlicensed doctoring and illicit distilling thrown in, was not by any means the future that he would have liked his oracle to predict for him. And though he forecast it accurately enough without the intervention of any soothsaying, this no more helped him to avoid it than if he had been an old-world tragical hero, whose friends were seeking by vain devices to circumvent the promulgated decrees of his destiny. Dan, indeed, took no steps of that sort. For him, as for most of us, the skirts of circumstance were as the meshes of the net in which Fate holds us, and his evil star was an object of which it seemed very hard to get a good grip. I have always wondered myself how people set about it. At any rate, Dan continued to walk under his; that is to say, if it were really bad luck that kept him at the forge. Upon this point there might be differences of opinion. Terence Kilfoyle, for instance, who dropped in to escape from a snow-shower in the course of that morning, would not, evidently, have taken such a view. For when Dan said something grumblingly about Lisconnel being "a slack sort of a place, where one didn't get much chance of doin' anythin' at all;" he replied, "Bedad now, if I'd the fine business you and your grandfather have to be puttin' me hand to, I wouldn't call the Queen me aunt."

In those times the district around our bogland was more thickly inhabited than it is at present, and the blacksmith's jobs were proportionately plentier. Nowadays the forge is liable to long spells of silence, but Dan, who as young Dan has been superseded, philosophises over them, and talks no more about chances. On this occasion his remarks were overheard by his grandfather, perhaps because the old man had begun to have thoughts of chances which made him sensitive to signs of discontent in his assistant. And by and by when Terence had gone, he said, " Terence said a very sinsible word; a lad might aisy get a worse start in life, ay indeed he might so, if it was twyste as slack. But anyhow there's them here that 'ud be hard set to make a shift for themselves if the two of us was out of it ; and I'm apt to be quittin' before Biddy at all events." To which Dan replied, " Why what talk was there of quittin'?" and the subject ceased out of the conversation. During the subsequent silence Dan thought, among other things, that it was "aisy for his grandfather to be talkin';" but in this he made a mistake. For old O'Beirne remembered vividly that he had once had his own restless ambitions, and his chances, too, of realising them, in times when he did more stirring things than merely forge pike-heads. Therefore he guessed what lent an unnecessary vehemence to his grandson's hammering, and if he could have thought of any consolatory remark, he would have made it. But it only occurred to him to say that the days would soon be len'thenin' now, anyway; and even to himself this seemed cold comfort. Dan replied, "Och, they're plinty long enough," and sent a thick swarm of fiery bees flitting up the dark-throated chimney.

That evening when Dan closed the broad-leaved forge doors, he shut himself out into a world as black and white as moonlight on turf and snow could make it. Though the morning's flutter of snow had left but a meagre sprinkling on that great bogland, the moonbeams touching every scattered flake, seemed to gather it all up widely in one stark spectral gleam. Far away towards the horizon this dulled off into a shadowy zone of mist, where the wind was muttering and moaning to itself, dimly heard across the hushed floor of the night. Beyond that Dan was aware wistfully of regions unknown, with all their possibilities fascinating and mysterious. But he had small scope for speculation about what he should find when he opened the house door fast by; and in fact he discovered everything and everybody just as he could have foretold. The fire-lit room was filled with the busy weaving of the web that ruddy gleams and russet shadows never got finished, swiftly as they glanced, and overhead the black spaces between the rafters gloomed down like inlets of a starless sky. There sat his great-grandmother smoking her dudeen in her nook by the hearth, and her big cloak—a very little of wizened old woman to a great many heavy, dark-blue folds. There, too, knitted her grey-haired daughter Bridget, who said, as she did every evening, "Well, Dan, so you're come in," and would have not much more to say for herself that night except the Rosary. And his grandfather, who had come in just before him, was lighting his pipe in the opposite chimney-corner. A year ago his brother Nicholas would have thrust a head, all eyes and rumpled hair, into a patch of bright flickerings, to pore over the tattered arithmetic-book; but by this time his absence had become a matter of course. The only at all unusual feature was Joe Denny, the blind fiddler, who had called in on his way home and had a drop of poteen and a farrel of wholemeal cake. Yet Joe was indeed a tolerably common incident, and his jokes altered not. He had begun his parting one, which was to the effect that sorra a man in the counthry of Connaught could see clearer than himself if the night was dark enough, when Dan's arrival interrupted him, and made him declare, taking out his fiddle, that 'twould be a poor case if the lad didn't get e'er a tune at all. Dan was not much in the humour for tunes, but he said, "Ay, Joe, give us a one, man-alive," and Joe struck up with twangle and squeak.

He was playing—

"Over the hills and far away,
Over the hills and beyond the say,
Over the hills and a great way off,
And the wind it blew—"

when a thudding knock on the door seemed to beat down the shriller sounds and stop the sliding bow. Dan went to see who it was, and found standing on the threshold a tall, lean old man in a long, ragged coat, with a thick, knotted blackthorn in his hand. A few hard-frozen granules pattered in at the opened door, which admitted a glimpse of the moon, tarnished by a thin drift of scudding cloud.

"God save all here," said the old man, who was a stranger.

"Good-evenin' to you kindly, sir," responded old Felix from his fireside corner; "and wudn't you be steppin' widin?"

"I'm on'y axin' me way to the place below there—Ballybrosna beyond Duffclane," said the old man; "it's the road I must be steppin', for I'm more than a thrifle late."

But he came slowly forward into the room as if lured by the fire, at which he looked hungrily. He stooped and limped very much, and when he took off his black caubeen, the sharp gleam of his white hair seemed to comment coldly on those infirmities.

"I'm widin a mile or so of it, or maybe less, by now, I should suppose," he said.

"Faix, then, it's the long mile," said the fiddler. "Put half a dozen to it, and you'll be nearer; and bedad it's aisier work doin' that in your head than on your feet. Be the same token I must be leggin' it, or they'll consait I'm lost at our place." And he stepped out darkly into the veiled moonlight.

"Wirrasthrew and weary on it," the old man said to himself; and then to the others, "Is it that far as he says?"

"Ay is it, every inch," said old O'Beirne. "And too long a thramp for you altogether, sir, if I might make so free."

"For the matther of that," said the ragged old

man, proudly, "I've walked the double of it, and more, times and agin, widout so much as considherin'. But your road's a bit heavy to-night, wid the snow—and could."

"That's the worst of the roads," said the little old woman, peering suddenly out of her corner; "the longer you walk them, the longer they'll grow on you, till you begin to think there's no ind to them. And after that, the best conthrivance is to keep off of them clivir and clane, the way I do. Then they're no len'th at all."

"Ah, ma'am, but 'twouldn't be very handy if the young folk took to thryin' that plan," the old man said. "*We*'re bound to keep steppin' out."

A short silence followed this remark, because the hearers felt uncertain whether he meant the pronoun for a jest. To evade the difficulty, old O'Beirne bade Dan fetch a mug for a drop of poteen, and meanwhile said to the stranger:

"Sit you down, sir, and take a taste of the fire. Where might you be thravellin' from this day?"

"I was livin' over at Innislone," said the old man, sitting down on a creepy stool.

"Musha, then, you didn't ever come that far all on ind—sure it's miles untould."

"'Twas the day afore yisterday I quit. Last night I slep' at Sallinbeg, and this mornin' I met a man who loaned me a grand lift in his cart."

"I used to know a man lived at Innislone," said old O'Beirne, "be the name of Brian English. He come by here of an odd while after the stuff."

"Ay, bedad, and a very dacint ould crathur he was. Meself's one of the Dermodys—young Christie they call me—but ould Christie that was me poor father's dead this while back. Thank you kindly, lad," the old man said to Dan, who now handed him a little delft mug half full of whisky. "Why, you're nigh as long a fellow as meself. Are you good at the wrestlin'?"

"Och, I'm no great things whatever," Dan replied with becoming modesty.

"There's not many heavy weights in the parish 'ud care to stand up to me," said this young Christie, holding the mug in a gaunt tremulous hand. "Faix, it's noways forrard they've been about it since the time I come near breakin' Rick Tighe's neck. I've noticed that. Begorrah, now, ivery sowl thought I had him massacred," he said, with a transient gleam of genuine complacency. "You might have heard tell of it, belike?"

"It 'ud ha' happint before my recollections,

sir, maybe," said Dan, looking at him perplexedly, "if 'twas apt to ha' been a longish while ago."

"'Twasn't long to say," said the old man. He drank the spirits lingeringly, in slow sips, and seemed to sit up straighter as he did so. Then he set down the empty mug on the table, and said, "*Boys' wages.*"

But he had scarcely uttered the words when he perceived that he had thought aloud irrelevantly, and made haste to cover the slip. "I'd better be gettin' on wid meself," he said, rising, "Thank you, kindly. That's an iligant fire you have." He looked at it regretfully, but turned resolutely towards the door, still open, and framing the broad dim whiteness out away to the bounding curtain of gloom. "It's a grand thing," he said defiantly, "to have all the world before you."

The sentiment was not accepted without qualification.

"That depinds," said old O'Beirne. "Somewhiles I question wud you find anythin' in it better than a warm corner and a pipe of 'baccy, if you thramped the whole of it. And you might happen on a dale worse. What do you say, mother?"

She was knocking ashes out of her pipe-bowl against the wall, and nodded in assent.

"It's no place for people that can keep shut of it," she said.

"If you've ne'er a chance of gettin' into it," said Dan, "I dunno what great good it does you bein' there afore or behind."

"Or if you knew there was nothin' left in it you wanted to be goin' after," said his great-aunt, half to herself.

"Well, whatever way you look at it," said the strange old man, "I've a notion I've a right to be gettin' somethin' more out of it be now than boys' wages. Ay, it's time I was. Boys' wages; the lyin' spalpeen."

"If you axed me, sir," said old O'Beirne, "I'd say 'twas time somebody else would be gettin' the wages. Isn't there any childer to be earnin' for you? Haven't you e'er a son, that you need be thrampin' the counthry that fashion, let alone talkin' about all the world, wild like?"

"I've a son, troth have I, if that was all," said the old man, turning away, angrily.

"Then it's that much better off than me you are. The only one I had, he took and died on me, himself, and his poor wife a couple of days after him—God be good to them—when the lad there wasn't scarce the height of that stool, and a less size on his brother, that's away now in the States gettin' all manner of a fine edication. Very dacint poor childer they always was, too; but it was a bad job."

"He might ha' done worse agin you than that," said Christie Dermody, "be the powers he might." He had retreated as far as the door, but now he faced round, and stood on the edge of the thin snow, leaning his right shoulder against the post, and looking in at the other old man by the fire. "He might ha' fooled you for years and years, and made a laughin'-stock of you wid everybody about the place—and me wid ne'er a thought of any such a thing—he might so, and bad luck to him. . . . 'Foostherin' about and consaitin' to be doin' a fair day's work, when he's the creep of a snail on him, and the stren'th of a rat.' That's what I heard Tim Reilly sayin' and I goin' home on the Saturday night. But if I come creepin' after him, the young baste, he'd maybe ha' ráison to remimber it. . . . And himself and the wife lettin' on there was nothin' like me; and he callin' me to come into his room—I heard him plain enough all the while, no fear, but I wudn't be lettin' on. There's ne'er a hap'orth ailin' him. Troth he may call till he's choked afore iver I'll come next or nigh him. And sendin' the little girl slutherin' to say her daddy wanted me. I tould her want might be his master. Sure they're all the one pack, and the widest width there is in this world I'll be keepin' between them and me. Shut of them I'll be for good and all— and I'll make me fortin' yet, and no thanks to him. What talk have they of ould men? Boys' wages. Good-night to you all."

To those in the room it seemed as if he dropped away back into the wan dusk behind him, and next moment they saw him in motion a few paces distant, limping fast, and gesticulating as though he were still carrying on his monologue.

"That old crathur's asthray in his mind, I misdoubt," said old O'Beirne, "and I wouldn't won'er if he was after gettin' bad thratement among his own people."

"Goodness pity him," said his sister Bridget. "It's a cruel perishin' night, and snowin' thicker. Where'll he get to at all? And carryin' nought but an old stick. We'd better ha' kep' him."

"Sure we couldn't ha' stopped him anyhow,"

said the blacksmith, "no more than one of them flustherin' blasts goin' by. When a body's took up wid onraisonable notions, you might as well be hammerin' could iron as offerin' to persuade him diff'rint. But he'll maybe turn in at the Gallahers'."

They watched him until the dark imprints of his receding steps in the thin snow-sheet could no longer be distinguished, and then Dan closed the door, shutting out the wide world and the fortune seeker. "Things is quare and conthráry," he said to himself.

Some two hours afterwards they were all sitting round the fire still. It was nearly nine o'clock, which is late in Lisconnel, but they found it hard to detach themselves from the cordial grasp of the warm glow. Bridget, however, had put by her needles, and begun to tell her beads, when another knock broke in upon them.

"He's come back belike," said old O'Beirne; but when Dan opened the door, the person who stood there, though likewise tall and gaunt and ragged, had grizzled black hair, and was not more than middle-aged. His face was hollow-cheeked and drawn, and his eyes glittered while he shivered and panted. The night had grown wilder as the moon sank low, and the snow went past the door like rapid wafts of ghostly smoke. This newcomer stumbled into the room without ceremony, as if half blinded, and said breathlessly—

"Did any of yous be chance see an ould man goin' this road to-day? An ould ancient man, somethin' lame; be the name of Christie Dermody?"

"Ay, sure enough, himself was in it not so long ago," said old O'Beirne. "If it hadn't been you, 'twas very apt to ha' been him come back."

In the man's face one trouble seemed to be relieved by another at the tidings.

"Glory be to goodness, then, that I've heard tell of him at last," he said. "But God help the crathur, what's to become of him streelin' about this freezin' night? The snow's as dhry as maildust. Perished he'll be. Och, he's the terrible man to go do such a thing on us. What way did he quit? It's me ould father, sir, that's over eighty years of age."

"And is he after strayin' away on you?" said old O'Beirne.

"Follyin' him since yesterday mornin' I am," said the other, "when it's in me bed I should be be rights, for I'm that distroyed wid the could on me chest I've scare a bit of breath in me body. But sure what matter if I can come be the crathur agin. Is it that a-way he went, did you notice?"

"You're bound to wait till the flurry of the win's gone by," said old O'Beirne, for his visitor pointed out into a shrieking whirl, shrilling higher and fiercer. "Sorra a minyit you'll lose, for you couldn't stir a step in that or see a stim. Sit you down a while. What was it set him rovin'?"

"Did he say anythin' agin us? Anythin' of bein' thrated bad?"

"Well, I wouldn't say he seemed altogether satisfied in himself," said old O'Beirne, remembering his suspicions. "Somethin' he said of bein' made a fool of, and tould lies to——"

"And gettin' boys' wages," said Dan.

"Ay, ay, wirrasthrew, that was the very notion he had, goodness help us. What will we do at all wid him? You see, sir, me father's a won'erful proud-minded man; he is that. And a great big man, and as strong as ten he was, ontil he got rael ould entirely. So it's cruel bad he thinks of not bein' able for everythin' the way he used to be; and he won't let on but he is, be no manner of manes he won't. 'Deed no, he sez he's as good a man as ever he was in his life."

"Belike now he's of the opinion the sun doesn't dhrop down out of the sky of an evenin'," said little old Mrs. O'Beirne, with sarcasm. "What does the ould body expec'?"

"I dunno, ma'am, I dunno. Sure it's agin nathur and raison. There's meself gettin' as grey as a badger, and noways that supple as I was. But me father's a terrible cliver man. You'd niver get the better of an argufyment wid him, for he wouldn't listen to a word you'd be sayin'. So you see the way of it was, the two of us is workin' this great while on Mr. Blake's lan', that's a dacint man enough; and it might be three year ago, he sez to me one Saturday night—for be good luck 'twas me and not me father he'd mostly be payin' —sez he to me, 'Look it here, Ned, it's the last time I'll be givin' man's wages to your father, for bedad an infant child 'ud do as much as he any day of the week. So I'll put him on boys' wages,' he sez, 'that'ill be three shillin's, and every penny as much as he's worth,' sez he. And sure I knew it was the truth he was sayin', but 'twould break me father's heart.

"So nought better could I do on'y to make out 'twas he would be gettin' the man's wages, and meself the boy's. Diff'rint raisons I conthrived," he said, with some natural pride in the details of his strategy, "but mostly I let on 'twas because of me bein' such a fool about the horses they couldn't trust me wid any except the ould ones. Anyway me father was contint enough; faix, some whiles he seemed a bit set up like, considherin' he had the pull over me, and he'd be sayin' what at all 'ud we do without him, and I such an omadhawn. Niver a cross word we had until last week I got laid up wid this mischancy could and the pain in me chest, so sorra a fut could I go to me work; and I well knew the whole thing 'ud come out, if he went when I didn't. Bedad I dhramed it all the night asleep and awake, till I was fairly moidhered in me head."

"Tub-be sure," said old O'Beirne, "that's the worst of lettin' on. If anythin' goes crooked, it's like the bottom bursted out of a sack of mail; you're carryin' about nothin' at all before you know what's happint you."

"Well, we done the best we could, me wife and me, to dispersuade him off of goin' on Saturday. Bad wid the could too, we said he was; but och not a fut of him but would go. So Barney McAuliffe was tellin' me wife, when the men was payin' in the yard, me father he ups and says to Mr. Blake :

"'Beg pardon, sir, but you're after givin' me no more than me son's money, and it's meself was workin' this week, not him.'

"And Mr. Blake sez, just goin' off in a hurry, 'What are you talkin' about, man? Whethen now, you don't suppose I've been payin' you full wages, that hasn't done a stroke of work worth namin' this half-dozen year? That'ill have to contint you till Ned's back agin.'

"And Barney sez my father had ne'er a word out of him, but just went home dazed like. And me wife sez when he come in, he sits down on the form be the door, and niver opens his lips. So she knew right well what ailed him, and she said iverythin' she could think of—how it's disthroyed we'd be on'y for him now I was laid up, and the won'erful man he was, and this way and that way. But niver a word he heeded, nor near the fire he wouldn't come, and had her heart-scalded seein' him sittin' there in the draught of the door. And I meself was tired callin' him to come in and spake to me, and I lyin' in bed, but next or nigh me he niver come, not even for little Maggie that he always thought a hape of. And the next mornin' if he wasn't quit out of it early, afore anybody knew, in the bitter black frost, and a quare threatinin' of snow. So then as soon as I heard tell, I up wid me and come after him. Troth, I left the wife frettin' wild, the crathur, thinkin' I'd get me death; but what else could I do? And now I must be steppin' on again. Och no, thank you, lad, if I took a dhrop of spirits, I'd be choked wid coughin'. But you might just set me on the right road."

"I'll go along wid him," said Dan, aside to his grandfather, "and if I can bring him, or the both of them, back here, I will. It's my belief he's as bad as he can stick together."

So Dan and old Dermody's son went out into the night. A lull in the wind had come, and the light of the moon, hung near the horizon's rim, flickered out dimly ever and anon as the edge of the drifting mist lapped up wave-like and touched her. It was piercingly cold. Ned Dermody leaned heavily on Dan as they walked, only till he fetched back his breath, he said, but it was slow in coming. They had not gone many hundred yards, yet vast tracts of solitude seemed to have folded round them, before Dan caught sight of something that somehow startled and shocked him—a group of boulders by the road, with a shadow under one of them strangely like a human form. A few paces further on he became aware that it really was a man—the old man—sitting huddled up under the big glimmering stone. Thus far had he carried his forlorn quest after Fortune, and mutiny against Fate. His snaggy stick lay at a little distance, a black line on the snow, and the sight of that made Dan's heart stumble. But Ned Dermody shouted out hoarsely and loud: "Be the Lord it's himself," and, as Dan afterwards used to tell, "took a flyin' lep at him, as if he'd a mind to ha' lep over the world."

"Musha now, and is it there you would be sittin' to catch your death of could?" he began, in a tone of gleeful reproach, shaking the old man by the shoulder. "Goodness forgive me for sayin' so, but it's yourself's the pernicious ould miscreant. Fine thrampin' over the counthry I've had after you—forby givin' us the greatest fright altogether. Sure I give you me word the whole of them at home was runnin' in and out of the house on Sunday mornin' like so many scared rabbits about a bank. And ne'er a man-jack of them, you persaive, had the wit to find out where you was off to till meself riz out of me bed to go look. And now, man-alive, git up wid yourself and come along, for it's mortal could here, and there's tons' weight of snow this instiant minyit ready to dhrop down on our heads. Come along. Sure it's niver disthressin' yourself you'd be about ould Blake and his wages? Musha sure Norah and meself was sayin' on'y on Saturday night that there wasn't many stookawns like me had fathers to be bringin' them home shillin's every week as regular as the clock, and givin' prisints to the childer, and all manner. There's little Maggie frettin' woful to be missin' you out of it. Don't be keepin' me standin' on me feet, there's a good man, for it's quare and bad I've been, and the doctor was sayin' he couldn't tell what ruination mightn't be on me if I didn't mind what I was at. And here's the dacint lad waitin' to show us the road. We're just comin' along this instant, boyo. Look-a-daddy, 'twas all a mistake, and we'll settle it up next week, when we're both workin' agin. Very belike Mr. Blake didn't rightly know what he was sayin'. Wake up and come along. . . . Daddy darlint, don't you hear what I'm teliin' you? It's raisin' your wages they'll be after Lent, I wouldn't won'er, raisin' them a shillin' belike—rael grand it'ill be—God Almighty!"

He stood up suddenly and looked towards Dan, but at neither him nor anything else. The moon began to shine clearer in a chink between two straight leaden bars, and the great white bog seemed to grow wider and stiller under the strengthening light. The very wind had forsaken them, and gone off keening into the far distance. It seemed to Dan that even a flake fluttering down would have been some company, but not a single one was in the air. He felt himself seized by a nameless panic, such as had not come over him since he was a small child a dozen years ago.

"What's the matter at all?" he said futilely to Ned Dermody, knowing well enough.

"Gone he is," said Ned, "the life was vexed out of him among us all. He's gone. And it's follyin' him I'd liefer be, on'y for them crathurs at home."

But in another moment he came staggering against Dan, and clutched his arm, saying wildly: "Ah, lend me a hand—for pity's sake—a hand for a minyit. Don't let go of me." And he leant such a heavy dead weight on him that all Dan could do was to let it slip down and down as softly as might be, until the snowy earth took it from him.

Ned had followed in spite of the crathurs at home.

CHAPTER X

CON THE QUARE ONE

AMONG the unfamiliar faces that show themselves now and then at Lisconnel, some make no second appearance, never coming our way again, but passing out of our ken as utterly as if their route lay along a tangent, or the branch of an hyperbola, or other such unreverting line. We seldom, it is true, get proof positive, as in the case of the Dermodys, father and son, that they will no more return. Generally their doing so any day may be supposed possible as long as anybody remembers to suppose it. But some come back at more or less regular intervals, like periodic comets, so that if a certain time elapses without bringing one of them, the neighbours say they wonder what's took him at all, while some reappear erratically enough to preclude any calculations upon the subject. Of this latter class was Con the Quare One, who, after his first arrival, on a summer's evening, now more than a quarter of a century since, became a rather frequent visitor, usually stopping for a few days at least, before he resumed his travels. It was conjectured that these were very extensive, though perhaps less so than Mad Bell's. But it was even more difficult to obtain a satisfactory report of them from him than from her. Mrs. M'Gurk said he was "so took up with his own notions, that he mostly knew no better where he'd been, or what he'd been doin', than a baste drivin' home from a fair; you might as soon be axin' questions of one as the other; though when Con chose to give his mind to it, he knew what he was about as well as anybody else. Sure if you wanted to know which way he was after comin', as likely as not he'd talk about nothin' on'y the sorts of clouds he'd been watchin' goin' by over his head; and 'twould take a cliver body to tell from that what road he might ha' had under his feet." This incommunicativeness made him a disappointing guest sometimes by the firesides, where he was finding a night's lodging; though he might eke out his conversation with a little twangling on his fiddle, in which the melody would be quite as vague as his narratives. As for his own earlier history, he never gave any clear account of it, probably having none to give, and the neighbours' speculations upon this point were somewhat wide of the mark, which was not surprising, as what stray hints he did let fall could be very deviously construed. The opinion most commonly received held that he had "took and run off from home, and he but a gossoon, be raison of doin' some quare bit of mischief, and had a mind yet to be keepin' out of his people's way; though, like enough, they weren't throublin' their heads about him be now;" a theory which was not entirely in accordance with facts.

Con was not, I believe, an especially quare one at his first start in life, begun under the thatch of a little white-washed cottage, dotted down among grass-fields beside a clear, brown river, which kept his mother busy exhorting him and his half-dozen brethren to not be falling in and drowning themselves on her. Her days were haunted by apprehensions of that catastrophe, which, however, was not included in the plot of her life's drama. Con's chosen bugbear was the bridge which bestrode the river close by, and beneath the arch of which he had once happened to be while a cart passed overhead. For the lumbering rumble had been an appalling experience, which he shuddered to repeat. Yet he lacked the moral courage to rouse his elders' derision by an avowal, so he followed, and did not let on, whenever their wading and dabbling brought them into the hollow-sounding shade. Despite this daily anxiety, Con spent his earliest years light-heartedly enough, with no stinting of pitaties—none at least that reached the childer—and ample scope for sports and pastimes. But when he was still very small, his grandmother, lately widowed and on her way to a new abode, stopped a night with her married daughter, and begged that she might bring home one of the grandchildren with her, "just to take the could edge off her lonesomeness," a request which could not well be refused. And Con seemed the appropriate person to go, as the old woman considered that "the dark head of hair he had on him was the moral of his poor grandfather's afore it turned white." Therefore the swiftly running mysteriously murmuring river flowed away out of his life, and with it vanished all the faces and voices and comradeship that had made up his world.

At first he fretted for them rather persistently, but after a time adapted himself to circumstances, and contented himself with the grass-bordered, hedge-muffled lane, which had become the scene of his adventures, fraternizing with the reserved fawn-coloured goat and demonstrative terrier, who alone took an intelligent interest in them. For his grandmother was satisfied with the sense of having him "playin' around handy," and could not be counted company.

But after nearly a twelvemonth had passed, Con seemed one day to be seized with a fresh fit of homesickness. It was a brilliant late summer morning, yet to old Mrs. Quin's perplexity, he continued to sit on his little stool, with his slice of griddle-cake half-crumbled in his lap, and answered her suggestions that he should finish his breakfast, and run out to play, by irrelevant requests for his own ould mammy. He wanted her cruel bad, he said, and there was nothin' ailed him, and he wouldn't like to look for blackberries along the hedge—or to throw stones for Bran—or even to be given a whole ha'penny to go buy himself a grand sugar-stick down at the shop—he only wanted his mammy. Such was his attitude and refrain all that day and the next. After which his grandmother said to her neighbour, Judy Ahern, that she couldn't tell what had come over the child, and he had her fairly distracted listening to him.

And Mrs. Ahern said: "Maybe he might be gettin' somethin'; there's a terrible dale of sickness about. But he doesn't look very bad to say. Arrah now, Con avic, why wouldn't you run out and play a bit this lovely mornin'? Wantin' your mammy? Sure that's foolish talk, and she nobody can tell how far away this minyit. It's just a notion you have. . . . 'Deed, ma'am, I dunno, but maybe you'd a right to let him home to her, or else he might get frettin' and mopin' himself into the fever. He's a poor little crathur; the face of him this instant isn't the width of a ha'penny herrin'."

"And he so continted," said Mrs. Quin, "until he took his fantigue. Rael quare it is."

"Most things do be quare and ugly these times," said Mrs. Ahern, "Goodness help us all. There's poor Mrs. Duff thravellin' off to-morra, to go stay wid her brother at Gortnakil. Very belike she'd take him along; and he'd be aisy landed home, once he'd got that far."

And on the morrow Con did actually set off with Mrs. Duff, feeling half appeased and half compunctious, as people do when they get what they have clamoured for; sorry a little to lose sight of Bran, staring open-mouthed after him down the lane; and relieved through all by a vague sense that he was going whither his heart-strings pulled. If he had been a more experienced traveller, he might have noticed some signs that things were, as Judy Ahern had said, out of joint. It was harvest-time, and the weather was not wet, though dull and chilly, but nobody was working in the fields. Nothing seemed to move in them, as they lay deserted, except trails of a white mist that drifted low among the furrows, where the potato-haulms looked strangely discoloured, speckled and blackened, as if a shrivelling flame had run through them all, charring and strewing pale ashes. The air was full of a peculiar odour, heavy and acrid, the very life-breath of decay. The roads were deserted too. For miles nobody would be met, and then a small stationary crowd of people would appear, collected it would seem without any more purpose than cattle huddled together in a storm, and as dumb as they, not giving so much as a " fine mornin' " to the passer-by. Other crowds they fell in with now and again, pacing slowly along, and these always had a heavy burden carried among them, and sometimes women keening. Once the car-horse shied violently at some dark, long thing, that was stretched out by the footpath, and Mrs. Duff crossed herself and said, "God be good to us," and the driver said without looking off his reins: "He's lyin' there since yesterday, and I seen another above about the four-roads, and I comin' past this mornin'."

Con did not give much heed to these incidents; but one scene in his journey impressed him strongly. It was at the small town where they slept the night, and it happened while they waited in the broad main street next morning for their car to pick them up, as Mrs. Duff travelled by a rather disjointed system of lifts in vehicles that were going her road. There were few people about, and Con was intensely admiring a gaudy tea-chest in the window of the shop before which they stood, when a great roar began to swell up round the corner, with a lumbering of wheels heard fitfully through it. Presently a large crowd came struggling into sight; a street full of men, women, and children, surrounding a blue, red-wheeled cart, piled high with dusty-looking white sacks. Half-a-dozen dark-uniformed policemen were trying to haul on the horse, and keep between the cart and the crowd, whose shout generally sounded like: "Divil a fut its to quit—divil a fut." It was a crowd that looked as if it had somehow got more than its due share of glittering eyes—in mistake, apparently, for other things.

As the cart came crawling past where Mrs. Duff and Con stood, a furious rush so tilted it over that the horse fell, breaking a shaft, and some of the topmost sacks tumbled off, dropping with dull thuds, like dead bodies, upon the damp cobblestone pavement. Con saw a little cloud of white dust rise up over each as it dumped down, and melt away on the air, making him wonder to himself: "Is it smokin' hot they are?" But in another moment they were hidden for a while by a wild wave of the crowd, which threw itself tumultuously upon them. One of the sacks burst, spilling the soft flour in flakes, and round it the jostling and writhing grew fiercest. The faces that got nearest to it looked hardly the whiter for their smears and powdering.

A young woman, all black eyes and elf locks, with a baby wrapped in her shawl, crouching low and making a desperate long arm, grasped a covetous handful, which spirted away wastefully between her clenched fingers. She moistened some of this in a puddle as she knelt, and held the paste to her baby's mouth. But its head was drooping wearily aside, and its lips did not move when she touched them. "Ait it up, me heart's jewel," she said; "ait it up, mother's little bird. 'Deed, then, but you're the conthráry little toad. It's breakin' me heart you'll be roarin' when I've ne'er a bit to give you, and sleepin' dead, when I've the chance to feed you." She was beginning to shake it, but a young man who stood behind her put his hand on her shoulder, saying: "Whisht, whisht, you crathur, for God's sake. It's done wid wantin' and cryin', and a good job for it too, the Lord knows." Then the girl shrieked again and again, and the people about her said from one to the other: "It's her child's starved on her." And an old man caught up the little body, and held it high over his head, shouting, "Boys, boys—look yous at that. There's the way Henderson's cartin' off the childer's bit of food to make his fine fortin in England." And the crowd shouted back through a surge of curses: "Divil a fut will he this day."

A very little old woman seized hold of an outlying sack and tried to lift it, a ludicrously impossible feat, at witnessing which a cripple leaner than his crutches laughed boisterously, saying, "Och, good luck to you, granny. You're makin' a great offer at it entirely. Is it often you do be liftin' up the Hill of Howth? More power to your elbow." And the crowd yelled with laughter too.

At this moment there was a prodigious clatter of hoofs on the stones, and round the corner whirled a squadron of hussars, all in their blue and yellow like a flight of macaws, coming to the rescue of Mr. Henderson's sacks. But Con saw scarcely more than the first confused onset, for somebody snatched him up and hurried him into a dark passage. The last sight he had of the fray was of a glossy black horse plunging frantically back from a cloud of the flour flung into his face, and rearing higher and higher, until he fell over with a terrific scrambling crash. Con particularly noticed the white gloves of the rider, and thought to himself, "He's been grabbin' the flour too." And the women about him said, "Och, murdher, the baste—the man's apt to be kilt!"

When Mrs. Duff and Con emerged again all was quiet in the street—two or three women had even stolen back, and were scraping up the white patches—and he was driven away on a car for what seemed to him a vast length of time. But at last, as he peered listlessly out on glimpses of the dreary, strange road caught between the shawled heads of two other passengers, his eyes suddenly fell on something delightfully familiar. It was a grey ruined mill which stood by the river, not many hundred yards from his home. All at once he seemed to be set down in the middle of his old life as if he had never left it, only with a charming freshness superadded. A delicious feeling came over him as he watched the clear, sky-glinting loops unwind themselves in the grass while the car jogged along. There were the big stones over the edges of which the brown water broke into dancing crests of crystal bubbles when the river was full, and the deep pools under the hollow banks where they had seen the trout that was the size of a young whale, and the twisted wild cherry tree from beneath which the eddies sometimes twirled away bearing fleets of frail, snowy petals. And Johnny and Katty and the rest might all come into view paddling round any corner. When the car stopped at the gap through which you got into the field just behind his cottage, he was almost beside himself with joy, as his fellow-travellers, who were less elated, lifted him down and handed him his bundle, and bade him run straight in to his mother like an iligant child.

He did run down the steep little footpath at the top of his speed, and round the corner of the house, and in through the open door. The room looked very dusk to him coming in from the mellow afternoon sunshine, and the first thing he noticed was that the fire had gone out. The hearth was a blackness sprinkled with white ashes, which made him think of the flour spilt on the dark ground. Next he saw his mother sitting on a stool by the hearth with her head leaned against the wall, and his father's old caubeen hanging on its nail above, a very unusual sight at that hour. Con rushed at her head-foremost, saying, "Och, mammy darlint, I'm come home this long way, and they was fightin' wid all the soldiers and spillin' the flour, and his horse rared up on his hind legs till he fell off his feet. And where's daddy if he isn't workin'? And musha what for is Nannie and Johnny in bed?" He pulled her shawl because she did not look round at him, and immediately she dropped down prone on the floor as heavily and helplessly as he had seen the white sacks fall. She had in truth been dead for hours, but Con ran out screaming that he was after killing his mammy, and nothing would persuade him otherwise. Vainly the neighbours averred that "the crathur was starvin' herself this great while to keep a bit for the childer, let alone her heart bein' broke frettin' after her poor husband and little Pat, who were took from her wid the fever, both of them the one day." Con's mind was shut fast into the dreadful moment when he had pulled her shawl and she had fallen down, and therein it abode, sorely afflicted, until a spell of brain fever intervening let it loose into a region of vaguer and more varied dreams.

And when he had struggled through this illness, nobody well knew how or why, he woke up to find his world swept very bare. Father, mother, and all his brethren, except little Katty, were vanished out of it, and as it came looming back to him thus depeopled, its aspect was immeasurably desolate. Nor did his loss end here, for from this time dated the springing up among his neighbours of a suspicion that he was not all there, a suspicion which developed into an accepted article of belief, the more readily, perhaps, because nobody remained for whom such a fact would have had a personal bitterness, the old grandmother having slipped away out of her lonesomeness before his recovery. It would not be easy to explain how it was that Con grew up into that privileged and disfranchised person who is spoken of as "a crathur," and whose proceedings are more or less exempt from criticism. People often said of him that he had plenty of sense *of his own*, and the remark was to some extent explanatory, as a certain singularity in his way of viewing things even more than an occasional inconsequence and flightiness in his sayings and doings tended to establish the reputation for eccentricity which followed him closely as a shadow, and set an impalpable barrier between himself and his kind. As he advanced in life this was strengthened by his increasing fondness for his own society, but he did not take to his solitary wanderings until after his sister Katty married young Peter Meehan and emigrated to New York. It was suggested to him that he should accompany them, but he sat looking meditative for a while, and then said, "How far might it be from this to the States?"

"I dunno rightly," said his informant, "but a goodish step it's apt to be, for people's better than a couple of weeks sailin' there, I'm tould."

Con meditated a little more before he put another question. "Would you be widin hearin' out there of the folk talkin' foolish?" he inquired.

"Why, tub-be sure, man, what 'ud hinder you that you wouldn't hear them talkin' same as anywheres else?"

"Bedad, then," said Con, "it seems a long way to be thravellin' to a counthry as close as that. Sure, if you take out for a stravade over the bog here, you'll be throubled wid nothin' the len'th of the day on'y the curlew, or maybe a couple of saygulls skirlin'—raisonable enough. I'll be apt to stay where I am."

Con, who was a person of many moods, happened to be in an unusually cynical one just then; however, he adhered to his resolution, and when his sister had gone he adopted a life of long tramps. Somebody had given him an old fiddle, and this he carried with him, though chiefly as a sort of badge, as his performances were but feeble, and he could turn his hand to many other things when he found it necessary to do so. His rovings had gone on for several years before they led him to Lisconnel. In those days he was a strange, small figure, who wore a coat too large for him, and a hat set so far back on his head that its brim made a sort of halo to frame his face, which had a curious way of looking fitfully young and old, with a shining of violet blue eyes and a puckering of fine-drawn wrinkles. A small boy and a little old ancient man would seem to change places half a dozen times in the course of a single conversation. Even his hair was a puzzle, regarded as an indication of age, because its black had become streaked with white in such a fashion that its apparent hue varied according to what came uppermost in accidents of ruffling and smoothing. A neighbour once said of him that he was the living moral of a little ould lepreehawn that they were after making a couple of sizes too big by mistake; and my own impression is that further opportunities for observing specimens of the race would be likely to bear out this statement.

The summer evening on which he was first seen at Lisconnel had followed a very fine day. In the heart of its golden afternoon Mrs. O'Driscoll trusted her youngest son Terence out on the bog with his brothers and sisters and some other children, the eldest of whom, Johanna Harvey, the Ryans' orphan niece, was credited with wit enough to keep the party out of the holes. They wandered off rather more widely than usual, along the foot of the hill, lured on by a sprinkling of dainty white mushrooms, which they found, generally with yells, studded here and there. At last they sat down on a bank to peel their delicate, pink-quilted buttons, all of them except Terence, who was not yet of an age to have acquired a taste for mushrooms. He had been carried most of the way, still he had toddled further than he was accustomed to do, and his unwonted exertions led him to curl himself up behind a sun-smitten rock and fall asleep with a quietness which presently brought upon him the fate of out of sight out of mind. After a while, however, Johanna did bethink herself of him, and was just on the point of wondering aloud where little Terence had gone to, when her cousin Thady turned her thoughts into a different channel by suddenly saying, "What was there in it before the beginnin' of everythin'?"

Thady was a small, anxious-looking child, whose pale and peaky face his mother often likened regretfully to a hap'orth of soap after a week's washing. He had spent a surprisingly considerable part of his six years in metaphysical speculations, and was always disposed to make a personal grievance of the difficulties in which they constantly landed him. His tone was now rather peremptory as he repeated, "What was there in it before the beginnin' of everythin'?"

"Sure, nothin' at all," said his elder brother Peter, to whom the answer seemed quite simple and satisfactory. But Johanna looked as if she had caught sight of some distant object which provoked hard staring.

"Then what was there before the beginnin' of nothin'?" pursued Thady.

"Dunno," said Peter, indifferently, "unless it was more nothin'."

"Sure not at all; that wouldn't be the way of it," Johanna said, dreamily, yet with decision. "If there was nothin' but nothin' in it, there'd ha' been apt to not be e'er an anythin' ever. Where'd it ha' come from? Don't be tellin' the child lies, Peter. Why, for one thing," she said, her tone sharpening polemically and taking a touch of triumph, "there was always God Almighty in it, and the Divil. Maybe that's what you call nothin'."

Peter evaded this point, saying, "Well, anyway, those times, if there was just the two of them in it, and no harm to be doin', let alone any good people to know the differ, it's on'y a quare sort of

Divil he'd get the chance of bein'. I wouldn't call him anythin' *much*."

" He wouldn't be so very long, you may depind," Johanna pronounced. "Musha, sure the Divil couldn't stay contint any while at all till he'd take to some manner of ould mischief 'ud soon show you the sort of crathur he was—it's his nathur. I should suppose the first thing he'd go do 'ud be makin' all the sorts of hijjis roarin' great bastes and snakes and riptiles that he could think of, and the disolit black wet bogs wid the could win' over them fit to cut you in two when you're sleepin' out at night," said Johanna, whose ten years of life had brought her into some rough places before her adoption by her Aunt Lizzie Ryan, "and the workhouses—bad luck to the whole of them—where there's rats in the cocoa, and mad people frightenin' you, and the cross matrons, and the pólis, and the say to dhrownd the fishin'-boats in, and dirty ould naygurs that put dacint people out of their little places——"

"If it had been me," said Peter, "I'd ha' been very apt to just hit him a crack on the head when I noticed what he was at, and bid him lave thim sort of consthructions alone."

"I dunno the rights of it entirely," Johanna admitted, "but it's a cruel pity he ever got the chance to be carryin' on the way he's done."

"Ah, sure it can't be helped now at all events," said Peter, who was for the time being not inclined to quarrel seriously with the scheme of things, as he basked on the warm grassy bank, where the wild bees were humming in the thyme, happily remote from the grim House and the hungry sea.

"Belike it can't," said Johanna; "but 'twould be real grand if it could. Suppose I was out on the hill there some fine evenin', and I not thinkin' of anythin' in partic'lar, and all of a suddint I'd see a great, big, ugly, black-lookin' baste of a feller, the size of forty, skytin' away wid himself along the light of the sky over yonder, where the sun was about goin' down, and his shadder the len'th of an awful tall tree slippin' streelin' after him, till it was off over the edge of the world like, and that same 'ud be just the Divil, that they were after bundlin' out of it body and bones, the way he wouldn't get meddlin' and makin' and annoyin' people any more. So wid that I'd take a race home and be tellin' you all the iligant thing was after happenin'. And in the middle of it who'd come landin' in but me father and mother, and little Dan. And then, if it isn't the grand cup of tay I'd be makin' her, ay begorra would I, and a sugarstick to stir it wid."

Johanna's vision of the millennium was broken in upon querulously by Thady. "Sure I know all about God Almighty and the Divil," he said comprehensively, "I was on'y axin' what was in it before the beginnin' of everythin', and you're not tellin' me that."

"There's a dale of things little spalpeens like you wouldn't be tould the rights of at all," said Peter, loftily, being rather annoyed at the interruption. He would have liked to hear some further details about the felicity to be inaugurated by that exquisite cup of tea. "Go on romancin', Han."

But Johanna, who felt that this assumption of superior knowledge was an uncandid subterfuge, and yet had not magnanimity enough to disclaim it on her own part, remained uneasily silent for a moment, and then only said: "Sure it's time we was gettin' home." This they accordingly proceeded to do, and had gone most of the distance before it occurred to anybody that little Terence O'Driscoll was not with them. Then, after a superficial and unproductive search among the scattered stones and bushes, they thought it expedient to run back in a fright, and report that the child had gone and got lost, unless by any odd chance he'd come home along wid himself.

Thus it was that when Terence wakened from his nap, he found himself deserted, and thrown completely upon his own resources. As he had not been quite three years in amassing these, they were on the whole but scanty. In fact, he was helplessly unable to realise a world with nothing in it except endlessly swelling up slopes of furzy grass, no Molly nor Micky for him to trot after, and to carry him wherever they were going, whenever he intimated the desirability of that step by abruptly plumping down on the way. So he set off in a great hurry to escape from such a wilderness. He still walked with a wobbling stagger, and his long frock of whity-brown homespun kept on tripping him up, which retarded his progress. But he was not at all long in mentally reaching the precincts of a wild panic which rose up and seized him in a grip never to be quite forgotten, though only a few desperate minutes ensued before he stumped blindly against Con's legs. It was so unutterable a relief to have come on somebody who could hear him roar, that Terence ceased roaring immediately, and let Con pick him up without demur. The appearance of Molly or Micky would, no doubt, have been more satisfactory, but this stranger man might serve well enough at a pinch to carry him home, which it was inconceivable that anybody of such a size could be unable or unwilling to do. As for Con, the inference he drew from Terence's dimensions was that his family and friends were probably not far to seek; and he recognised the shrewdness of the conjecture when he presently espied a shawled figure coming swiftly towards him over the edge of a slope, with the amber of the sunset glowing behind her, and her long shadow sliding on far below her, as if it were in an even greater hurry than herself.

Mrs. O'Driscoll's head was among the golden sunbeams, but her heart had gone down to the very bottom of the blackest and deepest hole in the bog. For towards that dreadful goal she had seen a small form toddling ever since the other children came home alarmingly late with the news that Terence had got lost on them, and they couldn't find a bit of him, high ways or low ways. She was so overjoyed at her rescue that her delighted gratitude cast a sort of glamour around Con, which never wholly faded away. Ever after the appearance of his queer figure called up in her mind a dim reminiscence of the moment when she had seen it for the first time come into view, laden with what she well knew was Terence sitting bolt upright in a manner that betokened him to have experienced neither drowning nor any other disaster.

As Con put the child into her arms, where it seemed to fit into a niche specially designed for it, he said: "Sure now, ma'am, when I seen him stumpin' along his lone, and he about the heighth of a sizable boholawn (ragweed), sez I to meself there was apt to be somebody lookin' after him. For bedad it seems to me mostwhiles the the littler a thing is the more people there'll be consaitin' they can't get on widout it; and that's lucky, belike, or else it might aisy get lost entirely, like a threepenny bit rowled away into a crack. But if you come to considher," Con said, hurrying on lest his allusion to the coin should be construed as a hint that he thought of payment for his services, "most people's lookin' out for somebody, or else somebody's lookin' out for them. It's on'y a few odd ones like meself that makes no differ here or there. I won'er now is the raison that it's after losin' ourselves we are in a manner

—I've me notions about that. For first I think I dunno if anythin's rightly lost that nobody's lookin' to find, and then I think I dunno but you might as well say you couldn't find anythin' you weren't after losin' and lookin' for, and that's not the truth be no manner of manes."

"And you after findin' the child," said Mrs. O'Driscoll.

"Sure not at all, ma'am," said Con, modestly, deprecating not the statement but the implied praise. "Small thanks to me for that, when the woful bawls of it you might have heard a mile o' ground. You could as aisy ha' missed a little clap of thunder, if a one was be chance comin' tatterin' along between the furzes, wid the head of it bobbin' up now and agin, and makin' all the noise it could conthrive. Troth it's the quare bawls *I* might be lettin' these times afore the rest of them 'ud hear me, for if it's lost I am, I'm strayin' a terrible long while; they're apt to disremimber they ever owned me. I do be thinkin', ma'am, that if you forgit what you've lost, 'tis maybe all the one thing as if you'd found it; and after that agin I do be thinkin' maybe 'twould be liker losin' it twyste over. It's quare the diff'rint notions there is about most things. And a good job too, or else what would you be considherin' in your mind, when you was thrampin' around? 'Deed now if you couldn't be supposin' they were this way and that way, and argufyin' over them wid yourself in your own mind, 'twould be like as if you took and swallied down a lump of 'baccy instead of chewin' it, and what sort of benefit or plisure 'ud you git out of that?"

This was Con's first bit of philosophising at Lisconnel, and it was not his last by many, as the place became one of his favourite resorts. His liking for it was perhaps partly due to the fact that its inhabitants received him on more equal terms than were generally accorded to him elsewhere; and this again may be largely attributed to the influence of Mrs. O'Driscoll. For her grateful feelings towards the restorer of Terence made her loth to recognise any deficiencies in him, and her neighbours, soon perceiving that she seemed vexed if Con was spoken of as cracked or crazy or "wantin' a corner," were ready enough to modify their language, and even their judgment, in accordance with her view. Still it was convenient to distinguish him from another resident Con, about whom there were no very striking features. Therefore her little Rose having been heard to say that she was "after seein' Con, not Con Ryan, but the quare one," they caught up and applied the epithet, which in Lisconnel is regarded as a safely colourless term, not likely to hurt the most sensitive feelings.

Con, on his part, formed the highest opinion of Mrs. O'Driscoll, and often took counsel with her about perplexing points which had presented themselves to him in the course of his meditations. In one practical matter, however, he showed an obstinacy that did not further her in her wish to uphold him on a footing with quite sensible people. This was his fancy for adorning the band of his broad-brimmed caubeen with a garnish of feathers and flowers. Mrs. O'Driscoll disapproved of the freak, rightly judging that it often created irrevocable first impressions, and fixed his standing at a glance. In this age and clime the Seven Sages could hardly maintain among them a reverend aspect, under the frivolity of a single flaunting blossom, much less the gaudy bunches and fantastic plumes upon which Con recklessly ventured. So at last, having hinted and remonstrated ineffectually, she contrived somehow to find time and stuff among her laborious days and scanty stores, and fashioned for him a round cloth cap of a severely plain design, which she thought would give no scope for any unseemly appendages. Upon being presented with this headgear, Con dutifully assumed it, and went about wearing it for a day or two in a depressed frame of mind. Then he appeared in the morning at the O'Driscolls', cheered, and crested with a remarkably long gannet's feather stuck upright in the crown of his cap, through which he had bored a hole to admit of the insertion. He was resolved to brazen out the matter, so he presently took off his cap, and twirling it round with an unconcerned air as he leaned against the door, said to Herself: "Well, ma'am, what do you think of that?"

"To tell you just the truth, Con," said Herself, whose countenance had fallen as she saw the failure of her little plot, "I was thinkin' it looked a dale better before you cocked that ould gazabo on top of it. 'Deed now it gives you the apparance of a head of cabbage that's sproutin' up and goin' to seed. Sure you niver see the other lads trapesin' about wid the like on them."

Con, who seemed rather cast down by this criticism, was about to reply, when young Ned Keogh took the cap out of his hand and affected to examine it closely, saying: "Glory be to goodness, what sort of thing is it at all at all? Bedad it's the won'erful conthrivance—ah, tub-be sure; *I* see what it is. He's about growin' a pair of wings for his wit to fly away wid. But musha good gracious, he needn't ha' throubled himself to be gettin' them that sizable. Somethin' the bigness of a hedge-sparrer's, or maybe a weeny white butterfly's, 'ud ha' plinty stren'th enough for the job, if that was all they had to do." Ned meant no harm, but his witticisms did not fall in with Con's humour, so he snatched back the cap and went off affronted, nor did he call at the O'Driscolls' again for some weeks.

The next time he came, however, Herself had espied him a bit down the road, and was standing at the door to receive him with his discarded caubeen in her hand. "You'd be better wearin' it, Con, after all," she said, "for the eyes are scorched out of your head under the sun widout e'er a scrap of brim." And as Con took it, he observed with glee that she had fastened into the band a dove-coloured kittiwake's wing-feather, a somewhat cherished possession of her own, which she used to keep over her best picture on the wall. Thus did she seek to make amends for the speech about the sprouting cabbage-head, which had been weighing heavily upon her conscience.

The kittiwake's feather had to weather rain and sunshine for many a year in Con the Quare One's old caubeen; but it is now on a room-wall again, the Kilfoyles' this time. Con brought it to Mrs. Kilfoyle one autumn evening in the year Mrs. O'Driscoll died. It was much longer than usual since he had wandered into Lisconnel, illness and one thing and another having detained him in the North for the last twelvemonth and more—all her blackest days of childless widowhood—so that this was his first visit since the departure of his earliest friend.

"Could you be keepin' it somewheres safe for me, ma'am?" he said, showing the soft grey feather to Mrs. Kilfoyle, who was sitting by the fire with her sons and her future daughter-in-law, and Ody Rafferty's aunt, and the Widow M'Gurk. "I'll be wearin' it no more. 'Twas she herself stuck it in for me, but sure I knew well enough all the while she'd liefer I wouldn't be goin' about wid such things on me head, and sorra a bit of me will agin."

"Whethen now but yourself's the quare man, Con," said Ody Rafferty's aunt, "to be takin' up wid that notion these times, when ne'er a differ it'ill make to her. There might ha' been some sinse in it, if you'd done it to plase her, but now you're more than a trifle too late wid that. A day after the fair you are. Sure she'll never set eyes on you or your old caubeen agin," she said, as if announcing some unthought-of discovery of her own, "no matter what ould thrash you might take and stick in it. You might be wearin' a young haystack on your head for anythin' she could tell."

"That may be or mayn't be," said Con. "But at all evints the next body that goes there out of this countryside 'ill be very apt to bring her word. Discoorsin' together they'll be of all the news, and as like as not he—or it might be she—'ill say to her—'I seen Con the Quare One goin' the road a while back, and he wid ne'er a thraneen of anythin' in his hat, good or bad; the same way the other boys are; lookin' rael dacint and sinsible.' Belike she might be axin' after me herself, and that 'ud put it in the other body's head. Yourself it may be, Moggy. Faix now, I wouldn't won'er a bit if it was, for there must be a terrible great age on you these times. Sure you looked to be an ould, ould woman the first day I ever beheld you, and that's better than a dozen year ago."

"Troth then there's plinty of oulder ould people than me, let me tell you," protested Moggy, who was about ninety, "that you need be settlin' I'm goin' anywheres next. Musha cock you up. And your own hair turned as white as sheep's wool on a blackthorn bush."

She seemed so much put out by Con's statement and inference that young Thady Kilfoyle, always a good-natured lad, sought to soothe her.

"Sure there's no settlin' any such a thing, and for the matter of goin', the young people often enough get their turn as fast as anybody else. It's meself," he said, "might be sooner than you bringin' news of yous all, and Con's ould caubeen, and everythin' else to Heaven the way he sez."

"I dunno if you've any call to be talkin' that fashion," said the Widdy M'Gurk, disapprovingly, "as if you could be walkin' permisc-yis into Heaven widout wid your lave or by your lave. Maybe it isn't there any of us'ill be bringin' our news."

"Might you know of e'er a better place then, ma'am?" said Con.

"Heard you ever the like of that?" said Ody

Rafferty's aunt, not unwillingly scandalised, "I should suppose nobody, unless it was a born haythen, 'ud know of any place better than Heaven."

"That's where she is then," said Con, stroking his feather. "For the best place ever was is none too good for her, God knows well."

"And thrue for you, man," said the Widdy M'Gurk. "But she's one thing, and we're another. It's not settin' ourselves up we should be to have the same chances."

"Ah, well, sure maybe we're none of us too outrageous altogether," said Mrs. Kilfoyle, looking hopefully round at her company. "And if they can put up wid us at all at all, they will. We'll get there yet, plase God. And anyway I'll be takin' good care of your feather, Con. Ay will I so; same as if it was dropped out of an angel's wing."

"So good-night to you kindly, ma'am," said he. "I'll be steppin' back to Laraghmena. I on'y looked in on you to bring you that, and give you news of Theresa. And I question will I ever set fut agin in Lisconnel."

He did not, however, leave it quite immediately. A little later, when Brian Kilfoyle was escorting Norah Finnegan home, they saw him sitting on the bank near the O'Driscolls' roofless cabin. Its mud walls were fast crumbling into ruin. Already the little window-square had lost its straight outline, and would soon be as shapeless as any hole burrowed in a bank. Con sat with his back turned to it until the dusk had muffled up everything in dimness, and then he stole an armful of turf-sods from the nearest stack, and groped his way in through the deserted door. The shadows within were folded so heavily that he could scarcely more than guess where the hearth had been. One of Con's peculiarities was a strange horror of a fireless hearth. At the sight of its hoarily sprinkled blackness he always felt as if he were standing on the verge of some frightful revelation; a vague reminiscence, no doubt, from the scene of his life's tragedy, all distinct memory of which had been blurred away by his illness. Now he piled and crumbled his sods with practised skill, and set them alight in well-chosen places. But he stayed only for a minute or so, till the little fluttering flames had fairly taken a hold, and were sending golden threads running along the netted fibres. Then he groped his way out again, and returned to his seat on the bank. Presently, as he watched, he saw a red light beginning to flicker through window and door, and growing steadier and stronger. When it was at its brightest, he got up and turned away. "That's the very way it would be shinin'," he said, "and I comin' along the road to see Herself and Himself and the childer—God be good to them all, wherever they may be. And that's the notion of it I'll keep in me mind."

And Con the Quare One came no more to Lisconnel.

CHAPTER XI

MAD BELL

NOT so very long before the sound of Con the Quare One's fiddle ceased to enliven Lisconnel any more, Mad Bell's singing had begun to be heard there occasionally, as it has been at intervals ever since she arrived with her two housemates, Big Anne and the Dummy, and took up her abode in the last of the cabins that you pass on the left hand, going towards Sallinbeg. Perhaps Lisconnel should not reckon her among its residents, so much of her time is spent on the tramp as an absentee. Still, she sometimes has tarried with us for a long while, and she is understood to have some property in the house-furniture, so it seems natural to consider the place her home.

From the first it appeared obvious to all that the dementedness which characterised the little wizened yellow-faced woman was of a much more pronounced type than Con the Quare One's.

Any attempt to spare people's feelings by ignoring the fact would have been very futile, and it was therefore lucky that the three new-comers, Mad Bell herself included, were quite content to accept the situation. The neighbours were at first inclined to commiserate Big Anne, who was pronounced to be "a dacint, sinsible, poor woman," for the oddities of her household, the incalculable flightiness of Mad Bell, and the impenetrable silence of the Dummy. But to their condoling remarks she was wont to reply in effect—"Ah sure, ma'am, that's the way I'm used to them, the crathurs. Why, if Mad Bell said anythin' over-sinsible, or poor Winnie said anythin' at all, it's wond'rin' I'd be what was goin' to happin us next." And Big Anne evidently looked upon this as an uncomfortable frame of mind. At first, too, they speculated much about the circumstances which had brought the curious trio together beneath one thatch, and found it especially hard to conjecture how the daft little vagrant had come into possession of sundry tables and chairs. All its members, however, being incommunicative persons, no satisfactory elucidation of these points was arrived at in Lisconnel.

The coalescence of Big Anne's and the Dummy's fortunes is a simple history enough. Anne Fannin, while yet a youngish woman, was left alone in the world to do for herself in her little wayside cabin. Without a dowry to recommend her rough-hewn features and large-boned ungainliness, she never had any suitors, and she found it as much as she could contrive to make out her single living by means of her "bit of poultry" and her pig. Nevertheless, when her nearest neighbours—the Golighers—died, leaving their daughter Winnie, "who had niver got her speech, the crathur," to live on charity or the rates, what else was a body to do except take her in? Anne would have put this question to you with a sincere want of resource. So Winnie Goligher transferred to Anne Fannin's house, herself and all her worldly goods, which consisted of the clothes she had on, and a prayer-book, and a lame duck, and thenceforward the two "got along the best way they could."

Mad Bell's history has more complications in it. They began one pleasant April day when she was only a slip of a lass, who had taken a little place at the Hunts' farm near her home, for the purpose of saving up a few pounds against her marriage with Richard McBirney. She had been given an unexpected holiday, and was running home across the fresh, spring-green grass-fields, thinking to take her people by surprise, when she came to a hedge-gap whence you look down into a steep-banked lane. And at the foot of the bank Richard McBirney was sitting with his arm round her sister Lizzie's waist.

To a dispassionate observer this transference of his attentions might have seemed a matter of small moment. Most of their acquaintances, for example, were just as well satisfied that he should court Eliza as Isabella. But the sight turned all the current of her life awry. For it set her off rushing away from it across the same sunny green fields, and she never came home again. Nor ever again would she settle down quietly anywhere. She had a strong, clear voice and a taste for music, and this led her to take to singing ballads about the country at markets and fairs. The harder she was thinking about fickle Richard McBirney, the louder and shriller she sang. A very few years of such wandering shrivelled up her plump "pig-beauty," so that in her little sallow, weather-beaten face her own mother would scarcely have recognised pretty Isabella Reid. Then, after a long spell of illness in a

Union infirmary, she began to grow noticeably odder and stranger in her looks and ways; until at length the children shouted "Mad Bell" as she passed, and that became her recognised style and title.

Such, briefly, had been her experience of life, when one September evening she came by chance to Big Anne and the Dummy's door. She had got a very bad cold, and felt hardly able to drag herself along between the berried hedges, and was so hoarse that she could with difficulty ask for the night's lodging, which they granted without demur. Their times had been unusually bad of late. In fact, their room was looking several sizes larger than they were accustomed to see it, because they had sold any articles of furniture for which "e'er a price at all" could be obtained. But to whatever accommodation this bareness permitted they made Mad Bell kindly welcome, the crathur being sick and crazy, and she stayed with them for three or four days. By that time, finding herself recovered, she resumed her journey, setting off early in the morning with the abruptness and absence of circumlocution which, as a rule, distinguished her proceedings. A friendly nod and grimace she made serve for announcement of departure and leavetaking all in one. As her hostesses watched her out of sight down the road, Big Anne said—

"Well, now, I never seen that quare little body in this counthry before, and we're very apt to not set eyes on her agin. God be good to us all, but the likes of her is to be pitied. She's worse off than the two of us. But bedad, Winnie, if thim hins there don't prisintly take to layin' a thrifle, it's in a tight houle we'll be ourselves. I dunno what's bewitchin' them. And the sorra an ould stick have we left in it that man or mortal 'ud give us the price of a pullet's egg for—and small blame to him, unless he was as deminted as herself that's quittin'."

Mad Bell's tramp that day was all along a sequence of lonesome winding lanes, where few dwellings were dotted among the green and gold of the fields. The bustle of the harvest, its reaping and binding, was over in them, and they lay without stir or sound. In some of them the stooks were still encamped, but some were smooth stubble, empty, except where a flock of turkeys filled it with dark, bunchy shapes. She walked steadily on the whole day without any adventure, but when the dew was beginning to fall through the twilight she came to a short, shady reach of lane, at the end of which stood, in a green nook, a small, prim white cottage with two peaked windows and a door to match. That, at least, is how it would under ordinary circumstances have presented itself to a passer-by. Just then, however, nobody would have noticed anything about it except the fact that out of the open door thick coils of woolly black smoke were rolling and rolling, stabbed through every now and again by thrusts of flame, which even in the lingering daylight gleamed strongly fierce and red. The house was evidently on fire. As Mad Bell drew nearer, she became aware of a wheaten-coloured terrier standing in front of it; and when he saw her he began to bark vehemently. She was used to being barked at, though not in this way, for howls were interspersed, and it was clearly meant not for a menace but an appeal. No other live creature was visible about the place, until she had come quite close to the surging door, when a small gossoon jumped up out of the ditch on the opposite side of the road and rushed across to her.

"What 'ill I do at all, then?" he said, whimperingly, catching hold of her shawl. "If them childer's burnt up widin there, Mr. Wogan 'ill be in a fine way. It's for killin' the whole of us he'll be. And it wasn't me set it afire. Sorra the match was I meddlin' wid, I could swear it. I wasn't out of it any time, gettin' a few ripe berries to pacify them childer, agin they would be wakin' and roarin', and when I come back, there it is all a smother of smoke. Divil a thing else was I doin' on'y mindin' them childer, and not meddlin' wid the matches, and goin' after a couple of blackberries. And Mr. Wogan himself's away to Ballymacartrican wid his boxes in the ass-cart. And all of them goin' to quit out of it to-morra, if it wasn't for them childer bein' burnt up inside—or maybe it's smothered they are. It's as unhandy as anythin'. It went afire of itself. And he'll be ragin'."

He bawled all this louder and louder in competition with the clamour of the dog, who kept on jumping up at each alternately, and evidently considered his remarks better entitled to a hearing. But Mad Bell merely replied, "Whisht gabbin', and hould that," thrusting, as she spoke, her little handkerchief bundle into his arms. And thereupon, making a sudden dive, she vanished among the flame-sheathing smoke.

Scarcely had she disappeared when an empty donkey-cart came round the turn of the lane, led by a rather dejected-looking middle-aged man, whose countenance, nevertheless, had for some time back been gradually clearing up at every wind of the way that brought him nearer to this particular point of view. But as he caught sight of the black smoke drifting and rolling, his aspect of reasonable melancholy changed to one of a despair that could not have been wilder if the reek of hell-mouth had blown into his face. He dropped the bridle, and hurled himself down the road like the distracted body that he well might be. For a twelvemonth ago he had lost his wife and both his elder children in one week, and his pair of two-year-old twins were now all that stood between himself and world-wide desolation. At the front door his frantic rush was met and baffled by a choking puff, which sent him fleeing round in hopes that entrance might be more possible through the back; and on the way he came face to face with the wrathful visages of his son and daughter, whom Mad Bell was carrying in the disregardful manner that betides a cumbrous load snatched up in a mortal hurry. She had escaped by the back door.

If the most radiant of guardian angels, in snowy plumes and golden tresses, had restored his children to him with a befitting speech, poor Matthew Wogan could not well have been more joyfully relieved from his terror than he was when this odd little yellow-faced woman, with a red handkerchief wisped round her head, and a singed grimness generally pervading her, handed over to him Minnie and Tom, casually remarking, " Bedad, it's the big heavy lumps they are." Minnie and Tom both were crying and coughing loudly, because the smoke had got into their eyes and throats, which they resented; and when their father returned with them to the front of the house, this noise was swelled by the gleeful yap-yapping of the terrier and the voices of a few other people who had appeared upon the scene— a matronly looking woman and two or three sun-burnt harvestmen. From Mrs. Massey's observations it could be gathered that she had been minding the Wogan twins by deputy, and further that she entertained the gloomiest views about the mental and moral qualities of her son little Larry, who replied to her animadversions with over-reaching protestations about matches and theories of spontaneous combustion. While they wrangled in the background, the young men inspected the conflagration, which proved to be less extensive than it looked, though undoubtedly serious enough to have soon put the sleeping children past waking, if rescue had not come. A heap of blankets and other bedding, that smouldered and blazed near the front door, was the source of the most stifling smoke; and when it had been subdued by many buckets of water, everybody began to drag what bits of the furniture they could out of harm's way. There was not much, because, as Wogan explained, he had sent "the marrow of it" to his sister at Ballymacartrican; and the legs of the largest table were charred so badly that it collapsed with a crash "the instiant minyit it set its four feet on the ground," as Mrs. Massey said. However, there were two smaller ones not much the worse, and three or four chairs, and a couple of stools, and some pots and pans, and a small clothes-horse, and a wagging clock, whose round white face glimmered through the dusk like a fallen moon as it lay flat on the grass. All these things made a little crowd on the plot of sward by the door.

"And what will you be doin' wid them now?"

said Mrs. Massey. "There's my place below you'd be welcome to stand them in as long as you plase. 'Deed would you, sir. The dear knows I'm not throubled wid too many sticks of furnitur'. That's a very handy-sized washin'-tub Larry's after carryin' out for you. I was noticin' to-day ours has a lake in it this long while back that dhrips over everythin'. I must get himself to thry mend it."

"That's a *lovely* table," suddenly said Mad Bell, who had hitherto made no remarks. "A rael grand one it is," she repeated, in a wistful sort of way, smoothing the leaf fondly with her hand.

"And very welcome you'd be to have it in a prisint, ma'am, if you've e'er a fancy for it; ay, or for the matter of that to the whole lot of them altogether," said Matthew Wogan, who, with his arms full of the smoky twins, felt a weight of gratitude which he would gladly have expressed in deeds. "Little vally there is on them—it's a small thing after what you're after doin' for us. I wouldn't like to be payin' away me bit of money from the childer, or else—— But if I auctioned them things off the way I was intindin' it's on'y a thrifle of a few shillin's they'd be bringin' me. Welcome you are to them, ma'am."

"Sure what use at all 'ud such a thing be to the likes of her?" put in Mrs. Massey. "It's on'y annoyed you'd be, woman, wid tables and chairs. And she thrampin' about, you may depind, wid ne'er a place to be bringin' them to, if she had them twyste over, let alone any way of movin' them. It's very convanient we are, just round the turn of the road."

"She might take the little cart and the ould ass along," said Matthew Wogan, looking at his equipage, which was straying towards them intermittently as the beast grazed the green border of the lane. "They're no use to me now. Then there'd be nothin' delayin' her that she couldn't be cleanin' out of it wid them right away—You needn't throuble yourself to be liftin' the little stool, Mrs. Massey. What wid fire and water, that'll be no place to sleep in," he said, pointing to the still smoking door. "The Mahonys 'ud take us in for to-night, and to-morra early we're off to me sister's and next day to Queenstown. 'Twill be a grand thing for the childer to be settled near their uncle Tom, that's doin' right well in New Jersey, in case anythin' happint me. So I'd as lief be shut of all that collection, supposin' they'd be any benefit to this crathur."

"Saints bless us, but you're givin' away all before you, Mr. Wogan," said Mrs. Massey, with a discomfited laugh.

"Have you e'er a house you could be puttin' them in?" one of the harvestmen asked of Mad Bell.

"Ay, bedad," she said. And with that she picked up a chair, and dumped it down into the cart, which had come to a halt at the door.

This promptitude on her part seemed to settle the question. Without more ado the rest of the salvage was loaded in, all except the handy-sized washing-tub, which by means of an adroitly taken up position Mrs. Massey contrived to have overlooked and left behind, when Mad Bell drove away with her newly acquired property.

On through the gloaming she drove, till the white dust flakes gathered up by the wheels grew damp and fragrant with dew, and till the moonlight was glimmering among the golden sheaves silverly, and till live embers were fanned out of the ashes low in the east. The small hours had a frosty chill, and old Ned's short steps were leisurely, and his halts for refreshment frequent; still Mad Bell continued to sit with serene patience. She was retracing her route of the day before, but at so much slower a rate of progress that the sun had been up for more than an hour when she stopped in front of Big Anne and the Dummy's little house. They were disturbed at their breakfast by the sound of the arrival, and when they came to the door, saw their visitor in the act of depositing a second chair upon the ground beside the cart.

"Whethen now and is it yourself back agin?" said Big Anne. "And what at all have you got there?"

"Inside they're goin'," said Mad Bell, pointing to the cart-load with an elated air. "It's a dale handier to have some chairs and tables."

This was a fact which Big Anne might well have admitted, considering that she had just been squatting on her heels to eat her plate of stir-about. However, she only continued her perplexed catechism: "Where at all was you after bringin' them things from, and who might be ownin' them?"

"Out of a house burnin' down," said Mad Bell.

"Och between us and harm. What house is it then? And how did it get burnin'?"

"Sure it's aisy enough settin' a house on fire,"

said Mad Bell with a grin, which to Big Anne who at this time was not familiar with her manners, looked rather sinisterly significant. "Flarin' up rael strong," she said, pushing towards her, as if in confirmation of the statement, the little wooden clothes-horse, whose rails were blackened and charred.

"Aisy it may be," Big Anne said, looking aghast at it, "but dreadful divilment it is to do such a thing, wid the misfort'nit people very apt to lose their lives, let alone everythin' else."

"There was nobody in it on'y the couple of fat little childer," said Mad Bell.

"The saints be among us all, woman," said Big Anne, "what sort of talk have you? It's not streelin' about the counthry you are, wid them ould sticks of furnitur', and lavin' the little childer in the house blazin' up? The Lord pity the crathurs, what 'ud become of them if they was left thataway? Burnt to cinders be now very belike."

"Stufficated," said Mad Bell, with a complacent nod.

Big Anne and the Dummy stared at one another in great horror. The Dummy could express her feelings only by crossing herself and gasping; but Big Anne spoke volubly: "May God forgive me for openin' me lips to the likes of you. Och but you're the unnatural wicked woman to go do such a thing, if you was twyste as cracked and crazy itself. Git along out of this, yourself and your ould cart, afore the pólis comes after you. Och the misfort'nit little crathurs. And don't be offerin' to darken our doors agin wid the ojis sight of you."

"Gimme a hand wid liftin' in them two tables," said Mad Bell. Whereupon Big Anne whisked away from her, and banged the door in her face.

Mad Bell, however, did not appear to be discouraged by this reception. She finished unloading the cart of all except the tables, which she found unwieldy single-handed. Then she unharnessed old Neddy, and went and seated herself on the low wall beside the house. She was seemingly quite content with the situation. But to the two women indoors it was a dreadful experience. Their minds were firmly persuaded that the daft little woman had designedly set fire to some dwelling, and made off with what household gear she could lay hands on, leaving the hapless children to perish amid the flames. It shocked and enraged them that their premises should be infested by the presence of such a criminal, and that her ill-gotten goods and chattels should be brought to their very threshold, not to speak of her outrageous proposal to harbour them under their roof. Big Anne declared that wid the legs of them chairs and tables glimpsing through the door, as if they were on'y turned out to be airin' a bit, she and the Dummy seemed as good as a pair of murderers.

Every now and then they went to the door and peered out, and the incendiary always greeted them with cheerful nods. On these occasions Big Anne sometimes said: "Oh, very well, me good woman. Just you sit brazenin' there till the patrol comes round this way, and then if I don't give you in charge as sure as the sun's shinin' crooked over our heads.—Begone out of that, and take them things out of litterin' about our place." Or she would remark loudly to her companion: "Just stop a minyit, Winnie, till I sling me ould shawl over me head, and run down to the barracks. It's not very long they'll be puttin' her out of it, and bundlin' her into jail, instead of to be sittin' there, wid ne'er a spark of shame in her, annoyin' dacint people." But neither mode of address produced any effect. The morning sunbeams still slanted down on the small pile of furniture, and old Neddy went on munching the blades off which they were drying the dew, and Mad Bell continued to sit upon the wall, as if placidly waiting for events.

Such was the posture of affairs until towards noon, when an outside-car came trotting quickly down the lane. On one side of it sat a black-whiskered man in his best clothes, with each hand tightly grasping a small, fat, wrigglesome child. And the three were Matthew, Tom, and Minnie Wogan. On catching sight of Mad Bell, he made the driver pull up.

"Well, ma'am," he called to her, "so you're after gettin' home. Bedad it's the fine long step you've took th'ould donkey; one while he'd be doin' it. And you're about gettin' in the few things? Very welcome she is to the whole of them," he continued to Big Anne, who had now emerged. "And begorrah nobody else had a better right to any trifle might be saved out of it. She'll ha' tould you, ma'am, the way the place was set on fire on me last night—some little divil of a spalpeen playin' wid matches it seems. But anyhow, there it was in blazes, and me galloppin' home like a deminted cow, consaitin' these two imps of the mischief here would be smotherin' inside it. And, troth, if herself over there hadn't them fetched out safe into the yard, when it was as much as your life was worth to put your head in at the door, for the stiflin' of the smoke. I dunno how she conthrived it. Maybe the crathur isn't altogether over sinsible," he said in a confidential tone; "but if she'd had all the wit ever was thought of, she couldn't ha' done better be the childer. So it's kindly welcome she is to the bits of furniture, and the ould baste. And dhrivin' on we must be. Good mornin' to yous all."

Mad Bell listened to this praise with the same equanimity as to Big Anne's threats and reproaches. But when the car had trotted on, she came up to her, saying just as before, "Gimme a hand wid liftin' in thim tables;" and Matthew Wogan, jogging down the long lane, may have caught the last glimpse of one of them as it vanished in at the doorway.

Thus it was that Mad Bell came to be domiciled with Big Anne and the Dummy in the pauses between her wanderings. The arrangement seemed equitable in view of her substantial contribution to the plenishing of the house. The donkey-cart, likewise, was found very serviceable, enabling them to turn a penny occasionally by fetching and carrying. And the coalition worked well upon the whole. But after a few years of such prosperity that they were seldom without a bit of food in the house, and sometimes had bacon on Sunday, things took a turn for the worse. Old Ned died under the burden of his many years, and a sort of murrain among the fowl cut off several promising pullets in the heyday of their youth. Then arose difficulties about "rint," while their landlord, who was new to the property, had a natural zeal for sweeping it clear of encumbering tenants. And the end of it was that the three women transferred themselves to Lisconnel, where they became not the least respected of its inhabitants.

But these particulars about their antecedents were never learned by the neighbours there; and the joint ownership of the furniture still presents itself as one of our unsolved problems. Another of them was propounded somewhat later, when Mad Bell returned from an unusually long ramble, during which she had crossed the Liffey by the spacious O'Connell Bridge, and had heard the boom of the big College bell, and with her wizened-lemon face had half-scared the smallest-sized children in villages round about Dublin. For she was wearing an elaborately fantastic piece of headgear, which moved everybody's curiosity so strongly that it cannot have been for want of wondering if we failed to find out how she had come thereby. Strangely incongruous it did undoubtedly look; yet the stages by which it had descended from its stand in the milliner's show-room and alighted upon the head of the little wandering-witted tramp, were much fewer than might have been supposed probable.

One blustery March morning when Mrs. M'Bean was on her way along by the low sea-wall to buy a bit of bacon at Donnelly's shop in Kilclone, the east wind did her the shrewd turn of whisking off her hat and dropping it into the water. It was a most shabby old black straw, rusty and battered, and torn, yet Mrs. M'Bean, a labourer's wife, who had nothing at all handsome about her, seemed to think it worth a serious risk. For she mounted on the broad wall-top, and thence made so unwary a snatch that she overbalanced herself and splashed headlong into the heaving high-tide, where she would very soon have perished beneath the cold olive-gray swell, had not the brothers

Denny, fishing for bass hard by, noticed the perilous accident, and pulled timely to the rescue.

When they disembarked her, gasping and dripping, at the nearest landing-place, she was understood to say, " Sure me heart's broke," a remark which Police-sergeant Young, who formed one of the group gathered by the disaster, considered sufficient grounds for marching her off to the handiest J.P. on a charge of attempted suicide. Mrs. M'Bean vehemently repelled the accusation. She explained that she had said her heart was broke only " because she had lost her ould hat, and every thread of a rag on her had been dhrenched and ruinated with the salt water. How could she go for to do such a sin as destroy herself, she urged, and she wid a houseful of little childer waitin' for her at home, the crathurs?" Her arguments proved convincing, and the charge was summarily dismissed, not without strictures upon Sergeant Young's excessive zeal, by which he, recking nothing of Talleyrand's maxim, felt himself puzzled and aggrieved.

The incident, however, brought some more agreeable consequences to Mrs. M'Bean, as the J.P.'s ladies, commiserating her half-drowned plight, sent her that same evening a goodly bundle of cast-off clothes, over which her eyes grew gleefully bright in her careworn face. At one of the articles included they widened with almost awe. This was an enormous hat made of white fluffy felt, with vast contorted brims, and great blue velvet rosettes and streamers. Its fabric was very stout and substantial, and withal quite new, for its original owner had speedily found it so stiff and heavy that to wear it gave her a headache and a crick in her neck. Mrs. M'Bean, for her part, could not entertain the idea of carrying anything so sumptuous upon her grizzled head; and when she tried it on her eldest daughter, it totally extinguished and nearly smothered the child. So she stowed it away in a corner, where it remained unseen for several weeks.

But next month, on the afternoon of Easter Day, Mrs. M'Bean had two visitors over from Ballyhoy: Annie Cassidy, elderly and rather grim, with her young friend Nelly Walsh.

"Nelly's bound to be havin' bad luck this year of her life," Annie observed in the course of conversation, "for not a new stitch has she put on her to-day, and it Easter. That's an unlucky thing, accordin' to the sayin'."

"Ne'er a bit am I afraid of me luck," averred

Nelly, cheerful and threadbare, not to say ragged. But Mrs. M'Bean was pricked by a sudden thought up the ladder to the little attic aloft, whence she creaked down again, bringing with her the great white hat. "There, Nelly," she said, "just clap that on your head, and then nobody can pass the remark that you didn't get the wear of somethin' new, any way."

Nelly took the hat, which struck her nearly dumb with admiration, but as she tried to catch a glimpse of it in the shred of looking-glass on the wall, her delighted expression waxed so eloquent that Mrs. M'Bean was impelled to say: "You're to keep it, girl alive, if you've e'er a fancy for it. Sure it's fitter for you than the likes of me, that 'ud look a quare old scarecrow if I offered to go about in such a thing." She had not at first intended this generosity, her worldly goods being so few that she could not lightly part with even a very unpromising possession.

Nelly, on her side, could hardly believe in her high fortune, when, after some polite demur, she found herself carrying off the splendid hat. To wear it on an ordinary walk would have seemed profane, so she held it under her old shawl all the way home to her cabin on the shore at the foot of the Black Banks, a good step beyond Ballyhoy. But when she reached the door, she could not forbear the pleasure of making her entrance in the glory of her new adornment. Her reception was altogether disappointing. For her mother's and grandmother's voices rose up shrill and shriller, demanding what at all hijjis gazabo she'd got on her. Billy, her eldest brother, said: "Musha, she's put a pair of blinkers on her like an ould horse;" and Larry, his junior, remarked with terse candour, "Och, the fright." More mortifying still, Joe Tierney, her sweetheart, who had called to conclude arrangements about the morrow's holiday, said in a disgusted tone: "Tare and ages! I hope to goodness, Nelly, you're not intindin' to make that show of yourself at the circus to-morra. Bedad, I niver seen such a conthrivance; you might as well be walkin' alongside some sort of deminted musharoon." This rather aptly described the effect of the huge white brim upon Nelly, who was small and short of stature; but it hurt her feelings badly.

The only upholder of the hat was Annie Cassidy, who is fond of controverting the opinions of other people, and who despises men. She said: "Don't be lettin' them put you out of consait with it,

Nelly; it suits you lovely. Sure if anyone doesn't think your app'arance is good enough for them, you needn't throuble them wid your company. Circuses, to my mind, is thrash—to be watchin' folks figurandyin' on a pack of ould horses' backs. There's a lot of us goin' over to-morra to Rathbeg, where they've merry-go-rounds you can ride in yourself, and all manner, if you'd just step down to the Junction station and come along wid us on the early train."

" 'Deed then I might," said Nelly; not that she had the least intention of doing any such thing, but because, being somewhat of a belle, she was unaccustomed to uncomplimentary criticisms and much affronted by them. Furthermore, for the same reason, she escorted Annie home, and stayed so long talking, that Joe before she returned had to go off about his milking, which annoyed him a good deal.

However, he had quite forgotten his vexation next morning, as he hurried through his early tasks with a day's pleasuring before him. He worked at the Kellys', whose land is bounded north and south by the Junction lane and the sea ; and as he walked about the fresh April fields he was in view of Howth, dark pansy-purple against the eastern amber, confronting the sweep of the Dublin mountains, outlined in wild hyacinth-coloured mist, across the dancing silver of the bay. The calves had been fed so expeditiously that Joe found he could spare time to stop at the starred bank under the hedge and pick a bunch of primroses, some of which Nelly's mother would proudly keep in a jam-pot on the window-stool, while Nelly herself might like to wear a few at the circus, brightening up her brown-striped shawl.

But when he was compressing a thick sheaf of the cool soft stalks in one hard hand, he chanced to look up, and saw what thrilled him with dismay. Bobbing along over the jagged edge of the wall, a short way down the lane went a gleaming white object, which he at once recognised as Nelly's new hat. He ran aghast to look through the gate, and despite intercepting road-curves and obstructive hedges, the hat it unmistakably was, making for the Junction station. So Nelly, intending a serious quarrel, had thrown him over and joined the Rathbeg party. A pleasure, hoarded in anticipation for many a month, shrivelled into dead leaves suddenly like fairy gold, as he perceived how certainly this must be the case.

His first angry impulse was a resort to Haskin's Public at Portbrendan, where he might spend his spoilt holiday taking drinks and making bets in the society of some cronies. What hindered him from immediately acting upon it was a compunctious forecast of the concern which would prevail in his family, if he absented himself contrary to expectation. "There's me mother's never aisy," he reflected, "unless she's persuadin' herself some of us are kilt on her." This made him resolve to postpone Portbrendan till after breakfast, and he turned lothfully homewards. As he passed along the Kellys' yard-wall, he relieved his feelings by tossing his nosegay over it at the place where he heard the grunting of their pigs, who on that occasion fared almost as delicately as Marvel's rose-lined fawn.

It was early still when he reached his cabin, one in the Walshes' row; and he sat down listlessly on a bank, to wait for nothing in particular. Presently Mrs. Walsh, senior, came by with a twinkling can of water. "Och, there you are, Joe," she said: "Nelly's been lookin' out for you this good while."

"Whethen it's quare lookin' out she had," said Joe, "and she took off wid herself to ould Annie Cassidy—bad manners to her for her interfarin'."

"What's the lad talkin' about at all?" said Mrs. Walsh, standing amazed; "Nelly's widin there this instiant of time, readyin' herself up."

"Maybe you'll tell me," said Joe, "that I didn't see her streelin' down the Junction lane afore I was lavin' Kellys'."

"And maybe *you*'ll tell *me*," said Nelly's grandmother, "that she wasn't just now callin' to me they were wantin' wather. It's a fine bawl she'd ha' had to let out of her, if I was to be hearin' her, and she up beyond Kellys'."

"There she was anyway," Joe said, doggedly. "Wouldn't I know that dad fetched-lookin' ould new caubeen she's stuck on her a mile o' ground?"

"You great gomeral," said Mrs. Walsh. "If that's all you might aisy enough ha' seen the big hat goin' the road—but have you the notion it's growin' on Nelly's head? Why, you omadhawn, you hadn't quit ten minyits last night, and Nelly was just after gettin' back, when who should come by but poor Mad Bell. Och now the raggedy objick the crathur was, wid nothin' over her misfort'nit head but an ould wisp as full of houles as a fishin'-net. So little Larry sez, jokin' like, 'Look here, Nelly,' sez he, 'you'd a right to be lettin' Mad Bell have a loan of your grand flappy hat to keep the sun out of her eyes.' But belike Nelly'd took a turn agin the thing wid the way they'd all been makin' fun of it; for sez she, 'Will you have it, Bell?' sez she, houldin' it out to her. And if she did, Mad Bell grabbed it in her two hands— it's not often she'll have a word for anybody— and no more talk about it, but cocked it on, and tied it firm under her chin wid the sthramers, as tasty as you plase. Musha good gracious, to see the len'th she drew the bow out on aich side of her bit of a yeller face, and the nod she gave her ould head when she'd got it done. So that's what's gone wid the hat. Goodness guide us, if she wasn't the poor crazy-witted body she is, 'twould be a sin to let her go makin' such a show of herself; but sure no one 'ud think to mind anythin' the likes of the crathur might have on her, the saints may pity her. Ay, bedad, them kind of quare consthructions do be fit for nothin' unless Quality and mad people," old Mrs. Walsh continued, without malice, soliloquising, as Joe had caught up the can, and was hurrying it with prodigal splashes towards his sweetheart's door.

The circus, with its flaring lights and whirl of tinselled prancing marvels, was so rapturous an experience to Nelly that she had not a regret for her discarded hat, which at this time was moving on beneath a soft dappled sky, between greening hedges, westward along quiet roads and lanes. It found shelter for the night under the ley of a tall hayrick near Santry, thus ending the first stage of Mad Bell's tramp home to the wide brown bog-land of Lisconnel.

CHAPTER XII

A FLITTING

AMONG the latest of the strangers that have visited Lisconnel were some who came at a time when the neighbours stood rather in need of distraction. For the summer following Mrs. Kilfoyle's death was, between one thing and another, a drearyish season with us. That little old woman had left a great gap; and then there were many long spells of gloomy bad weather, which seemed to beat people's troubles down upon them as the damp drove the turf-reek back through their smoke-holes into the dark rooms, where they could scarcely see how dense the blue haze was growing. Stacey Doyne's marriage also had removed something young and pleasant, and at times, when the thatch dripped without and within, neighbours were apt to talk about her in tones of commiseration, and say, "Sure, her poor mother's lost entirely." So that towards autumn the diversion of some new residents' arrival happened opportunely enough. It was made possible by the fact that Big Anne had given up her holding and entered into partnership with the widow M'Gurk, thus leaving her late abode empty for another tenant, who appeared much sooner than any one might have anticipated from the aspect of the cabin.

Except as a fresh topic of conversation, however, the strangers gave small promise of proving an acquisition to the community. Lisconnel did not like their appearance by any means, and further acquaintance failed to modify unfavourable first impressions. These were mainly received in the course of the day after their arrival, which took place on a night too black for anything beyond a shadowy counting of heads, and a perception that the bulk of the newcomers' household stuff had jogged up on one donkey, and must therefore be small. A portion of Big Anne's furniture had remained behind her in the cabin, owing to certain arrears of rent. Her heart was scalded, she said, wid the prices she'd only get for her early chuckens, and they the weight of the world, if you'd feel them in your hand; and poor

Mad Bell, that 'ud mostly bring home a few odd shillin's wid her, was away since afore last Christmas, and might never show her face there agin, the crathur; and the poor Dummy gone, that was great at the knittin' if she got the chance—a bit of narration which would look funny enough in anybody's rental. Mrs. Quigley, who went to the door with the offer of a seed of fire, found it shut, and a voice inside called, "as onmannerly as you plase,". "No, we've got matches;" whereupon another voice, further in the interior, quavered, "Thank'ee kindly, ma'am." So she departed little wiser than she had come. But daylight showed that the party consisted of an old man, and his son, and his son's wife, and her sister, and three small children, besides some cochin-china fowl, and a black cat with vividly green eyes. This much was apparent on the surface. Also that the old man was frail, bent, shrivelled, and civil spoken, that the son was "a big soft gomeral of a fellow," that both the women were sandily flaxen-haired, with broad, flat cheeks and light eyes, and that two of the children resembled them, while the third—a girl a trifle older—was a dark-haired, disconsolate-looking little thing, "wid her face," Mrs. Brian said, "not the width of the palm of your hand, and the eyes of her sunk in her head." As for the fowl, there could be no doubt that their "onnathural, long, fluffety legs were fit to make a body's flesh creep," and the cat looked "as like an ould divil as anythin' you ever witnessed, sittin' blinkin' atop of the turf-stack."

Other less self-evident facts came out by degrees—more slowly than might have been expected, as the strangers were generally close and chary of speech. They came from the north, where their affairs had not prospered—in fact, they had been "sold up and put out of it," as the young man divulged one day to Brian Kilfoyle. They were a somewhat intricately connected family, by the name, predominantly, of Patman. The sister-in-law was Tishy M'Crum, which seemed simple enough, but the two light-haired boys were Greens, Mrs. Patman having been a widow, while the little girl was the child of a wife whom Tom Patman had already buried; for though he looked full young to have embarked upon matrimony at all, this was his second venture. "And it's a quare comether she must ha' been after puttin' on him," quoth Mrs. Quigley, "afore he took up wid herself, that's as ugly as if she was bespoke, and half a dozen year oulder than the young bosthoon, if she's a minyit." It is true that at the time when Mrs. Quigley expressed this unflattering opinion she and her neighbours had been exasperated by an impolite speech of Mrs. Patman, who had said loudly in their hearing, "Well, for sartin if I'd had a notion of the blamed little dog-hole he was bringin' us into, sorra the sole of a fut 'ud I ha' set inside it;" and had then proceeded to congratulate herself upon having prudently left "all her dacint bits of furniture up above at her mother's, so that she needn't be bothered wid cartin' them away out of a place that didn't look to have had ever e'er a thing in it worth the throuble of movin', not if it stood there until it dropped to pieces wid dirt." Mrs. Quigley rejoined (to Judy Ryan) that "it would be a great pity if any people sted in a place that wasn't good enough for them, supposin' all the while they was used to anythin' a thraneen better—maybe they might, in coorse, and maybe they mightn't. It was won'erful to hear the talk some folks had, and they wid every ould stick they owned an aisy loadin' for Reilly's little ass." But Judy Ryan, with a flight of sarcastic fancy, hoped that Mrs. Patman and her family "were about goin' on a visit prisintly to the Lady

Lifftinant, because it was much if they'd find any place else where there'd be grandeur accordin' to their high-up notions."

Skirmishes such as this, however, were a symptom rather than a cause of the Patmans' unpopularity. That sprang from several roots. For one thing, both the women had harsh, scolding voices, and it was even chances that if you passed within earshot of their cabin you would hear them giving tongue. Their objurgations were, as a rule, addressed to the young man or the old, the latter of whom soon grew into an object of local compassion as "a harmless, dacint, poor crathur," while his son came in for the frank-eyed looking-down-upon which is the portion of an able-bodied man, shrew-ridden through sheer supineness and "polthroonery." But what Lisconnel often said that it "thought badder of" was the stepmotherly treatment which seemed to be the lot of the little girl Katty. Of course the situation was one which, under the circumstances, would have made people believe in such a state of things upon the slenderest evidence. Still, even to unprejudiced eyes, it was clear that Katty's rags were raggeder than those of her small step-brothers, and that she crept about with the mien of a creature which has conceived reasonable doubts respecting the reception it is likely to meet in society. When the autumn weather began to grow wintry, little Katty Patman, "perishin' about out there in the freezin' win'," became a spectacle which was viewed with indignant sympathy from dark doorways whence she received many an invitation to step in and be warmin' herself. Her hostesses opined that she was fairly starved just for a taste of the fire, and didn't believe she was ever let next or nigh it in her own place. Often, too, the consideration that she had no more flesh on her bones than a March chucken led to the bestowal of a steaming potato or a piece of griddlebread; but the result of this was sometimes unsatisfactory to the giver, Katty being apt to dart away with her refreshments, which she might presently be seen sharing among Bobby and Stevie, for whom she entertained a strong and apparently unreciprocated regard.

"I wouldn't go for to be sayin' anythin' to set her agin them," Mrs. Brian Kilfoyle remarked on some such occasion. "But, goodness forgive me! I've no likin' for them two little brats. I'd misthrust them."

"Ah, sure they've no sinse," said Biddy Ryan.

"Where'd they git it? And the biggest of them, I'd suppose, under four year ould."

"Sinse!" said Mrs. Quigley. "Bedad, then, if sinse was all that ailed them, the pair of them is as 'cute as a couple of young foxes. I mind on'y a day or so after they'd been in it, I met the laste one on the road, and I comin' home wid be chance a sugarstick in me basket. So, just to be makin' friends like, I gave it a bit for itself, and a bit for the other that I seen comin' along. Well, now, ma'am, if it had took and ate up the both of the bits, I'd ha' thought ne'er a pin's point of harm—'twould ha' been nathural enough to the size of it. But I give you me word, when it seen it couldn't get the two of them swallied down afore its brother come by, what did it go do but clap the one of them into a crevice in the wall, and cover it under a blackberry laif. And wid that down it squats, and begins sayin', 'Creely-crawly snail—where's the creely-crawly snail I'm after huntin' out of its houle?'—lettin' on to be lookin' for somethin' creepin' in the grass. And a while after it come slinkin' back, when it thought nobody was mindin', to poke the bit out of the wall where I was gatherin' dandelions under the bank. So while it was fumblin' about, missin' the right crevice, sez I, poppin' up, thinkin' to shame it, 'Maybe the crawly snail's after aitin' it on you,' sez I. 'Och, yis; I seen it,' sez the spalpeen, as brazen as brass. 'Gimme 'noder bit instid.' There's a schemin' young rapscallion for you!"

"They're too like their mother altogether to plase me," said Judy Ryan. "The corners of their eyes do be as sharp as if they were cut out wid a pair of scissors. Not that I'd mind if they'd e'er a sthrake of good-nathur in them; but I misdoubt they have. The little girl, now, is as diff'rint as day and night."

"If *she* takes after her father, she's a right to want the wit powerful, misfort'nit little imp," said Mrs. Brian. "For if he isn't a great stupid gomeral and an ass, just get me one. Why, if he was worth the dust blowin' along the road, he'd purvint of his own child bein' put upon."

"Och, they have him *frighted*," said Mrs. Quigley, with scornful emphasis. "They won't let him take an atom of notice of her, they're that jealous. Sure, if he gets talkin' to her outside the house there, one of them 'ill let a bawl and send him off to be carryin' in turf or wather. I've seen it times and agin."

"If he'd take and sling it about their ears some fine day he'd be doin' right, and it might larn them to behave themselves," said Judy.

"But the ould man would disgust you," pursued Mrs. Quigley, "wid the romancin' he has out of him about his son Tom. You'd suppose, to listen to him, that the omadhawn's aquil never stepped. He'll deive you wid it till you're fairly bothered. Troth, he thinks the young fellow's doin' somethin' out of the way if he just walks down the street, and expec's everybody to stand watchin' him goin' along. It's surprisin' the foolery there does be in people."

"Och, murdher, women alive!" said Ody Rafferty, whose pipe went out at this moment, "there's no contintin' yous at all. It's too cute they are, and too foolish they are. Musha, very belike they're not so much off the common if you'd a thrifle more exparience of them; there's nothin' to match that for evenin' people. Bedad, now, there's some people *I* know so well that I can scarce tell the one from the other."

Lisconnel, however, generally declined to fall in with Ody's philosophical views, and the Patmans, whether suspected of excessive cuteness or folly, remained persistently unpopular. There was only one exception to this rule. The widow M'Gurk has a certain fibre of perversity in her which sometimes twists itself round unlikely objects, for no apparent reason save that they are left clear by her neighbours, and this peculiarity renders her prone upon occasion to undertake the part of Devil's Advocate. When, therefore, she had once delivered herself of the opinion that the new-comers were "very dacint folks," she did not feel called upon to abandon it because it stood alone. As grounds for it she commonly alleged that they were "rael hard-workin' and industhrious," which was obviously true enough, since Mrs. Patman and her sister might constantly be seen tilling their little field with an energy far beyond the capacity of its late tenant. Her neighbours' unimpressed rejoinder, "Well, and supposin' they are itself?" did not in the least disconcert the widdy, nor yet their absence of enthusiasm when she stated that it was "a sight to behould Tishy M'Crum diggin' over a bit of ground; she'd lift as much on her spade as any two strong men." As for little Katty, "she'd never seen anybody doin' anythin' agin the child; it might happen by nature to be one of those little *crowls* of childer that 'ud always look hungry-like and pinin', the crathurs, if you were able to keep feedin' them wid the best as long as the sun was in the sky." In short, something more than talk was usually needed to put the widow M'Gurk out of conceit with any notion she had taken up. Perhaps the comparative aloofness of her hillside cabin helped to maintain the Patmans at their original high level in her estimation. At any rate they had not sunk from it by the time that they had been nearly three months in Lisconnel, and when Mrs. Patman and her sister were on terms of the very glummest civility with all the other women in the place. Even towards the widow M'Gurk they were tolerant rather than expansive. She said "they had done right enough to not be leppin' down people's throats."

One morning not long after Christmas, the widow, being bound on an errand down below, called in at the Patmans' with a view to possible commissions. Meal was wanted, and, while Tishy M'Crum stitched up a rent in the bag, Mrs. M'Gurk noticed where little Katty, who had been "took bad wid a could these three days," rustled uncomfortably among wisps of rushes and rags in an obscure corner. Fever made her bold and self-assertive, for she was wishing nothing less than that her daddy would get her an orange—"An or'nge wid yeller peel round it"—Katty laid stress upon this point—"like the one her mammy got her a long time ago. And daddy'd be a good daddy and get her another now. And she'd keep a bit for Bobby and Stevie and all of them—a big yeller or'nge." Katty's eyes blazed with excitement as she reiterated these extravagant desires.

"She's got an oncommon fancy for a one," said her daddy, looking wistfully from the child to his wife.

"They have them down below," suggested the widow, "pence apiece."

Mrs. Patman's hand was slipping towards her pocket. "If it was just for wunst," she had begun, when Tishy tweaked her sleeve viciously and interpolated a rapid whisper, "It wont *be*; there'll be no ind to it if you begin humourin' them," so the sentence was badly dislocated. "She'll do a dale better widout any such thrash," Mrs. Patman concluded, and walked off to throw sods on the fire.

Just then the widow became aware that old Joe Patman was grimacing at her from a corner fast by in a way that might have startled her had she not been familiar with such modes of beckoning.

But when she obeyed his summons, what she saw did astound her outright, for Joe was stooping low over a leathern pouch which he had drawn from a wall-cranny, and which seemed to contain marvellous depths of silver money, with here and there a golden gleam among it, as he warily stirred it up, circling a hurried forefinger. She had only the briefest glimpse ere he shoved back the pouch and thrust a sixpence into her hand, muttering, "Git her the orange—don't be lettin' on for your life."

As she turned away with a reassuring nod, she perceived that Tishy M'Crum was standing unexpectedly near, and looking towards them over the top of the meal-bag. Tishy was bitting off a loose end of thread, which gave her a determined and ferocious expression, but whether she could have seen anything or not the widow felt uncertain. She thought not.

About ten days after this Mrs. M'Gurk was roused at a very early hour by a thumping on her door. When she opened it she found some difficulty in recognising her visitor, as the dawn had scarcely done more than dim a few stars far away in the east, which is an ineffective form of illumination. "Whethen, now, Joe Patman, is it yourself?" she said, peeringly. "And what's brought you out at all afore you can see a step or a stim? Is the little girl took worse?" For Katty's illness still continued, and had grown rather serious.

"Sure, no," said the old man; "Katty's just pretty middlin'. But it's waitin' I've been the len'th of the mornin', till 'twould turn broad daylight, before I'd be disturbin' of you, ma'am, to tell you the quare sort of a joke they're after playin' on me down yonder."

"Saints above, man, what talk have you of jokin' at this hour of the day or night?" said Mrs. M'Gurk, feeling the unseasonableness acutely as a bitter gust came swooping up the slope and indiscriminatingly ruffled the rime-dusted grass-tufts and her own grizzled locks.

"Och, bejabbers, it's a great joke they have agin me whatever," said old Patman, who was shivering much, with cold partly, and partly perhaps with amusement. "You see the way of it was, last night, no great while after we'd all gone asleep, I woke up suddint, like as if wid the crake of a door or somethin', but, whatever it might be, 'twas slipped beyond me hearin' afore I'd got a hould of me sinses rightly. So I listened a goodish bit, and somehow everythin' seemed unnathural quiet, till I heard Katty fidgettin', and I went over to see would she take a dhrink of wather. The Lord presarve us and keep us, ma'am, if all the rest of them hadn't quit—quit out of it they have, and left us cliver and clane."

"Ah, now, don't be romancin' man," said the widow, remonstrantly. "What in the name of the nation 'ud bewitch any people to go rovin' out of their house in the middle of the black night, wid the frost thick on the ground?"

"Quit they are," said the old man. "Tom's gone, and the wife, and every man-jack of them. They've took the couple of chuckens I noticed Tishy killin' of yesterday. Begorrah, I believe they've took Tib the cat, for ne'er a sign of it I see about the place, that would mostly be sittin' cocked up atop of the dresser. Goodness guide us, sorra a sowl there is in the house but the two of us, me and the child, and she's rael bad. It's a quare ould joke."

"It 'ud be the joke of a set of ravin' mad people," said the widow.

"But the best of it is," he went on, "do you mind, ma'am"—he looked round him suspiciously and lowered his voice—"the leather pouch you might ha' seen wid me the other day?"

"Whoo!" said Mrs. M'Gurk, "are they after takin' that on you? Sure, man, I thought you had it unbeknownst."

"Aye, it's took," old Patman said: "but how she grabbed it I dunno, onless, I was thinkin', be any chance you mentioned somethin' about it?"

"Divil a bit of me did," the widow averred, with truth, which her hearer accepted. "And how much might you have had in it at all?"

"Troth, I couldn't be tellin' you," he said; "I never thought to count it. 'Tis just for a pleasure to meself I keep it. This long while back I've put ne'er a penny in it, but when we used to be livin' up at Portnafoyle I'd slip in the odd shillin's now and agin, and sometimes I'd think 'twould be handy for buryin' me, and other times I'd think I'd give it to Tom as soon as I'd gathered a thrifle more, on'y some way the thought of partin' wid it 'ud seem to go agin me, and since poor Tom made a match with Martha M'Crum 'tis worse agin me it goes. 'Tis that good-for-nought weasel of a slieveen Tishy's after conthrivin' it on me, I well know, and bad luck to her," quoth the old man, with a sudden spasm of resentment. "Tom 'ud never play such a thrick—I mane it wasn't he invinted the joke; he doesn't throuble himself wid much jokin'; he's too sinsible, and steady, and perspicuous, and oncommon set on me and the child, all the while. There's no better son in Ireland. Och, but the rest of them mane no harm wid it; they're just schemin' to dhrop in prisintly and be risin' a laugh on me."

Steps which were promptly taken to verify old Joe Patman's strange story proved it to be correct in every particular. The only fresh fact which investigations brought to light was the presence of a five-shilling piece lying on the dresser, where Joe had overlooked it in the early dusk. All the other inmates, chuckens and cat included, had disappeared, and with them most of the few movables, the old man and the sick child being left as forlorn fixtures. Lisconnel at large was neither slow nor circumlocutory in forming and expressing its opinion as touching the nature of the joke, a firm belief in which old Joe resolutely opposed to his troubles as they thickened around him. For no tidings came from the absentees, nor were any heard of them, while Katty's fever ran so high that it seemed likely her grandfather would be at small further charges on her account—a prospect which, however financially sound for a capitalist of five shillings or under, none the less filled his soul with grief. Then, one night, when Katty was at her worst, a great gale came rushing and roaring across the bog, and when the day broke it discovered the Patmans' brown thatch-slope interrupted by a gaping crevasse, over which a quick-plashing rain-sheet quivered.

The widow M'Gurk had less spare room than heretofore at her disposal now that she harboured a co-tenant, with a slight accession of tables and chairs. Yet she made out a dry corner for the child and her grandfather, who accepted these quarters in preference to any others, because the widow, whatever may have been her private views, was prevented by a mixture of contrariness and magnanimity from joining in the general denunciation of her former allies, compromising as were the circumstances under which they had elected to take their departure. In her society, therefore, he was not obliged to overhear trenchant criticisms upon his Tom's behaviour, and could dilate, at least uncontradicted, upon those gifts and graces in the young man, which recent events had certainly placed in some need of exposition.

Other disquieting voices there were, however, which he could not dodge, and they spoke louder every day. For his five shillings were melting, dwindling—had vanished; and Lisconnel, with the best will in the world, could ill brook a burden of two incapables more laid upon its winter penury. No word on the subject had reached the old man's outer ears; but as Katty struggled slowly and fractiously towards convalescence, it became clearer in his mind that unless something happened, she must, when well enough to be moved, seek change of air away at the big House. Perhaps this prospect was now more constantly before him than even the thought of Tom's filial virtues, as he sat drearily on the bank by the widow M'Gurk's door. He might often be seen to shake his head despondently, and then he was probably saying to himself: "Belike he thought bad of me, keepin' the bit of money unbeknownst."

By that time he had abandoned the joke theory, and fixed his hopes upon the arrival of a letter to explain the mysterious nocturnal flitting, and say whither they had betaken themselves after passing through Duffclane, the furthest point to which the detective forces of the district had tracked the party. Young Dan O'Beirne, whose work brought him daily up from down below to the forge a long way on the road toward Lisconnel, had safely promised to convey this letter so far whenever it came; and on many a day the neighbours nodded commiseratingly to one another as they saw "the ould crathur, goodness may pity him, settin' off wid himself" in quest of it. The prompt January dusk would have already fallen before he struggled up the Knockawn, to be greeted by the widow in the tone of marked congratulation which our friends sometimes adopt when all reason for it is conspicuously absent: "Well, man alive, there wouldn't be ere a letter in it this day anyway."

"Och tub-be sure, not at all," he would answer cheerfully, "I wouldn't look to there bein' e'er a one sooner than to-morra. I hadn't the notion of expectin' a letter whatever. 'Twas just for the enjoyment of the bit of a walk I went."

"Why tub-be sure it was. But be comin' in, man, for you're fit to dhrop, and be gettin' your ould brogues dhried. Och man, you're dhrownded entirely; 'tis a mighty soft evenin' it's turnin' out."

"And here's Katty lookin' out for you this great while," Big Anne would say, "she's finely this evenin', glory be to goodness."

CHAPTER XIII.

A RETURN.

AFFAIRS were much in this posture, when the widow M'Gurk was one day perplexed by the occurrence of two small incidents. In the first place, as she was starting on an expedition to the Town she saw at a little distance something run across the road which looked uncommonly like the Patmans' black cat Tib. Lisconnel owns no other cats for which she might have mistaken it; still, as she was puzzled to think how the creature should have hidden itself away for more than a fortnight, she concluded that she had been deceived by some fluttering bird or glancing shadow. In the next place, she happened in the Town upon one Larry Donnelly, who in the course of conversation remarked: "So you've that young Patman back wid yous agin. What took him to be leggin' off wid himself that way?"

"And what put that in your head at all?" said the widow. " Light nor sight we've seen of him, or a one of them, or likely to. It's off out of the counthry he is belike, and he after robbin' his ould father, that's niver done talkin' foolish about him, and lavin' his innicent child to go starvin' into the Union—bad luck to him." She found a free expression of her sentiments rather refreshing after the restrictions under which she was placed at home.

"Well now," said Donnelly, "I'd ha' bet me best brogues I seen that chap a couple of nights ago streelin' along the road down about our place; but 'twas darkish enough, and I might aisy be mistook."

The widow pondered much over this statement on her homeward way, but had the forbearance to say nothing about it. She was still undecided whether or no she would communicate it to anybody, when, next morning, on her way for a can of water, she saw the black cat, unmistakable this time, run across the road, and, as on the day before, make off over the bog towards the little river. Widow M'Gurk stood staring after it for a few minutes, and came to a resolution. Then she looked about her, and was aware of Andy Sheridan's head leaning against his doorpost. Of Andy her opinion was, as we have seen, rather low, but she could descry no other person available for her purpose, so she called to him: "Andy, lad, I'm goin' after me two pullets that's strayed on me; come and be givin' me a hand." Andy lounged over to her goodnaturedly, and they turned into the bog, where Ody Rafferty presently joined them. The widow thought her fowl might be among the broken ground, where the stream runs at the back of the Knockawn, and the three went in that direction. It was a mild soft grey morning, and they met with neither stir nor sound, till they came abruptly upon a grassy hollow, shut in by furzy banks, and fronted by the running water, and then the widow, who alone had been expecting the unexpected, uttered a suppressed screech, and said: "Och, boys dear, goodness gracious guide us!"

What they saw was the figure of a man in a long great-coat, "crooched all of a hape" under the bank. Near him were ranged in a row half a dozen oranges, strikin' up a wonderful golden glow. A small grimy scrap of paper was spread out near them, covered with several piles of shillings and pennies, and a silver thimble. Beside these Tib the black cat sat severely tucked up, apparently dissatisfied, and irked by the situation. At the widow's exclamation the man raised his head, and was seen to be Tom Patman, looking haggard and dazed, and as hollow-eyed as little Katty herself. Widow M'Gurk and Ody and Andy stood in a line facing him.

"Whethen now, Tom Patman," said Ody, "and what might *you* be doin' wid yourself?"

"I'm sittin' here," said Tom.

"Och musha, tell us somethin' we don't know then. Sittin' there you are, sure enough, but what the mischief are you after, might I politefully ax? or what you mane *by* it at all at all?"

"I'm sittin' here," said Tom again, "and starvin' I am; and sittin' and starvin' I'll be morebetoken till the ind of me ould life. Sure what else 'ud I be doin', and meself to thank for it, wid niver a sowl left belongin' me in the mortal world, nor a place to be goin' to?"

"Well tub-be sure," said Mrs. M'Gurk, "if that talk doesn't bate all that iver I heard! And himself after trapesin' off as permisc-yis as an ould hin that won't sit on her eggs, and lavin' his own flesh and blood behind him as if they were the dust on the road. And then he ups and gives chat about niver a sowl bein' left him."

"'Twas Tishy—bad cess to her," said Tom. "Och, but it's the mischievious ould divil-skins is Tishy M'Crum, and it's herself stirred up Martha, that wouldn't be too bad altogether if she'd be let alone, till the two of them had me torminted wid tellin' me th' ould man had pots of money he'd niver spend as long as he had us to be livin' on; and that we'd all do a dale better if some of us slipped away aisy widout risin' a row, and left him for a bit, while we'd be sellin' Martha's things, and seein' about gettin' into a dacint little place, instid of the whole of us to be starvin' alive up at Lisconnel, that's nothin' more than a bog bewitched; and he after lettin' us be sold up, they said, and all the while ownin' mints of money, so that we'd no call to be overly partic'lar about lavin' him to make a shift along wid the child, if 'twas a convanience; on'y he'd be risin' a quare whillabaloo, if he knew we were goin' off anywheres. Troth, I couldn't tell you all the gabbin' they had day and night—and showin' me the place he kep' his bag hidden in, and this way and that way. Och bedad themselves 'ud persuade the hair on your head it grew wrong side out, if they'd a mind to it."

"They might so," said Ody, "supposin' I was great gomeral enough to be mindin' a word they'd say, or the likes of them." In his subsequent reports of the interview, Ody always alleged that he had replied: "Aye, very belike, supposin' it grew on the head of an ass," which was certainly neater. But Ody Rafferty's repartees, like those of other people, are occasionally belated in this way.

"So the ind of it was," Tom went on, "nothin' else 'ud suit them except gettin' all readied up for us to be slinkin' out in the evenin' late. Faith, I'd twenty minds in me heart agin quittin' little Katty, and she that bad. Howane'er they swore black and white that me father'd be spendin' all manner of money on her when he got us out of it, and we were to be writin' for them to come after us as soon as we were settled, and iverythin' agreeable—so I went along. But if I did, ma'am, sure when they'd got the bits of furniture sold, the on'y notion they had was to be settin' off to make fortins in the States, and ne'er a word about Katty and th' ould man. Och they had me disthracted; outrageous they were; and that ould thief of the world, Tishy, allowin' me sorra a penny, so as I mightn't ha' been bound to stop wheriver they was. But one day they thought they had me asleep in the room-corner, and the two of them was colloguin' away at the table, so all of suddint Tishy whips out me poor father's bag, that I knew the look of right well, when he used to keep his 'baccy in it, and down she slaps it, and it jinglin' wid money. 'What's that for you?' sez she, and: 'The laws bless us,' sez Martha, 'is it after takin' that you are? And what's to become of them crathurs up at Lisconnel?' 'Och blathers,' sez Tishy, 'you needn't be lettin' on you didn't well know all this while I had it. Sure th' ould one might ha' plinty more hidden away on us. Anyway, I left them somethin' to get along wid,' sez she."

"The five shillin's," said the widow. "Och but that one's a caution."

"Rael hard-workin' and industhrious she is," observed Andy.

Tom resumed his narrative: "'Them two'll do as well inside as out,' sez Tishy. 'I'll just be countin' the bit of silver,' sez she. But bedad I was fairly past me patience, and up I leps, and I grabbed a hould of the little bag. Och it's a quare fright I gave them that time, and they not thinkin' I was mindin', rael terrified they were," said Tom, sitting up more erect, and recalling this rare experience with evident complacency. "And 'Lave that, you omadhawn,' sez Tishy, wid the look of a divil on her, 'what foolery are you at now?' 'You thievin' miscreant,' sez I to her, 'it's shankin' off to the pólis I'll be, and layin' a heavy charge agin you for robbin' and stealin', and you after lavin' the innicent child there and th' ould man to starve widout a penny to their names,' sez I. 'Faugh!' sez she, 'for that matter the fever's liker to have took her off agin now wid no throuble to be starvin', and maybe a good job too for iverybody.' And 'Be this and be that,' sez I, 'if I thought there was e'er a fear of it, 'tis wringin' your ugly neck round I'd be this instiant.' 'Let go of that bag,' sez she, sweepin' up some of the shillin's that was spilt. 'The pólis,' sez I, 'and a heavy charge, if there's another word out of your hijjis head.' 'I vow and declare,' sez Martha, 'I believe 'twould be the chapest thing we could do wid him, to let him take it and go. Sure he'd be divil a ha'porth more use for an immigrant than the ould cat there I was ape enough to bring along to pacify the childer.' So then

Tishy gave some more impidence, but the last ind of it was we come to an agreement that I'd take the note and the silver, and they'd keep what bits of gould was in it, and they'd go off wid themselves wheriver they plased at all, and I'd thramp straight back here to be lookin' after the child and th' ould man. Ay, bedad, we settled it up civil enough. And afore I went Martha handed me out th' ould thimble, and bid me bring it to Katty. ''Twas her mother's,' sez she, 'I was keepin' for her; and thick it is wid houles be the same token; but don't say I'd be robbin' it off her.' And they tould me to take Tib along, or else they'd be lavin' her to run wild; so I put her in the basket. Begorrah, I believe Bobby had a notion to be comin' wid me and the cat, for he was lettin' sorrowful bawls the last thing I heard of him.

"So away I come wid the best of me haste; och I knocked the quare walkin' out of meself entirely. And I stopped at the last big place I was passin' to get Katty the oranges. And I was thrampin' it all the night after, till just when there was a sthrake of the mornin' over the bog, I come into Lisconnel. But och wirra wirra—the roof's off of the house—och the look of the black houle wid the rafters stickin' thro' it, and ne'er a breath of smoke, till me heart was sick watchin' to see might there be an odd one; and the door clap-clappin'. Sure be that I well knew the child was dead, and me father quit out of it, or maybe buried himself, and I after lavin' them dyin' and starvin'. So for 'fraid somebody'd be comin' out and tellin' me, off I run away into the bog, till I was treadin' here in the could wather. And then I tumbled th' ould cat out of the basket, that was scrawmin' and yowlin' disp'rit, and I took and slung the basket into the sthrame—there's the handle among them rushes—and down I sat under the bank. I dunno how many nights and days it is at all—but here I'll stop; niver a fut I'll stir to be lookin' for bite or sup, or lettin' on I'm in it— and anybody may take the bit of money and welcome; I'd as lief be pickin' up the dirt on the road—for I'll just give me life a chance to ind out of the world's misery and disolation."

"Now, may goodness forgive you," said the widow M'Gurk, "it's a poor case to want the wit. Troth, and yourself's the quare ould child-desertin', mane-spirited, aisy-frighted slieveen of a young bosthoon; but what sort of a conthrivance is it you have on you at all at all be way of a head that you couldn't have the sinse to considher the roof blowin' off a body's house 'ud be raison enough for them to be quittin' out of it, and no signs of dyin' in the matter? D' you think the win' was apt to be waitin' till there happened to be nobody widin, afore it got scatterin' the thatch? God help us all, you've little to do to be squattin' there talkin' about disolations and miseries, wid the two of them this instiant minyit sittin' be the fire up at my place, and sorra a hand's turn ailin' them, forby Katty's a thrifle conthráry now and agin, thro' not bein' entirely strong yet."

"And bedad at that hearin'," reports of the occurrence used to proceed from this point, " the lep he gathered himself up wid, and the rate he legged it off—musha, he was over the hill while we were pickin' up his things for him. And as for th' ould cat that he tripped over, it rowled three perch of ground before it got a hould of its four feet."

"Sure we were sittin' there as quite as could be consaived"—the conclusion of this precipitate rush was thus recounted—" when all of a suddint we couldn't tell what come bouncin' in at the door, as if it had been shot out of the inds of the earth, and had us all jumpin' up and screechin', till we seen it was on'y Tom Patman, and he in such a takin' you might suppose he thought somethin' 'ud swally up ould Joe and the child on him before he could get at them."

Lisconnel's opinion was divided as to whether Tom would actually have stayed and starved in his hiding-place had he not been discovered. Mrs. M'Gurk thought it likely enough. "The cat goin' back and for'ards that way," she said, "gave her an idee there was somethin' amiss in it, and that was why she took Andy along. 'Deed and she got a quare turn when first she spied the chap croochin' under the bank—she couldn't tell but he might ha' been a corp."

Brian Kilfoyle's view was: "Divil a much! Sure if he'd had e'er a notion to be doin' anythin' agin himself, there was plinty of deep bog-houles handy for him to sling himself into, and have done wid it." Whereupon Mrs. Sheridan crossed herself and said deprecatingly: "Ah, sure, belike the crathur wouldn't have the wickedness in him to go do such a thing." Her husband didn't know but he might. "Them soft sort of fellers 'ud sometimes stick to anythin' they took into their heads, the same as a dab of morthar agin a wall."

And Ody Rafferty supposed the fact of the matter was, "that if be any odd chance they got a notion of their own, they mistook it for somebody else's."

On one point, however, the neighbours, Mrs. M'Gurk not excepted, were practically unanimous, the utter flagitiousness, namely, of Tishy M'Crum. There was a tendency to begrudge her the trivial merit of having voluntarily left behind her the five-shilling piece. For this marred that perfect symmetry of iniquity which is so pleasant to the eye when displayed by people of whom we "have no opinion." Only Mrs. Brian said it was a mercy she had that much good nature in her itself. But even she added that the fewer of them kind of folks she saw comin' about the place, the better she'd be pleased, and she hoped they'd got shut of them for good and all.

This aspiration seemed the more likely to be fulfilled, when within a week or so the Patmans heard from the family of Tom's first wife, who held out prospects of work for himself, and a home for Katty and his father—a proposal which was gladly accepted. Their departure left as the single trace of their sojourn in Lisconnel, Tib the cat, which remained behind, a somewhat unwelcome bequest to the widow M'Gurk. Indeed, I fear the creature became a source of some annoyance to her, because Andy Sheridan contracted a habit of addressing it by the name of Tishy, and bestowing upon it the same laudatory epithets with which the widow had been wont to justify her admiration for the energetic sisters.

It was on a hushed February morning that the Patmans finally departed. The smell of spring was in the air, and filmy silvery mist had begun to float off the dark bogland in vanishing wreaths, soft and dim as the frail sloe-blossom, already stolen out over the writhen black branches up on the ridge. A jewel had been left in the heart of every groundling trefoil and clover-leaf, and the long rays that twinkled to them were still just tinged with rose. Here and there a flake of gold seemed to have lit upon the clump of sombre green furze-bushes, by which neighbours in a small knot stood watching the three generations of Patmans dwindle away down the road with its narrow dewy grass-border, threading the vast sweep of sky-rimmed brown. Father and son walked, while little Katty bobbed along, balanced in a swaying donkey-pannier. The widow M'Gurk, who felt a good deal of concern about the destiny of her late lodgers, hoped "they were goin' to dacint people, for there wasn't as much sinse among the three of them as you'd put on a fourpenny bit." And Mrs. Quigley thought "'twould be hard to say which the young man or ould one was the foolishest; for the blathers ould Joe talked about Tom, and the gaby Tom made of himself over the child, now that he had his own way wid her, was past belief."

"And I can tell you," said Ody Rafferty, "there's folks goin' about that you'll want all the wits you iver had, and maybe a thrifle tacked on, to get the better of rightly."

"Augh, I question will they iver do any great things, goodness help them," said Mrs. Sheridan. "'Twill be much if he keeps them outside the House."

"Well, anyway," said Biddy Ryan, "I'd liefer be in their coats, for fortin or no fortin, than like them two ugly-tempered women, settin' off to the dear knows where, after robbin' and plunderin' all before them."

"Thrue for you, then, Biddy," said Mrs. Brian, turning away from her wide outlook, " we're none so badly off, when we're stoppin' where we are, instid of streelin' about wid the notion of such black villinies in our minds. For sure enough," she said, as she faced round towards the grey-peaked end-walls, and smoke-plumed thatch of Lisconnel, "the world's a quare place to get thravellin' thro', take it as you will."

CHAPTER XIV

GOOD LUCK

ALTHOUGH Laraghmena is no great distance from Lisconnel as the crow flies, but little intercourse takes place between the two hamlets. For the crow's flight would be over a rugged mountain ridge, sinking into a trackless expanse of bog, which often spreads rough and wet walking before wayfarers who have to experience it at closer quarters than those who merely throw down a flapping shadow as they pass. And round by the road is a good long tramp, not to be lightly undertaken. So it does not happen half a dozen times in the year, perhaps, that anybody comes from thence to Lisconnel, and our visits thither are fewer still. The neighbours say that the people up there do be very poor entirely, and are wont to use a commiserating tone when speaking of them. But their knowledge of the locality and its inhabitants is by no means intimate, and would be even less so, were it not that Theresa Joyce and her brother Mick, the remnant of Mrs. Kilfoyle's family, are now living there, which makes a connecting link.

Laraghmena is scattered rather wildly over the slopes of a grey mountain that shoulders the sea at the point where its foam comes nearest to Lisconnel. Some of the cabins stand so low along the shore that the shingle knocks clatteringly at their doors when the tide is full and rough; and other some are perched so high up on the hillside that they constantly disappear from view behind a curtain of the pale mists which haunt its summit, creeping to and fro. When one of these little white dwellings, with its field-fleck beside it, emerges from the clouds, you feel as if the slightly improbable had happened, since at such a height you would have expected nothing but the appropriate rocks and swampy patches. There was once a French princess who would no doubt have wondered why on earth any people should choose to live and farm in such unchancy places. Rather than that she would have ploughed herself up a little bit of the rich green land which spreads in broad tracts round about, with sometimes sheep nibbling over it, and here and there a few deer. But the views of this young lady are represented as having been so far in advance of her age that she seems hardly possible as an historical personage, and withdraws into the myth-mists. To that region certainly belongs the ancient chronicle in which we read how the Irish Nemedians, revolting against the intolerable deal of cream and butter and wheaten meal exacted from them by their oppressors, the Fomorians, those ferocious African pirates, emigrated to Hellas, in hope of better things, but were at last driven back home to escape the heavier yoke of the Athenians, who compelled them to: "Dig clay in the valleys, and carry it in leathern bags to the top of the highest mountains, and the most craggy rocks, in order to form a soil upon those barren places, and make them fruitful, and able to bear corn." That history should repeat itself is, of course, to be recognised as merely a commonplace fact; but a myth reproducing itself in the shape of events happening visibly before our eyes, is a rarer phenomenon. And it seems to be occurring whenever a string of Laraghmenians come plodding up their winding mountain-path under the burden of heavy creels filled with earth, or oftener with slippery brown sea-wrack and leathery weed. For it is in this way that whatever scanty foothold their starveling crops may find, has been fashioned and maintained in the stony little fields. Year by year, as the blustery days of late autumn darken into winter, the steep-ledged path is wetted all along with sea-water, and bestrewn with dark trails and tough tawny pods out of the dripping creels, until it grows as sharply ocean-odorous as the beach, while the many bare feet are continually toiling slowly up and quickly pattering down it. Yet their efforts are rewarded by only meagre and stunted growths; so intractable is the material upon which they are expended. Micky Joyce has been heard to declare, as he took a despondent bird's-eye view of his holding, that "you might as well be thryin' to raise crops in the crevices of the stone walls."

However, as we were just now shown, these dwellers at Laraghmena have another resource to fall back upon. In fact, they have nothing less than the wide sea as a supplement to their bit of land. The queer small boats hauled up on the strand, and the dark-brown net festooning the rafters, betoken that, as does also the bit of salt-fish hung against the wall, pallid and juiceless, a shadowy, wraith-like looking viand. But the bounty of the sea has limits; it does not yield up its stores for nothing, but takes as well as gives. And it helps itself sometimes on a liberal scale. Some years ago, for instance, it took poor Thady Joyce and several of his companions, who had gone off in a couple of luggers after the herrings. The event is remembered with awe at Laraghmena, because in that wild March gloaming Con the Quare One had met Thady himself face to face stepping up the winding path, and had given him good evening, and asked him how he had got all dripping wet, just at the very time when the unlucky lad must have been lying drowned miles and miles from there, among the surges of Galway Bay. Other such toll has often been levied since then; for the curraghs and pookawns in which Laraghmena goes to sea are frail craft to cope with the billows come rolling, maybe, from the fogbanks of Newfoundland, and blasts that have cooled their breath among hills of ice before they sweep across the Atlantic. Now and then a boat comes to grief even on the short voyage made for the purpose of cutting wrack from the shelves of the black-reef that lies a bit off the shore. So, on the whole, the inhabitants of

Laraghmena may be considered to pay dearly for their supplies of fish and seaweed; and we at Lisconnel, though we live beyond reach of such things, and have few substitutes for them, are not far wrong in speaking of the people up there as " rael poor entirely."

Yet they themselves would not by any means have it supposed that they " think bad," as they call it, of their fortunes and habitation. On the contrary, whatever their private opinion may be, they are disposed to uphold the merits of the place in public, and to prove themselves sudden and quick in resentment of any outsiders' disparaging criticism. The most deadly insult that can be offered to a Laraghmenian as such, is an allusion to the libellous report which has somehow become current to the effect that his Riverence at Drumroe, the nearest parish, always sends over a special messenger on Saturday night to remind them of the morrow's Mass; the innuendo being that Laraghmena's out-of-the-way situation, and general want of culture, preclude its inhabitants from knowing the day of the week. This is why an innocent-seeming remark such as, " Well, boys, it's Tuesday this mornin'," has been known to set blackthorns whirling wildly.

Something of the sort occurred at Sallenmore fair, one day in last September, when Matt Doyne and Andy Sheridan from Lisconnel fell in with their acquaintances, Larry Sullivan and Felix Morrough, from Laraghmena. After they had fought as long as seemed good to them, they exchanged what news they had. The most important piece was that Larry and Felix were presently setting off to the States. They were rather urgent in advising the other two lads to join their party; but Andy said that everything would go to sticks at home if he was out of it, and Matt averred that his mother would be of the opinion she was lost and kilt entirely, if he so much as mentioned any such an idea. "And herself wid your brother Terence at home to be keepin' her company," objected Felix. "Sure there's me mother wid ne'er another crathur in the world, you may say, but meself, and she's never done this last six months persuadin' me to go along."

"Then it's the quare woman she must be, bedad," said Matt, "unless it's yourself's the quare bosthoon on her entirely, and maybe that's liker;" a rejoinder which brought on a renewal of hostilities.

Just at this time a spell of fine weather, very

bright and serene, had been brooding over Lisconnel. It was the early spring of autumn, when leaves and berries here and there were taking a blossom-like vividness; the frost-touched briersprays seemed to have found and dipped in the same red that had dyed the young buds and shoots of April. The air was so still that the seeded dandelions stood day after day with their fairy globes unbereft of a single downy dart, like little puffs of vapour among the grasses. A soft mist rounded off all the bogland, holding in a drowse the sunbeams that steeped it, and letting them waken to their full golden glory at the very heart of noon. But one morning the haze began to thicken and darken on the horizon, as if wafts of murky smoke were blown through it, and towards evening massy shapes of black clouds came slowly lifting themselves up, some with outlines curved like bosky clumps of wood, some ruggedly ledged and angled like a drift of begrimed icebergs. By sunset the far west was all a sullen gloom veined with lurid, tawny streaks, and mottled with deeper stains. Old Peter Sheridan, who is reputed to have "a great eye for the weather," turned it forebodingly upon the prospect, and said the sky was "the moral for all the world of the back of an ould brindled bull, and he'd never known any good come of that manner of apparance."

And true for him. Before sunrise next morning Lisconnel was roused by the réveille of a crashing thunder-peal, which preluded a violent storm. It is seldom that one booms and rattles so loudly over our bogland, or glares with so fierce a flame. Brian Kilfoyle, taking a rapid observation through his door, said, " Be the powers of smoke, I never seen the aquil of that. You might think they was after whitewashin' the whole place wid blindin' fire. Here's out of it, sez I." And he retreated blinking to his dark corner. At the height of it, even Andy Sheridan, who is probably our freest thinker, felt secretly relieved to know that his stepmother and his sisters were saying their prayers. The arrangement seemed to give him a sense of security without claiming any concessions from his superior strength of mind. But in the end the perilous clouds rolled away growling and gleaming towards the mountains and the sea, leaving only one victim behind—the Quigley's little goat, who had been struck dead by a lightning flash, to the sorrow of her owners, and the awe of all Lisconnel in contemplation of the black and white body stretched out still on her wide grazing-ground.

The storm, however, seemed to have broken up the fair weather, and the days that followed it were blustery and rainy. On the next of them Larry Sullivan and Felix Morrough were seen passing through Lisconnel, evidently equipped for a journey. Larry, who had parted from no near friends, was apparently in good spirits; but Felix looked so much cast down that his contemporaries refrained from any references to the days of the week, and the pair went on their way unmolested amongst the lengthening shadows. They reported the storm to have been terrific altogether up at Laraghmena. The Widdy Bourke's thatch was set in a blaze, "and it was a livin' miracle that the whole of them wasn't frizzled up like a pan of fryin' herrin's."

It may have been ten days or so after this that a good many of the neighbours had dropped in one evening at Mrs. Doyne's. She had been ailing of late, and old Dan O'Beirne had stepped up from the forge to prescribe for her, and cheer her with accounts of how finely young Dan and her daughter Stacey were getting on at their place down below in Duffclane. The rest of the party had assembled merely for company and conversation. It included members of nearly all our families—Kilfoyles and Quigleys and Ryans and Raffertys and the Widdy M'Gurk and Big Anne. Presently Judy Ryan, who was looking out of the door, had an announcement to make.

"Whethen now, and who might yous be when you're at home? There's two women comin' along the road from Sallinbeg ways, I dunno the looks of at all, I should say; but the rain's mistin' thick between me and them. Carryin' bundles they are. If they're not any of the Tinkers we're right enough. One of them's a little ould body, and the other's a good size bigger. Strangers they are. Och, mercy on me, have I eyes in me head at all? How strange she is! Sure it's Theresa Joyce herself. But we haven't seen her this great while, and who she has along wid her I couldn't be tellin' you. A feeble sort of crathur she looks to be, accordin' to the way she's foostherin' along."

When these two travellers arrived at the Doynes' door, nobody failed to recognise Theresa Joyce, notwithstanding the estrangement of a long absence; and she hastened to introduce her unknown companion, who kept a tight clutch on her arm, as if afraid to let go, and looked at nobody's face, but seemed to listen from one to the other. She was, it appeared, the widow Morrough from Laraghmena, who had been struck blind by the lightning in the great storm Friday was a week— the sight of her eyes clean destroyed with one flash as she was throwing a bit of food to the fowl at her door. And the last child she had belonging to her set off the next morning to the States. And now she herself was going into the Union down at Moynalone, for what else could she be doing, that couldn't see her hand before her face? So Theresa was bringing her down, and they thought they might have got as far as Duffclane against night; but the creature wasn't well used yet to walking in the dark, so they were slow coming, and they'd hardly do it.

Such was the outline of Mrs. Morrough's history up to date, and its rehearsal had at once the effect of arousing a sympathetic bustle about her, which did not subside until she sat a wet and wayworn guest, in the most comfortable hearth-corner, and had been provided with a cup of the tea that Mrs. Doyne had made herself in her character of an invalid. She now sat on one side of the blind woman, and stirred her tea for her, and on the other Dan O'Beirne shook his head in regretful confirmation of the opinion pronounced by the Drumroe doctor, which was reported to be that mortal man couldn't do her a thraneen of good. Meanwhile Theresa Joyce, who was likewise bedrenched and weary, found a seat in the opposite corner, where her nearest neighbours were Ody Rafferty, and her niece-in-law, Mrs. Brian Kilfoyle, with her daughter Rose.

"Well, Theresa, it's the long while since you've stepped over to see us," Ody said, starting the conversation, "and it's the soft evenin' you've chose to be comin'. Your shawl's dhreeped. Take it off, and I'll give it a shake above the fire. Bedad, Theresa, the two of us has been wearin' the dusty male-bags on our heads since the time I seen you first. As black as a sloe you was; but now it's liker the blossom it's turned."

"And time for it," said Theresa. "Sure I'm over sivinty year of age now, any way, every day of it—and the long days there was among them, God knows."

"But wid all that, ne'er a one of them was long enough for you to be findin' a man to your mind in it," said Ody. "And I declare to goodness I dunno but maybe it's the very sinsible woman you were for that same. Sure meself was a great while afore ever I thought of axin' Biddy, and for anythin' I can tell I might ha' done better if I'd held me tongue a bit longer and then said nothin', as the sayin' is. I was ould enough to know me own mind any way. But, musha, for that matter, Rose there 'ill prisintly be settin' up to think she's ould enough to know hers, and it's twenty chances if she has as much wit as you."

"And why would she," said Theresa, "or anybody be wishin' it to her? Oh, let that alone. There's a dale of diff'rint sorts of wit, and no raison why one of them shouldn't be as good as another. Look at her grandmother, me sister Bessy, it's plinty of paice and comfort she had wid her marryin'."

This was quite true, as although she had been rather early widowed, and her only daughter had married an emigrant, her son and his wife had taken such care of her, and made so much of her, that the neighbours had never thought of calling her the widdy, a title reserved for a woman left struggling alone; and she had remained Mrs. Kilfoyle to the end of her days.

"And look at the poor crathur there, what she's

come to," said Ody, instancing the tragical figure of the widow Morrough.

"Ah, the saints may pity her," said Theresa. "But the likes of such bad luck happins few people married or single, thank God."

"It's a quare unnathural young villin her son must be," said Mrs. Brian, "to skyte off and lave her that-a-way. Sorra the bit he can be good for."

"'Deed, now, Norah woman, that's the very notion is disthressin' me," said Theresa, "for I dunno but it's after usin' him ill, I am. You see the way of it was the poor sowl—poor Mrs. Morrough—had the great dread of the say upon her, be raison of her husband and her father gettin' dhrowned at the fishin', so she'd always the fear in her mind of the same thing happ'nin' her couple of boys. Howane'er, the eldest of them went off to California a good few years back, and was doin' pretty middlin' well out there the last she heard of him, but that's a long while ago now; about gettin' married he was. But Felix, the lad she had at home wid her until the other day, often enough he was bound to be on the wather, after the fish and the sayweed, if he was to get his livin' at all. And disthracted she was seein' him goin' out in their ould boat, that's laiks enough in her to sink the biggest ship ever set sail, and herself wid scarce the width to hould a sizable flounder. Sez I to Felix one wild evenin', when we was argufyin' wid him, that sure the little loadin' he could be puttin' in her 'ud never be worth losin' his life for. But sez he to me, the bit of food they'd put in their mouths was littler agin, and yet they might be losin' their lives for want of it. And ne'er a word had I to say to that. But one night last winter he was as nearly lost as anythin' in a squall, and after that his mother would be tormintin' herself worse than she was before. So she set her heart entirely on gettin' him to take off to the States, and be out of the way of fishin' and dhrowndin'. She'd ha' gone wid him herself, on'y they said she was too ould, and spoilin' his chances she'd be. A long while it was before he'd hear any talk of it. The whole summer she was persuadin' him; but at last he made up his mind he would. 'Twas no notion of his own to be lavin' her, I'll say that for him."

"Whethen now, but that was as curious a plan as ever I heard tell of for keepin' a person from dhrowndin'," said Ody; "to be sendin' him off over the rowlin' says, sailin' goodness can tell you how many hunderds and tousands of miles. What was she dhramin' of at all at all to go do such a thing?"

"Ah, but sure it's a diff'rint sort of sailin'," said Theresa. "Why, they say one of them big stamers 'ud carry a couple of our little boats along wid her, and you'd scarce notice she had them on board. Terrible safe they must be if they're that size."

"And morebetoken," said Mrs. Brian, "there's such a sight of ships comin' and goin' between this and the States, wouldn't you think that agin now they'd ha' got a kind of track line, crossin' over, as if it was a manner of road they was follyin' that nothin's apt to happen them on, and not sthrayin' about permisc-yis in the storms?"

"*Thrack?*" said Ody, shrilly. "Bedad, then, its the quare thrack, and the quare places it brings them into. D'you know that, for one thing, they go slap through the Bay of Bisky?"

"And is that an ugly bay?" said Mrs. Brian.

"You may call it that. I wouldn't be sayin' so to herself over there," said Ody, with much careful mystery. "For it might be on'y discouragin' the crathur worse than she is already. But it's the place where the Seven Oceans of the World meet. Ay, indeed, ma'am—but don't be lettin' on to her. I was spakin' to a man who had a brother went through it, and he said the ragin' and tearin' of them all flowin' together 'ud terrify the sinses out of King Solomon. They had the great big stamer he was in whirlin' round and round and round, the same as if it was a float on one of its own paddlewheels, he couldn't tell how many days and nights. Thracks, how are you. It's a very ready one there is in it to the bottom of the say."

"Still a good few people gets through it safe enough," said Theresa, "ay, and comes back through it of an odd while."

· "But how many's lost in it that you never hear tell of?" said Ody. "And besides that, the man I was talkin' to tould me his brother was never right in his head after the tossin' he got. It's a poor case to be landin' ravin' mad in a sthrange counthry, supposin' you get there itself. But me own notion is that if people's well off, they've a right to stop where they are, and if they're misfort'nit, they've a chance any way of better bad luck stayin' at home."

Ody stated his own notion authoritatively, and

Theresa looked depressed by the dilemma in which it seemed to place the emigrant.

"'Deed, now, maybe it's a bad turn I'm after doin' the two of them," she said; "but poor Mrs. Morrough, many a time she sez to me it 'ud be the greatest comfort to her at all to get quit of the fear she was in continyal wheniver he went out wid the ould boat. Sure she might be a bit lonesome, she'd say, but after all what great company was he to her when half the time she would be drowndin' him under the rowl of the say, like his poor father and grandfather? And wid the most he could do it's hard set he was to make what 'ud keep him. So she'd planned she'd be able to conthrive well enough wid her hins and her spriggin' work, till Felix could be sendin' her over a thrifle. A very cliver woman she was at the spriggin'; the handkercher corners she'd work was rael iligant. Pence a-piece she got for them, and I've known her finish a dozen in three days.

"Och, but I got a turn on the Friday mornin' when I stepped down to her place to see what way they were after the storm, and there she was sittin' crouched up in a corner, and screechin' to me to know who was comin' in, and I standin' before her eyes in the middle of a sun-bame. And 'Glory be to God,' sez she, 'that it's yourself, for you'll have the sinse to give me a hand wid endeavourin' to keep the knowledge of what's after happenin' me from Felix, the way he won't be purvinted of goin' to-morra. Sorra a fut would he if he knew aught ailed me; and then sure he might stay at home for good and all; and dhrownded he'll be, and meself 'ill go deminted.' And sure I thought it was maybe no thing to be doin', and so I said to her. But it seemed the heart of her was to be broke altogether if anythin' 'ud hinder him gettin' out of it. And then I was mindin' the father and grandfather of him, the way they went, and me brother, poor Thady, and I couldn't tell but I might ha' raison to think bad of biddin' him stay; and if he did, sure perhaps he couldn't be keepin' her at all, and she so helpless; it's better able he might be to help her out in the States. And sorry I'd ha' been to disappoint the crathur of the first wish she'd took a thought of sittin' in the dark of her misfortin. So the ind of it was I settled I'd stop wid her for that day, and thry could we let on there was nothin' amiss when Felix come in, that was out somewhere since early in the mornin' before the storm began.

"But 'deed now it was the quare conthrivin' we had after he'd come home. And where'd he been but off down to Drumroe gettin' her an iligant big taypot for a keepsake? So the sorra a stim of it, in coorse, could she see; and I done me best biddin' her look at the grand gilt handle, and the wrathe of pink roses on it, and she'd say the same thing after me; but sure its noways very aisy to fall into an admiration of a taypot you've never set eyes on; and I misdoubt the poor lad thought she wasn't so much plased with it as he expected. And then he'd be walkin' in and out, and axin' for this and that he was to put in his bundle; and she could on'y be tellin' him where to look for them, instid of readyin' them up for him herself. And the pair of socks she'd promised him she couldn't get to finish—rael fretted she was wid it all. Howsome'er one way or the other we made a shift, till poor Felix went off in the grey of the mornin' wid ne'er a notion of anythin'. Sez he to her: 'You'll be seein' me steppin' in agin one of these days;' and sez she: 'Ay will I—as sure as I'll see the sun shinin';' so he consaited she was well enough contint—but the two of them was thinkin' diff'rint things.

"Ne'er a word of it we said to anybody before

Felix was gone, or else somebody 'ud ha been safe to ha' tould him, for there's plinty of people couldn't be goin' about widout tellin' everythin' they hear any more than a wasp could fly widout buzzin' its wings. And then we got the docther to her, but he couldn't do e'er a hand's turn. Sure what could anybody do agin the lightnin', that's a sort of miracle, you may say, unless it was wid another one?"

"And I dunno has people any call to be settin' themselves up to thry do them," said Mrs. Brian. "We'd better lave the like to Them that understands the nathur of such things."

"Ah, I should suppose we'd a right to be thryin' whativer we get the chance to," said Theresa, "and that's little enough, the Lord knows. Plinty of things there is kep' up out of the raich of our meddlin' wid them."

"Ay bedad, or else it's the quare regulatin' we'd be givin' them now and agin—we would so," said Ody, regretfully. "Och, but there's an odd few good jobs I'd give more than a thrifle to be puttin' me hand to this minyit if I could get a hould of them."

"And that's the way it is, I'm afeared, wid the lightnin'-blindin'," said Theresa. "Howane'er, up at Laraghmena we'd ha' done the best we could for her, if she'd ha' been contint to ha' sted there; we'd ha' conthrived among us all to keep her well enough. But not a bit of her would for all we could do or say. She wouldn't be a burden on the neighbours she said. You see she's proud in her mind, the crathur, that's what it is, goodness help her."

"And when a body has that sort of a notion," said Ody, "you might as aisy crack an egg indways as get it out of their head."

"So that's the way of it," said Theresa. "But if you could be tellin' me whether it's wrong I done or right, you know more than meself. Felix 'ud be for killin' me if he knew, that's sartin, and small blame to him I was thinkin' part of the while comin' along. For bad work there's apt to ha' been, sure enough, in anythin' that inds in landin' a body in the Union."

The blind woman in her corner across the hearth seemed to have caught the last word, for she abruptly said, "Ay, ay, it's there I'm goin', and the first of the Morroughs iver wint on the rates, or the Conroys aither. But I'm not takin' their name along wid me; troth no; sorra the Ellen Morrough 'ill they find in it."

"Sure not at all, woman dear," said Theresa. "Why, Mrs. Doyne, it's great work the two of us had this day comin' along the road, plannin' a fine name for Mrs. Morrough to have in the Union, for she sez it's none any dacint poor people own she'll be bringin' into it. So we've settled she's to be Mrs. Skeffington Yelverton. That's an iligant soundin' one, isn't it, ma'am?"

Everybody expressed admiration, and a forlorn glimmer of complacency at the arrangement passed over even the sorrowful countenance of Mrs. Skeffington Yelverton herself, as she sat in her ragged old wisp of a shawl. She was holding under it her grand new delft teapot, whose beauties she should never see; though by this time much fingering had made her familiar with the outlines of its raised pink-rose wreath. Then Theresa Joyce said, "We ought to be steppin' on wid ourselves, if we're to get to Duffclane before dark. The evenin's took up a bit. I see the sky there turnin' like goulden glass agin the windy-pane." But the neighbours protested against their setting forward again; and it was agreed that they should sleep the night at the Kilfoyles'.

When this point had been decided, Mrs. Morrough said, " Would that be the say—the rustlin' I hear outside there?"

Upon this people looked ruefully at her and at each other, as if the question had given them a glimpse into the darkness in which she was sitting.

"Ah, no, ma'am," said Mrs. Doyne, "that's on'y the sedge-laves in the win' round the big pool just back of the house. Few days of the year there is, summer or winter, but they'll be shoosh-sooin' that way. A dhrary sort of noise it is to my mind. I do be tired listenin' to it in the night sometimes."

"Sure there's ne'er a dhrop of say-wather nearer us, ma'am, than the place you're after quittin' out of," said Judy Ryan, "it's the quare whillaloo it 'ud have to be risin' before we'd hear it that far."

"Well, well," said the blind woman, "yous are the very lucky people, I'm thinkin', all of yous, that see the shinin' of the sun, and live beyond the sound of the say."

Her remark was followed by a short silence, during which her hearers were, perhaps, questing for consolatory rejoinders rather than congratulating themselves upon their own luckiness. It was Big Anne who broke the pause, saying, with the best intentions, "Ah, sure, ma'am dear, plase God, *you* won't be so, and *we* won't be so;" a sentiment which apparently did not meet with the approval of Ody Rafferty, as he frowned bushily at her and said in a testy undertone, "Musha, good gracious, woman, what talk have you out of you at all?"

Just at this moment sounds, the nature of which could not easily be mistaken, rose up close by—shouts and laughter and thumps and trampling of feet. People who ran quickly to the door were in time to see a knot of youths fall confusedly out of the house over the way—the Quigleys'—obviously, to judge by their subsequent proceedings, for the purpose of continuing a scuffle with ampler elbow room. But it was only for a very brief space that their wrestling and skirmishing among the puddles held anybody's attention. That was speedily diverted to the far more extraordinary and astonishing behaviour of their visitor, Mrs. Morrough. For she suddenly sprang up off her chair, exclaiming, "Saints above—it's Paddy—that's Paddy's voice—him that I haven't set eyes on for nine year next Easter—and there's Felix yellin' too! The both of them's come back, glory be to God!"

And so saying out of the house she ran, and across the road as straight as a dart, she who not an hour before had been led gropingly in, and would have put her foot among the glowing hearth-sods, if her guides had not pulled her away.

The neighbours could at first look on in only mute amazement, but in any case the two boys and she were for some time so intricately entangled that any attempt to elicit any explanation would have been futile. When at last questions and answers were possible, no very lucid account of the matter was forthcoming. To the many voices that demanded: "Is it seein' you are, woman alive? Is it seein' you are?" all Mrs. Morrough could answer was: "Ay, bedad am I, and as well as iver I done in me life—praise be to goodness. Sure I dunno what way it was, but me sight came back to me all of a flash, the same as it went, just the very minyit I was hearin' the lads shoutin'. Och, Paddy, avic, but you're the grand man grown; and Felix, och now, to be seein' you agin, and everythin' else as clear as clear. It's meself's the lucky woman this day—glory be to God and Mary."

In short, the marvellous restoration of her sight

is to this day a miracle, very freshly in remembrance at Lisconnel and Laraghmena, where the inhabitants know little about paralysed optic nerves, and might perhaps continue to wonder none the less even if they knew more. Beside it the unexpected reappearance of the two young Morroughs seemed almost a commonplace incident, though Paddy's fine new suit and gold watch-chain were, indeed, very exceptional things at Lisconnel. His story ran that he had prospered highly of late out in California, having made enough to set him up grandly on a good bit of land in the old country, and give Felix a fair start, and keep the old mother in comfort all the rest of her life. With which objects in view they had landed at Queenstown, he and his wife, a girl belonging to very respectable, decent people in the county Wicklow. "So next mornin', walkin' along the Quay, who should I see but me gintleman there, and another chap along with him, and both of them lookin' as wild as if they'd been caught. And says I to Sally, 'You bet, that's Felix from our place at home;' and right I was, and just slick in time to stop him goin' on board." Paddy had then left his wife with her family in Wicklow, where he had seen a promising farm: and he and Felix were now on their way to fetch their mother thither.

"And it's in the quare consternation you'd ha' been," said Theresa Joyce, "if you'd landed up at Laraghmena, and found her quit out of it the way she was."

"And that would ha' happint us," said Felix, "if it hadn't been for young Dan Ryan in there just now passin' the remark that we couldn't expec' Father Martin to be sendin' us notices all the way to the County Cork, and supposin' I'd very belike missed the right day for the stamer be raison of it. For if we hadn't got fightin' and tumblin' out of the house, you might aisy ha' gone along wid yourselves, and niver known we were in the place at all. 'Twas great luck entirely."

Fortune, in truth, had seemingly taken Mrs. Morrough and her affairs into the highest favour. Even the luck-insurance of a trivial loss was not wanting to her, as in her hasty exit she had dropped her new teapot, which broke into many pieces on Mrs. Doyne's floor. So that, as has been said, she never beheld it in its beauty. But the very skies had cleared above her head, swept by a waft of wind that scattered the clouds faster and further than a drift of withered leaves, and the sinking sun broadened in splendour before the eyes that had lost sight of him through ten interminable days. The wet stones on the road glistened like jewels, and the shallowest pools between them held unfathomed deeps of blue, when the Morroughs set off for Laraghmena, where they intended to sleep the night, and bid their friends farewell. "And if it's themselves won't be in the fine astonishment when they set eyes upon you, woman dear!" said Theresa Joyce, "for if you'd been twenty year away thravellin' the world crooked and straight, you couldn't ha' come back a diff'rinter crathur from what you were, and we settin' out this woeful mornin'. Little notion you had what was comin' to you, and it all the while runnin' up your road, so to spake, like the sun racin' the shadows on a windy day. 'Deed now, I'd be goin' along wid you to hear what they'll say to it, but I'm ould you see, and ivery step I've thramped I have the feel of in ivery bone of me body; so I'll stop this night up at Brian's."

"And bedad, ma'am, it's well off you are, if you've the feel of nothin' worse in them," said the querulous voice of old Peter Sheridan, whose acquaintances describe him as being "terrible gathered up with the rheumatism this great while," so great, in fact, that everybody except himself has by this time become accustomed to his condition.

For the most part, however, they were rather pleased faces that watched the three strangers out of sight, the last long beams from the sunset making blink the eyes of nearly all Lisconnel. The west dispread its fiery golden bloom wider every moment as the swelling scarlet disc wheeled lower, burning with orbed flame a hollow path through the kindled haze. One laggard cloud, a great, soft nest of snow, drifted into the heart of it, and out of it again, flushed and glistering, and sailed on, a radiant shape, to meet and eclipse the misty white ghost-moon, faint and dim in the east. Far away over the level bog the light was stealing about in streams like water spilt on a floor.

"Well now, I declare," said Mrs. Brian, "it does one's heart good to see a bit of luck like that happenin' to a body."

"Ay, does it," said Judy Ryan, "the crathur to be gettin' back her sight just in the right minyit of time to see her son comin' home to her. Sure now one might take a plisure in plannin' such a thing, if one had the managin' of them."

"Ah, dear, but I wish somebody 'ud be conthrivin' a bit of good luck for us then," said Mrs. Quigley.

" Maybe there's plinty more where that's comin' from," suggested Brian Kilfoyle, hopefully.

"It's apt to stay there, then," quoth Mrs. Quigley, "for any signs I can see."

"Ay, ma'am, that's me own notion," said Peter Sheridan, bitterly; "I'm thinkin' we'll have to be goin' there, wheriver it is, and lookin' after it for ourselves, if it's good luck we're a-wantin'."

"And I dunno what better we could be doin'," said Theresa Joyce, "than goin' where it is, when we get the chance. Ah, there's the last of the sun," she said, as a quivering red shaft shot up suddenly, and trembled away into nothing on the air. "Ay, for sure, he goes down a great way off out on the bog; the crathur 'ud ha' been plased to see it. 'Deed no, I dunno anythin' better we could be doin' than goin' after our good luck."

So all through that gathering twilight Mrs. Morrough and her two sons were journeying away with their high fortune to Laraghmena. They were still on the road long after the clear moon had filled the air with shimmering silver, and sent their shadows stretching darkly far over the frosted grass. But Lisconnel had gone to seek, for the time being, its good luck in the land of dreams.

www.ingramcontent.com/pod-product-compliance
Lightning Source LLC
Chambersburg PA
CBHW030405230426
43664CB00007BB/759